THE ART OF KNITTING

Edited by Eve Harlow

Jederman sey vnterthan der Obri
nun wider die Obrigkeit setzet der
widerstrebet Gottes ordnung etc. Rom. 13. Anno 1674

THE
ART OF
KNITTING
COLLINS
Glasgow and London

Introduction

Knitting has a rich, fascinating, and mysterious past. The origins are unknown but, as far as we can tell, they lie somewhere in the Middle East – "the cradle of the world" – and they date back almost 3000 years.

In this book, we can re-trace the spread of knitting from the Middle East, through many countries both to the east and to the west. Different cultures have influenced the development of the craft, from simple peasants living in remote lands to the centres of European culture at the height of the Renaissance.

But the picture is, for all that, incomplete. In ancient times, knitting was practised to make practical rather than beautiful items and these garments were rarely treasured. Most of the examples which illustrate this book survived only because they were of archaeological interest or demonstrated an unusual technique.

The few fragments and examples of knitting which exist in museums and private collections cannot be said to be a comprehensive representation of the craft but there is still enough to provide us with a glimpse of the richness and variety of its past.

A word about colours

The patterns in this book have been inspired by some of the most beautiful and interesting pieces of knitting in the world. The designer has attempted to match the colours of the original yarns used but, sadly, modern dye colours cannot exactly reproduce the subtleties of the vegetable dyes which were used and the colours vary to a minor degree. If you decide to change the colour schemes given, then we suggest you select colours in sympathy with the tonal qualities of the originals, since these are often an integral part of the beauty of the knitted fabric. If colours are brightened, the contrasts may mask the patterning and change a subtle effect for one which may look crude.

This is a book for everyone who loves knitting. For those who find relaxation and satisfaction in this simple craft, there are new and fascinating patterns. For those who are interested in the origins of handcrafts and trade, this book provides a glimpse of a colourful history.

But for the adventurous knitter, the book is also an opportunity to reproduce some of the beauty of the past, perhaps re-establishing a link with those hand-knitters who lived so long ago and whose skill has made this unique collection of knitting patterns possible.

First published in 1977

Published by William Collins Sons and Company Limited
Glasgow and London

Created and designed by Berkeley Publishers Limited, London

Printed in Great Britain
ISBN 0 00 434601 7

Contents

SECTION I – The history of knitting

SECTION II – The landscape of knitting

SECTION III – The patterns

Introducing...the girls who

Anne Gordon and Jane Rapley, the creators of this book, were at London's Royal College of Art together and it was there that the idea for this book was born.

Anne had already spent three years at the Gloucestershire College of Art in Cheltenham. There, and later at the Royal College, she studied for degrees in textile and fashion design.

Jane Rapley, now a merchandising manager for a major knitwear firm, was doing a thesis at the College in the history of hand-frame knitting. She, too, had gained a degree in fashion and textile design.

The two girls became friends and Anne, also, soon became absorbed in the knitting styles and fashions of earlier times.

She began to doodle on her drawing board and to wonder whether some of the ancient patterns and motifs they both admired so much could be adapted for modern usage. And, there, for the time being, the matter rested. Jane completed her thesis and eventually joined the knitwear firm.

By now Anne Gordon was working as a designer and a move to Jane's firm seemed a logical development. She joined as a knitwear designer and a designer of printed textiles and was put to work in developing the company's colour ranges.

Anne also renewed her interest in historic knitting.

"I was particularly fascinated by the colours", she explains. "Some of the surviving specimens were still remarkably fresh. And the designs were often extremely beautiful.

"I went back to my doodling and soon found that certain motifs began to suggest specific garments. It *was* possible to adapt them and soon the most apparently unpromising originals began to take on exciting new shapes.

"A party dress from a prayer panel may seem slightly irreverent – but then it was only a 'Prayer to Parliament' so I didn't think that mattered!

"And then came the man's sweater, derived from what was – to me at any rate – a most entrancingly designed 18th-century Alsace carpet."

One by one the collection in Anne's scrapbook began to grow. A Dutch embossed petticoat underwent an exhilarating metamorphosis into a serviceable scarf, Charles I's silk shirt became a theme for a smock and – curiouser and curiouser

On these and the next two pages we show some of their first rough sketches as they travelled through time. Jane Rapley (left) and Anne Gordon at work on their garments for today from patterns of the past.

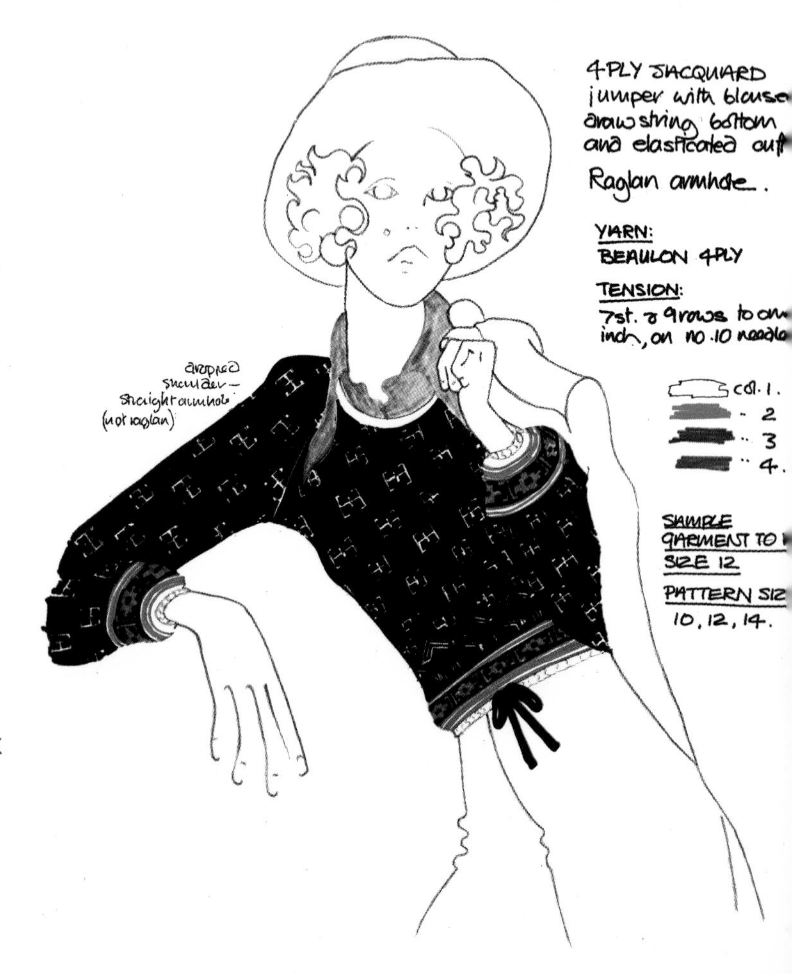

caught a stitch in time

Introducing...the girls who caught a stitch in time

– a pin cushion in the Victoria and Albert Museum became a girl's dress and cardigan.

Anne began to feel an enormous rapport with these early knitters. There was, she explains, a sense of continuity. Knitting has often been used in literature as a synonym for Time – Shakespeare's "ravelled sleeve", for example – and Anne began to feel that in a sense she was handing on the vitality and inventive abundance of these early craftsmen.

"That probably sounds pretentious", she says, "for their work is often extremely beautiful. But I did begin to feel that the origins of my designs gave the end product a certain fascination. For instance, I remember thinking to myself – wouldn't Charles the First have been surprised! And there seemed something divinely reassuring – almost a protection in itself – in turning a design used in a pair of Spanish altar gloves into a man's vest."

Soon Anne's collection of designs – inspired originally by Jane's thesis – had built up into a considerable portfolio. This book contains a selection we found the most appropriate. Here, truly, we have genuine and highly original garments for today from patterns of the past.

And what about Jane Rapley? She believes there is endless fun to be had for expert knitters in selecting their own inspirational knitting motifs. Jane shares Anne's admiration for the skill and quality shown in their work and would like to see this sort of pride in craftsmanship revived today.

"Once you have developed the habit", she says, "art galleries and museums take on an extra dimension. There is always the possibility that the odd corner of some lovely old piece of knitting can be made to blossom into a new and entirely fresh existence."

Well, we think this book proves the point. Moreover, today's advanced knitting machines have considerably enlarged the area of the possible. And even in this machine area the past breaks through. For all our modern machines trace their ancestry back to that inventive and ingenious parson Lee who wanted to ease his wife's tasks some 400 years ago (page 54).

Yes, knitting in every sense can be said to be part of the substance of our social history.

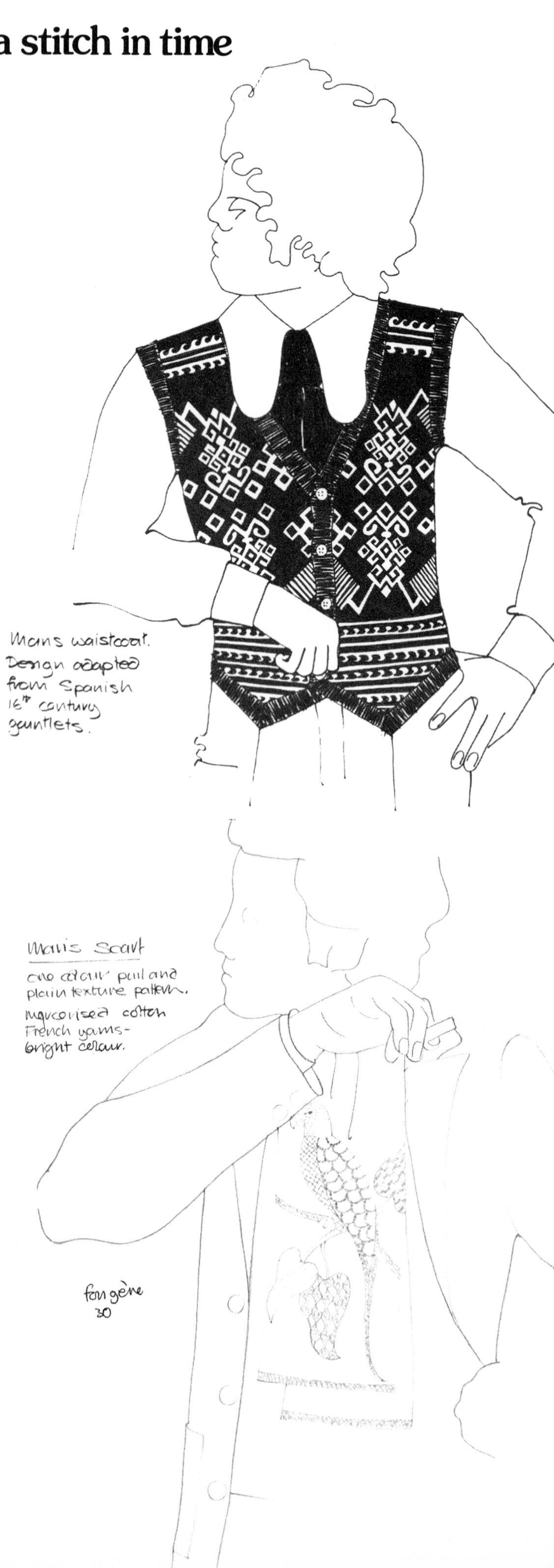

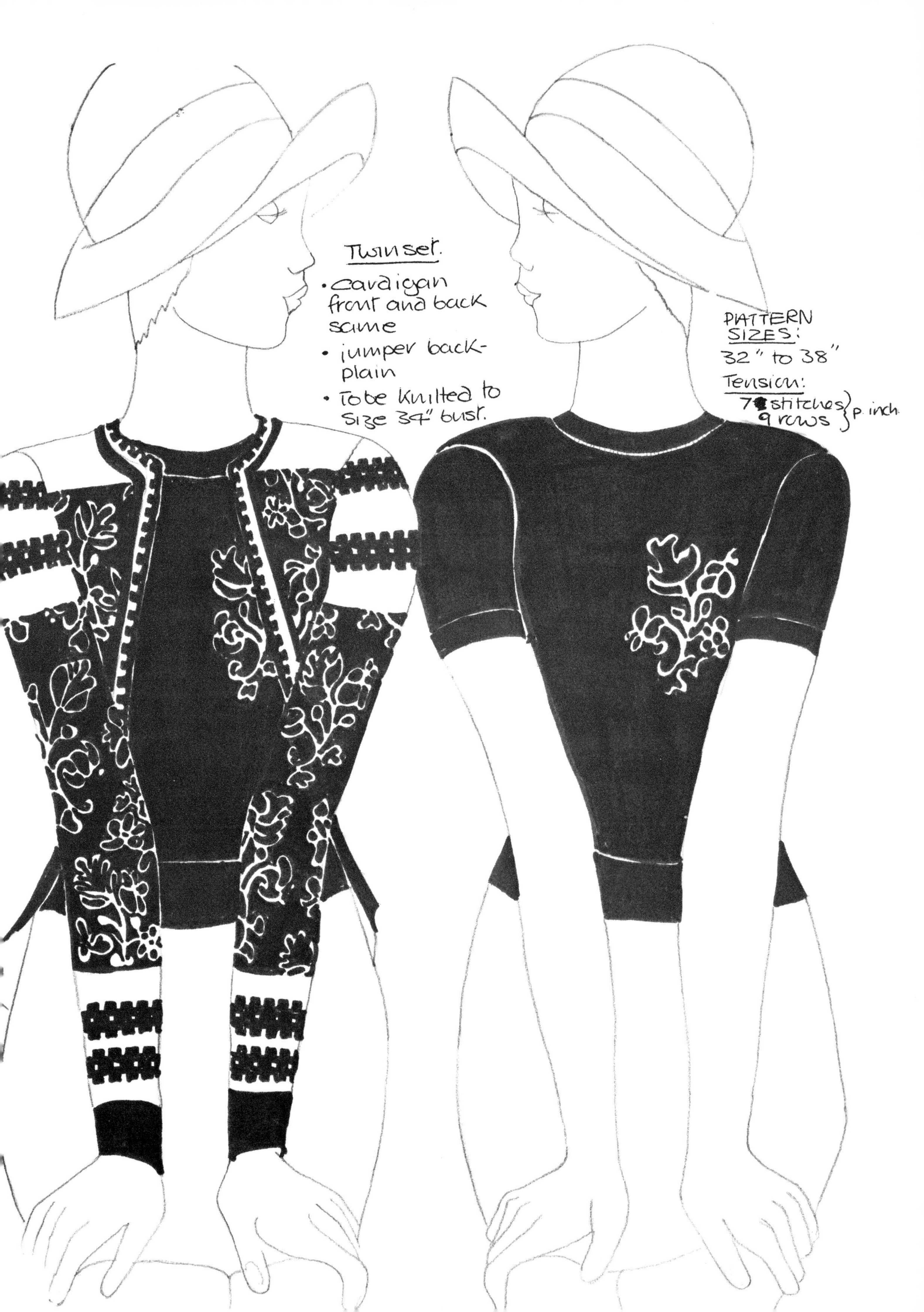
Twinset.
• cardigan front and back same
• jumper back-plain
• To be knitted to size 34" bust.
PATTERN SIZES:
32" to 38"
Tension:
7 stitches
9 rows } p. inch

'NAHYAT,' the story of an ancient craft

Legend has it that even Eve could knit – and that Joseph's famous coat was knitted. But these, of course, are simply folk myths. Nevertheless, the craft or art of knitting has ancient origins. This is the story of that craft throughout the centuries.

The origins of knitting are not known for certain, but from the scant archaeological evidence that exists knitting appears to be a comparatively modern accomplishment between 2000 and 3000 years old. The word "knitting" is derived from a Sanskrit word "Nahyat" meaning net or weave. In Anglo-Saxon it appears as cynttan, knetten, netten, chitten and knotten, each word being used in the context of uniting firmly or interlocking. Tradition suggests that knitting came from the Middle East. In the ancient city of Yemen, known as Shabiva, the city of the Queen of Sheba, the art is said to have been known for ever and that Eve knitted the pattern on the serpent's back.

Some authorities claim that Joseph's coat of many colours was knitted, others that Christ's garment worn at his crucifixion must have been knitted since it was described as being without seams. There is also a tradition that the fishermen who followed the apostle Peter wore knitted caps. Scholars question whether the fabrics mentioned in the *Iliad* and the *Odyssey* were perhaps knitting rather than weaving. In the *Iliad*, Helen wove a mighty web.

"Here, in her palace at her loom she found,
The golden web her own sad story crown'd
The Trojan wars she weaved, herself the prize."

The web was described:

"It shines like fire, was rich and full of size
The work of both sides being alike, in which
She did comprise the many labours warlike
Troy endured."

It has been suggested that such a complex work would require a loom too large and cumbersome for a queen to use but that she could have done it on a peg knitting frame.

The story in the *Odyssey* says that Penelope wove a web during the day which she then unravelled at night. Had she in fact been weaving she would have had very little sleep, for unravelling a woven fabric is a long job. Knitting on the other hand unravels all too easily.

It is unlikely that the truth of such legends will ever be known but the fact that such stories exist adds mystery to the story of knitting. The Greeks of the

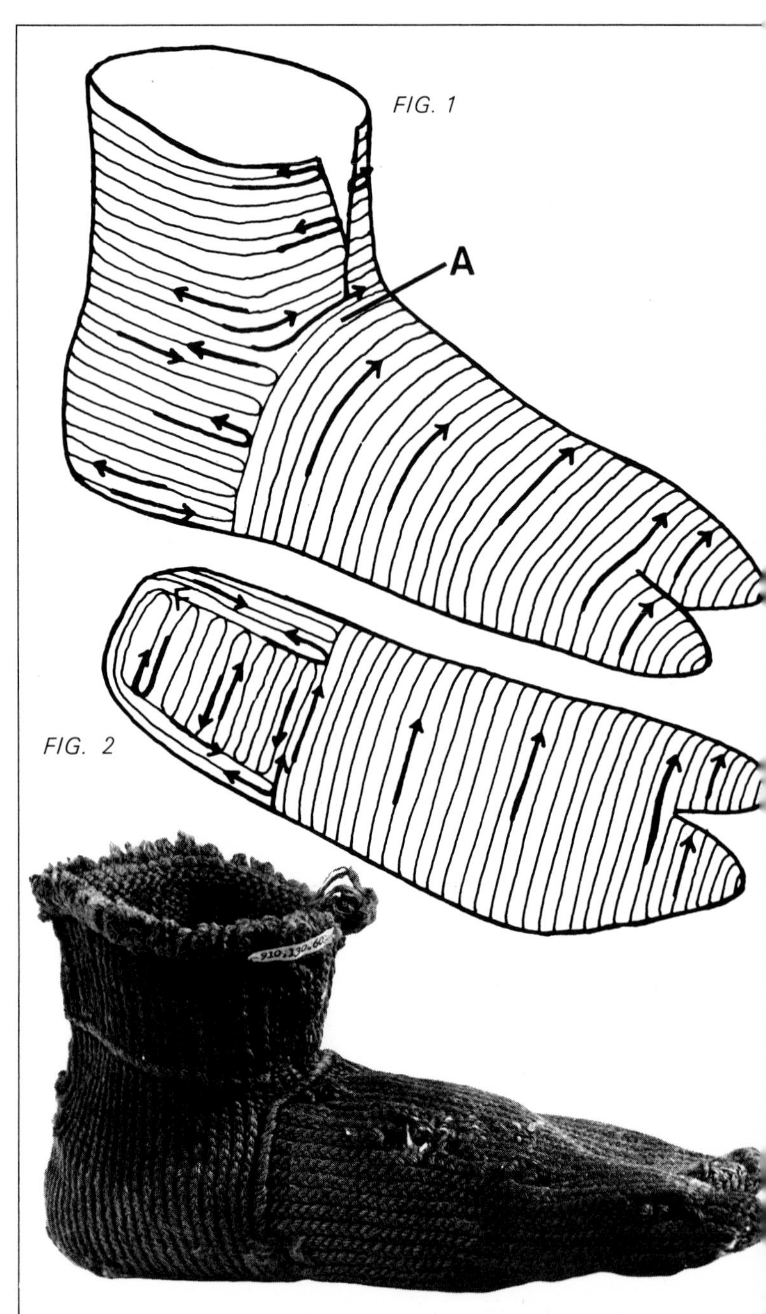

These diagrams show the techniques used to produce the typical Coptic knitted sock. The end product is shown immediately above and the stages in its creation are indicated in the two diagrams. The foot was gradually shaped until the point where it was divided to make one section for the big toe and another for the remaining toes. These were knitted separately, both in the round.

RIGHT: An alternative Coptic technique which used only a single needle. Its great advantage was that "laddering" did not occur.

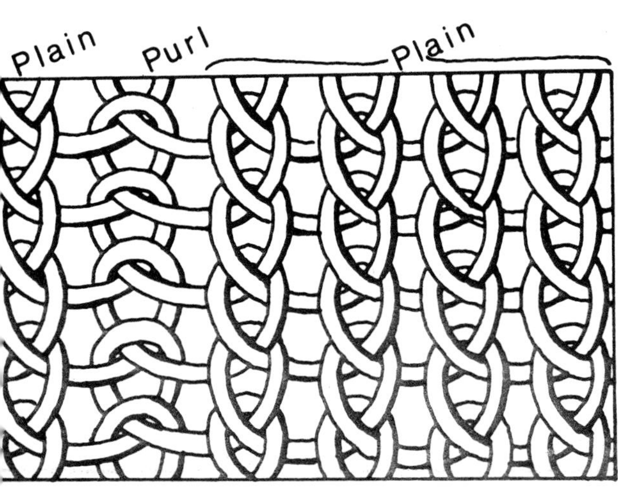

Relics from the dawn of knitting – these knitted objects are believed to have been produced by the Christian sect known as the Copts. The doll is particularly interesting since it shows the widespread popularity of knitting as a household craft in those early times. The doll's cap is seen at the top of the picture, the small bag is below it and the striped sock is at the bottom on the right. The socks are not unlike mittens in the sense that they have a separate big toe.

period, and later the Romans, were certainly skilful weavers and were capable of mastering the art, but it is not until a later date, 1000 BC, that the first knitted type of structure – Sprang – appeared, and in countries as far apart as Egypt and Scandinavia.

The Middle East

Sprang was made in two different ways. In one method a blunt needle and yarn were used to make a chain up a set of warp threads, interlacing the stitch of the chain from the previous warp thread. When the area was completely covered the warp was removed. This method was called "needle sprang". The alternative technique was called "plaited sprang". In this, a chain was made using a continuous thread which was wrapped back and forth on a frame. These threads were then twisted or plaited round each other, starting in the middle, and as each row was completed it was pushed to the top or bottom of the frame and held in position by a stick threaded through the warp, while the next row was plaited. There were several quite elaborate variants to the basic twist.

The major evidence of knitting in the Middle East comes from Egypt, where several knitted garments dated between the 4th and 5th centuries have been discovered at Bahnasa. These, it is believed, were knitted by a Christian sect known as the Copts. Among the items were a doll's cap, a pair of child's socks in blue and white stripes, a small bag and several pairs of sandal socks. These socks have a separate piece for the big toe, rather like a mitten with a separate thumb piece enabling thonged sandals to be worn in comfort. During the second half of the 19th century, Doctor Jaeger of Munich revived the sandal sock as part of his "healthy" clothing campaign. His "health-socks", however, had five little pockets, one for each toe.

This collection from Bahnasa represents a well established technique. Whether it was real knitting has recently been contested. It was previously thought that the sock was knitted from the top down on two needles to the end of the opening and then in the round to the instep where stitches were cast off for the top of the foot. The remainder were knitted still on two needles backwards and forwards to form the back and sides of the heel. When the bottom of the heel was reached, the stitches were divided into three and the central group continued to form the under-heel, picking up the side sections in progress. All the stitches around A in figure 1 (Page 10) plus those previously cast off for the top of the foot were all picked up and

Loop knitting frame

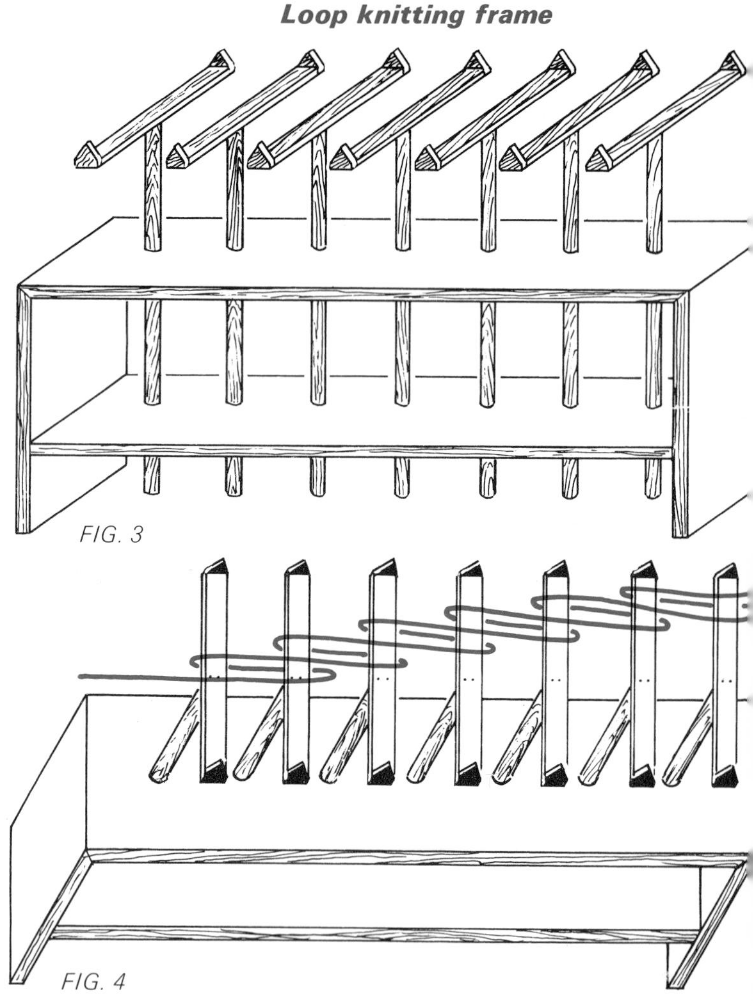

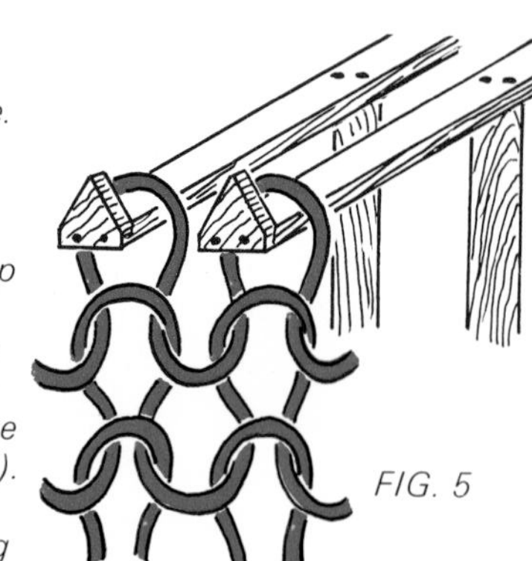

One rather complex frame was known as the loop knitting frame. This consisted of two planks of wood set apart, rather like a modern shelf unit. Narrow strips of wood were attached to the top of rods piercing the unit and these strips had triangular blocks set at each end (Fig. 3). Casting on was achieved by wrapping the yarn around the top strips (Fig 4). The yarn was then taken across the T-shape and the first winding was looped off the end, over the triangles to form the stitch (Fig. 5).

In the early ring frame the first stitches were cast on by winding the yarn around each peg in turn until the first peg was reached again (Fig. 6). Fig. 7 shows the winding for casting on and for close stitch. Fig. 8 shows the winding for casting on a 1×1 rib. Fig. 9 shows the winding for a 1×1 rib. Fig. 10 shows the winding for casting on a 2×2 rib. Fig. 11 shows the winding for a 2×2 rib.

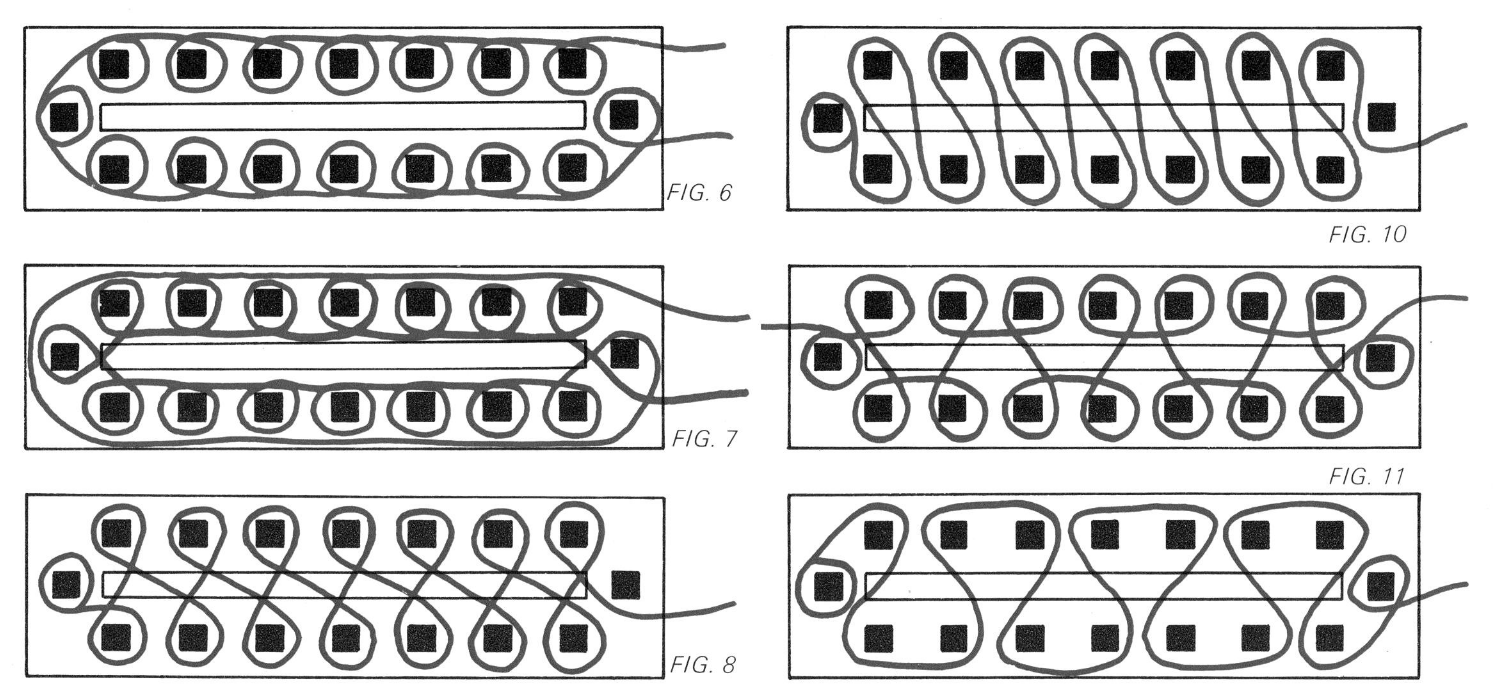

the knitting began in the round again. The foot was shaped gradually until the point where it split in two, one section for the big toe and the other for the remaining toes. These were knitted separately, both in the round.

More recently an alternative technique was used which started at the toes and progressed up the foot to the heel. The method is represented by figure 2 (Page 10) which, like sprang, used only a single needle. True knitting would, in fact be faster than this method but the major advantage of this single needle technique is that there was no laddering, rather like the modern non-run tights.

The next recorded knitting examples were also found in Egypt, this time at Fostat. These tiny fragments – probably of socks – are dated about the 10th century and there are also some more dated about the 12th century. An interesting feature of these pieces is that they are knitted with bands in geometric designs in two or more colours. The vogue for this coloured knitting seems to have been popular in the East and these patterns form the basis of almost all types of folk knitting.

It is very difficult to trace when and exactly how the craft of knitting spread from the Middle East to other countries. It appears to have spread first towards Syria and Persia and possibly from there to Afghanistan and Tibet. Apart from the north coast there is no trace of knitting in any other part of Africa.

In 1272, while travelling in the East, Marco Polo visited the monastery of Barsarno near Tabrey in Persia. Here the monks knitted woollen girdles as part of their work. These were blessed and were said to have magical powers which relieved body pains in their wearers. When the monks went begging for alms the girdles were presented to the peasants and landowners.

The spread of knitting to Europe is assumed to have taken two forms. The most popular theory is that the Arabs, after conquering Egypt and most of North Africa, learned the art from the native Mohammedans and Christian Copts and took the skill with them right across North Africa until their conquest of Spain in the 8th century. Alternatively, the craft might have spread through the Copts themselves who probably sent missionaries to convert the pagan lords of Europe to Christianity. There is some evidence that knitting was done in various religious settlements in Europe at a later date. The truth probably lies in a combination of these two theories.

Tools and Implements

Like the origins of knitting, the earliest implements used for the craft are unknown. The logical assumption is that a form of knitting was first worked on the fingers of one hand. The yarn could have been wound in and out of the fingers so that three threads were on each. The bottom thread was then taken over the top

'NAHYAT,' the story of an ancient craft

of the other two and off the finger. The Red Indians of Canada were supposed to have used five sticks in the same way to construct a mesh.

A later method that was certainly practised for a long time in Europe used a frame. These were variously known as Ring, Box, Bung, Spool, Reel or Peg frames. The straight variety was made of an oblong block of wood with an oblong hole cut in the centre through which the work fell as it was fabricated. Wooden or bone pegs were fitted into the wood around the edge of this opening. The pegs were regular in height and size and were equally spaced. For coarse work they were large, strong and set far apart, whereas for finer work the pegs were thin and set close together. The same principle was used to make circular frames, commonly known as "Cap" or "Ring" frames. Here the pegs were set at the edge of a round opening in a block of wood. The ring frames were mainly used to knit tubular fabric, for making such articles as scarves, caps, stockings and silk cords such as the monks used for girdles. The tasselled caps worn by French revolutionaries were reputedly made on such frames. The Egyptian fez and the French beret were probably also made by this method and the fabrics felted, so that they became unrecognizable as knitting.

Ring frames fell into disuse by the mid-19th century and their only surviving descendant is the little "bobinette" that children are still occasionally given. Frames were worked on the same principle as the bobinette or the five sticks of the Indians (see diagrams on Page 13). The first stitches were cast on by winding the yarn around each peg in turn until the first peg was reached again. The way the second winding was made decided the type of stitch and pattern. For plain, close knit fabric, the yarn was laid round the outside of the pegs and the first winding was slipped over the top, using a hooked needle. For loose, open, fabric the second winding was wrapped round the pegs in the same way as when casting on (figure 6). Figures 8, 9, 10 and 11 (Page 13) show how a one-by-one rib or a two-by-two rib is constructed. Vertical stripes can be produced by winding alternate pegs with one colour then the other pegs with a second and third colour. The width of the stripes is determined by the number of adjacent pegs wound in any one colour. Horizontal stripes are achieved simply by varying the colour of each winding. An open fabric is made by missing certain pegs in the sequence. Casting off is done on the same principle as in normal hand knitting, that is by transferring one stitch to the next peg, etc.

This Russian peasant doll is particularly interesting. It consists of small patches of knitting and crochet in brightly coloured wools and silks and is trimmed with tatting and embroidery. This is a traditional toy. The knitting of the face is most ingenious. Increasings each side of the centre four stitches form the chin and give shape to the cheeks and then the same four stitches are purled to suggest the nose.

RIGHT: A rare picture of knitting in practice – in this case an abbey altar piece known as "The Visit of the Angels", painted between 1390 and 1400. The knitter, of course, is the Virgin Mary which makes the picture all the more appealing. She is using four needles to pick up stitches at the neck of a vest.

'NAHYAT,' the story of an ancient craft

Another, more complex, frame is the "loop knitting frame". This consists of two planks of wood set apart as in a modern shelf unit. Each plank has a row of holes along its length, exactly parallel to one another and through these are placed rods about 12ins. (30·5cm.) high. At the top of each rod is a narrow strip of wood, with triangular blocks set at each end (figure 3). Casting on is done by wrapping yarn round the strips of wood (figure 4, Page 12). The yarn is then taken straight across the top of the "T" shape and the first winding is looped off the end over the triangles to form the stitch (figure 5). Depending on whether it is looped backwards or to the front a plain or purl fabric is produced. If the stitch on alternate rods is looped back and the rest to the front then a one-by-one rib is produced. The knitted loops are formed round the upright rods and when sufficient work has built up the rods are removed from their holes to release it and then put back in again. If the yarn is placed near the edge of the "T" shape a small stitch is formed, whereas if it is placed in the centre near the upright rods a big stitch is formed. This frame is complicated in operation and was probably not in common use.

The implements used to manipulate the loops were hooked needles and the first straight knitting needles also had hooks at one end. It is probable that all the pieces of early knitting were made with this type of needle. The Arabs probably made them from wood, bone, briar or copper wire.

Hooked needles are still used in countries such as Bolivia, where Spanish influence is strong. The tradition for making hooked needles from whatever material is available appears to continue, for it is said that the knitting shepherds of Landes in the South of France use old umbrella ribs, five to a set, to make their hooked needles. There is no evidence that the hooked needle was ever used in England apart from the type used for Afghan knitting.

There are basically only two stitches in knitting – the plain or knit stitch and the purl stitch. When the plain stitch is used throughout on straight knitting this is called garter stitch, but when used throughout on circular knitting where the work is not turned and turned about, it has a different result, which is called stocking or stockinette stitch.

The basic method of knitting in the Middle East differed slightly from that now in use in Europe. In the east the yarn was wrapped around the needle in a different direction depending whether it was a purl stitch or a knit stitch. This would have been easy using

Knitting sheaths, once commonly used in the Border counties of England and Scotland. These knitting sheaths and sticks had a hole at one end in which to place one of the needles when knitting. The sheath was kept in position on the right side of the user by being slipped into the waistband or passed twice round the apron string. They were often carved by village boys as presents to their sweethearts. The chip carving was mostly done with a pocket knife. Some were inlaid with ivory, metal or mother-of-pearl. They were made in many different shapes and sizes, according to the whim or taste of the maker. Scimitar shaped sheaths were the earliest forms. The heart-shaped varieties were usually fastened upon cloth with edges broad enough to pin to the dress.

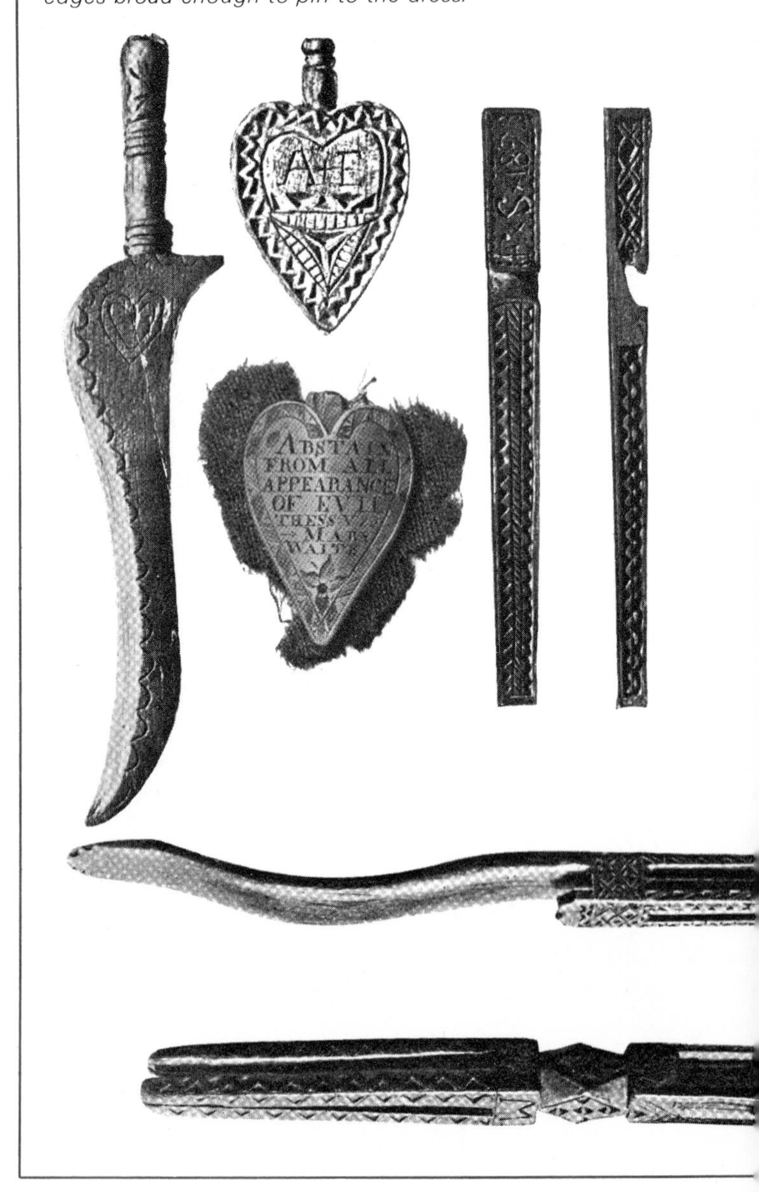

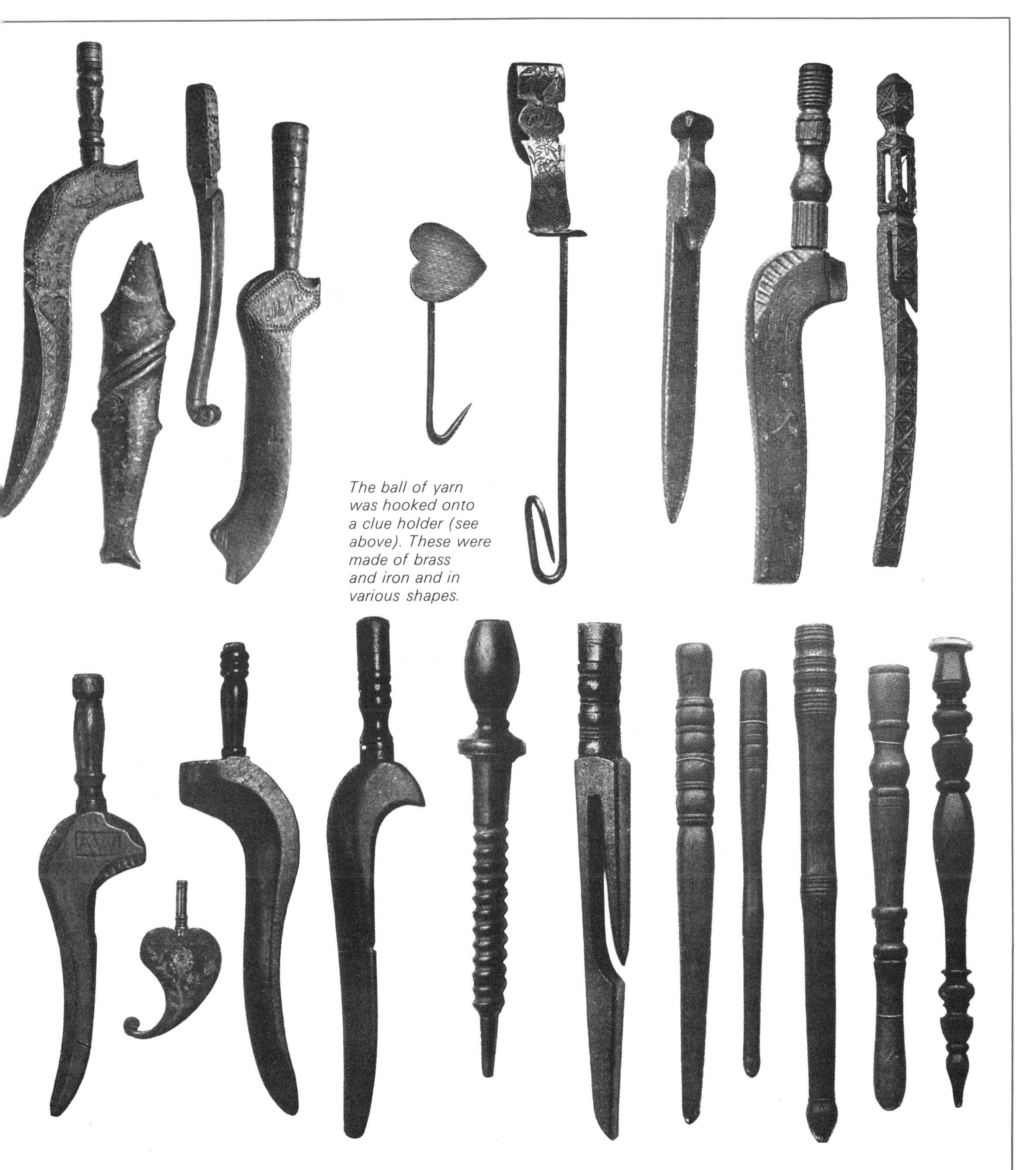

The ball of yarn was hooked onto a clue holder (see above). These were made of brass and iron and in various shapes.

hook needles. A very popular structure in early knitting was the crossed stitch. This made a close fabric with a slightly different texture. The combination of the Eastern and European knit stitch is found in the folk knitting of the Balkan states of the U.S.S.R.

The straight knitting needle with points at either one or both ends was probably a European invention. In one of the very few pictorial representations of knitting, the 14th-century painting of the "Visit of the Angels" taken from the Buxtehude altar-piece, this type of knitting needle is seen being used by the Virgin Mary (page 15).

Knitting needles have been made from a multitude of materials – wood, briar, bone, bamboo, copper wire, iron, amber, tortoiseshell, steel, nickel-plated steel, lacquered aluminium and, latterly, various types of plastic – and stiff or flexible according to the knitter's preference. Although more comfortable to use, flexible needles have to be handled very lightly to get an even fabric. The really fast, highly skilled, knitter nearly always used a rigid needle, essential when using a knitting "sheath" (see previous page).

These sheaths also seem to be European in origin. They contribute greatly to the speed and evenness of work. A longer sheath was known as a knitting stick, the sheath or stick being stuck into a belt. Some were made scimitar shape to fit round the body comfortably. A hole was bored in the centre of the narrow end of the sheath and the knitting needle was balanced in this hole. This left the right hand free to work the yarn and stitches up to the point of the needle and back with great speed. Knitting sticks were often carved and decorated with mottos, initials and motifs such as fish, dolphins, love-hearts and flowers.

Some sheaths had chains attached to the wider end, with a hook at the end of the chain. The chain went round to the back of the body and the hook was attached to the end of the knitting. This not only kept the work under tension, thus also helping the speed, but it meant that the actual knitting could be dropped at any moment and would not fall to the ground but would dangle from the waist.

The Great Schools – Spain and Italy

Sometime before the 9th century knitting appears to have been introduced into Spain by the Moors, and then to isolated religious settlements by missionaries. The spread across the rest of Europe was slow but steady.

There is a 13th-century written reference that Pope Innocent IV was clothed in knitted gloves at his burial in 1254. Such "altar gloves", which had been introduced as part of the church regalia by St Augustine, must have been very elaborate and beautiful to be included in the regalia of the Pope. It is probable that these were imported from Spain which was famous for this type of glove. Another such glove was found in the mid-14th-century tomb of a bishop at the cathedral church of Ross. Sixteenth-century examples of such knitted gloves are evidence of a well established craft as they are on the whole beautifully made, knitted in silk and gilt thread on fine needles.

An altar glove probably imported from Spain, which was famous for this type of glove. 16th century examples of these knitted gloves show that the craft was well established since they are on the whole beautifully made. Most examples are knitted in silk and gilt thread on fine needles.

Knitted gloves were knitted in the round although the method of knitting the thumb varies. The gauntlet and the hand part and sometimes even the thumb are lined with silk. In some examples the hand is decorated even further with embroidery or lace. From the 15th century, knitted gloves became an important accessory for the rich, as well as church dignitaries, and in many men's portraits from this date they appear being worn or held as a sign of wealth.

This development of fine silk and gilt thread work

'NAHYAT,' the story of an ancient craft

spread to Italy. The Italian jackets of the 17th century represent one of the heights of hand knitting. The garments themselves are not consistent in their standard of make but the ambitious floral patterns of the fabric show great knitting skill. It is likely that the fabric was produced in panels, the pattern always being knitted by the same person. Panels of different designs were bought and put together by tailors or dressmakers to produce waistcoats, jackets and capes. In addition to the colour brocaded look, as seen on the Spanish gloves, a number of pattern pieces were made using purl stitches to form the pattern. This was sometimes outlined afterwards with embroidery.

Skill in French Knitting

It is supposed that knitting spread from Spain to France and a sizeable industry grew up on the fine, highly skilled work which was produced. The French tended to concentrate on stockings using worsted and linen yarns but it was not until the mid 16th century, when silk came into common use, that great knitting skills were developed. Henry II of France wore silk stockings when he married Catherine de Medici in 1533 and this seems to have started a fashion for silk stockings amongst the monarchs of Europe. Henry VIII of England certainly had some imported from France. After 1560 the French courtiers began to wear silk stockings and the trade in both silk and worsted stockings was founded in Paris on August 16th 1527. This was the biggest of many guilds of hand knitters which were to develop all over Europe. Eventually the invention of the knitting machine destroyed the trade in France as it did in England. Hand knitting survived only at the domestic fireside or in the folk traditions of the remoter regions.

From Spain the craft also spread to Holland, Austria, Germany and Switzerland.

Germany and Austria

In Germany, knitting thrived, again introduced by the religious orders. In the abbey altar piece entitled "The Visit of the Angels", mentioned before, the Virgin Mary is shown knitting using four needles to pick up stitches at the neck of a simple vest or overshirt. It is possible that the nuns and monks of the abbey were well-known for their knitting and that this was the reason for the Virgin being shown at such an unusual occupation.

As the skill spread outside the monasteries and convents it developed in a very different form from that of the southern European countries. Whereas Italy became associated with knitted jackets, Spain with gloves and hose and France with fine, fancy stockings, German and Austrian knitters were known for a heavier, coarser type of knitting, always in wool and sometimes embroidered in bright colours. However, it is for the magnificent knitted carpets which were used as wall hangings that Germany and Austria are famous.

There were two distinct styles from different districts. The carpets from Silesia had a floral border with a text surrounding a central panel of figures and landscapes, usually with a religious theme. These carpets were sometimes felted. The carpets of the upper Rhine and Alsace were square and floral and often included the double-headed eagle of the Hapsburgs, who granted the charters of the guilds in the area.

The German knitting guilds were numerous and influential in raising the standard of work. The conditions of each guild varied but the general rule was that a boy was apprenticed for up to seven years. Three years were spent with a master, three more travelling and gaining experience. In the seventh year the apprentice demonstrated his skill by producing, in only thirteen weeks, a beret, a shirt, a pair of stockings with Spanish clocks at the ankle, a cap and, most important of all, a carpet, the design of which was to contain flowers, foliage, birds and animals. The carpet was made in one piece, probably on a peg-frame.

It is thought that the art of knitting was taken from Holland to Scandinavia in the early 16th century by a Dutch family who went to live near Copenhagen at the request of the King of Denmark, who liked knitted stockings.

Knitting for the Russian army

Felted knitted caps from Holland were also found in the wardrobe of Peter I of Russia and a hand knitting trade developed round Moscow. Silk stockings and gloves, very similar in design to those of Spain, were made by the Russian knitters but were inferior in quality. They also produced "klobuki" – a type of hood worn by the priests. This tied under the chin and was often embroidered with a bird with a human face, representing the Holy Spirit. The Russian knitters also produced sword sashes for the army. These were worn over the soldiers' tunics either round the waist or over the shoulder, like a "Sam Brown" belt. They were made in strong thread in an elastic structure and doubled as stretchers for moving the wounded in battle.

Knitting spreads to England

The precise date when knitting was introduced into England is unknown. The first written reference, dated between 1452–56, appears in the accounts of the Chapter of the Collegiate Church of Saints Peter and Wilfred in Ripon, Yorkshire, where "One knyt gyrdll" is mentioned.

Garments were knitted but especially popular were knitted caps. The knitted fabric was soaked in dye for about five days to thicken it. It was then blocked into shape and brushed with a teasel. After this process the fabric could be cut without unravelling and was durable and waterproof. In 1488 Henry VII passed a Sumptuary Law fixing the price of such hats at one shilling and eight pence while that of "knytted woollen caps be two shillings". By Henry VIII's reign these hats were even more popular.

By 1552, the hand knitting industry had taken shape and recognized centres had begun to appear in Leicester and Nottingham, the counties of Surrey, Yorkshire, Norfolk and throughout Scotland. A law of this time mentions "knitte hose, knitte petticoats, knitte gloves, knitte slieves". There was a growing interest in everything connected with clothes during this period, instigated by Queen Elizabeth I, whose enormous vanity gave her an insatiable interest in personal adornment. Knitting schools were officially set up by the parish councils, to train the poor, giving them a means of making a livelihood. When Queen Elizabeth visited Norwich in 1579, children were brought before her, some of whom had been taught to spin worsted yarn, others to knit hose. The Norwich Court Book of 1630 states that a Knitting School dame was to be provided for every Parish "to sitte poore children and other poore to work".

The Queen's Stockings

In the third year of her reign Elizabeth's silk woman, Mrs Montague, gave her a pair of hand-knit silk stockings. The story of these stockings and their reception by the Queen was quaintly told in a pamphlet published some years later by a John Alexandre, a printer and machine knitter. The Queen apparently received the gift in the presence of her leading statesman, Lord Burleigh, and her favourite suitor, the Earl of Leicester. She was surprised that something so fine and delicate could be worn. When asked his opinion, Leicester replied "My gracious Majesty is all beautiful; in fact a fairy queen wanting but this gossamer wear to perfect fairy attire". Burleigh's comment was that cloth hose was good enough and that if Elizabeth took to silk hose she would upset the cloth hose trade and encourage extravagant dressing. He also thought that it was impossible for a human leg to get into such a narrow fragile thing! Goaded, the Queen tried on the stockings and pronounced "Gentlemen, the silk stockings fit me right well and I like them much, because they are pleasant, fine and delicate; and henceforth I will wear no more cloth stockings".

Ultimately, the Queen's preference for fine hose did bring about the end of the cloth stocking trade. Philip Stubb's "The Anatomy of Abuses", published in 1583 states, "Then have they nether stock in these gay hosen, (not of clothe, though everso fine, for that is thought too base) but of jarnsey worsted, silk-thread and the like, so curiously knit with open seams down the leg, with quirks and clocks above the ankles and sometimes haply laced with gold and silver thread as is beautiful to behold. And so much insolence and outrage is not given, everyone (almost) though otherwise verie poor, having scarce fortie shillings of wages by the yeare will sure to have 2 or 3 paire of these silk nether stocks, or else of the finest yarn that may be got, though the price of these be a Royal, or twentie shillings, as commonly it is! For how can they be less when the very knitting is worth a noble, or a Royal or much more. The time hath been when one might have clothed his body well, from top to toe for less than a paire of nether stocks."

The knitting trade provided a great deal of work especially in the towns and villages around London. To help the trade, Queen Elizabeth passed Sumptuary Laws to create demand which in turn created work for her subjects. In 1565 a law decreed that "No person shall make or cause to be made any cap or any other thing of felt, but only hats. Nor shall they make any cap of woollen cloth not knitte." Another law stated "Every person above the age of 7 shall wear upon the Sabbath or holyday (unless in the time of their travel out of town) upon their head a cap of wool knitted, thickened and dressed in England."

Continued on P.24 ▶

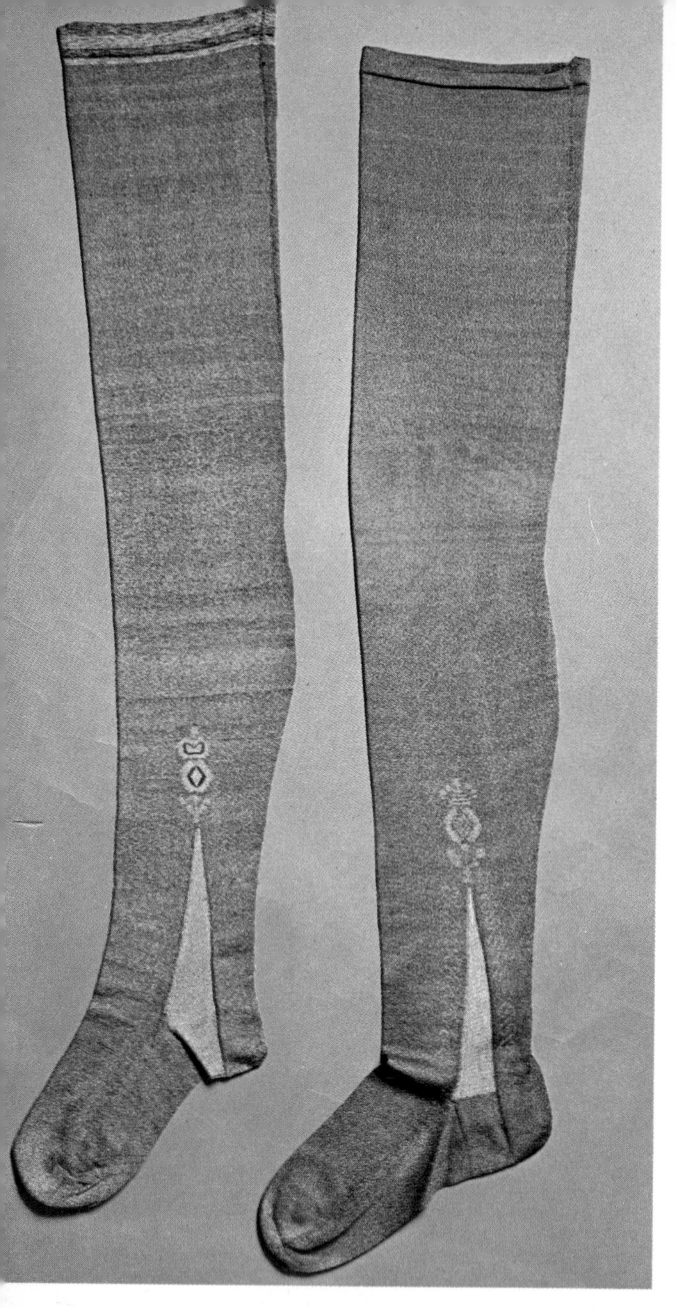

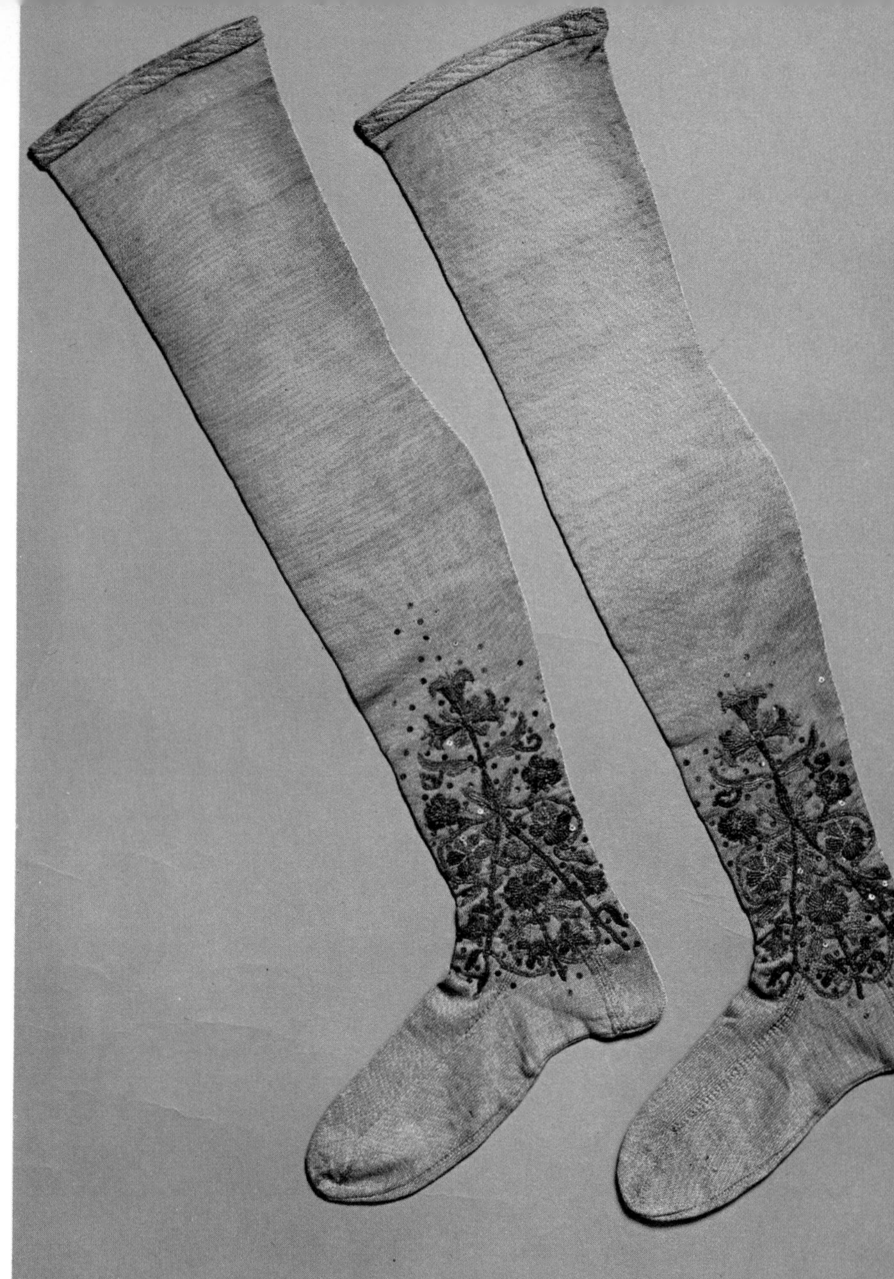

An early example of machine-made stockings (above left). This sort of knitwear was produced by machines similar to the first machine invented by Parson Lee in 1589. These boy's stockings are knitted in silk and have embroidered clocks. They date from c. 1600–25.

An example of the finely worked stockings (above right) worn at Court in the 17th century. These stockings have an English-style foot and are beautifully embroidered with silver gilt and gold thread. They were almost certainly made in London or at any rate not far from the capital.

This Tudor knitted cap (right) is typical of the types of hats worn in Holbein's picture of "The Ambassadors". However, the hats in the Holbein painting may be of cloth.

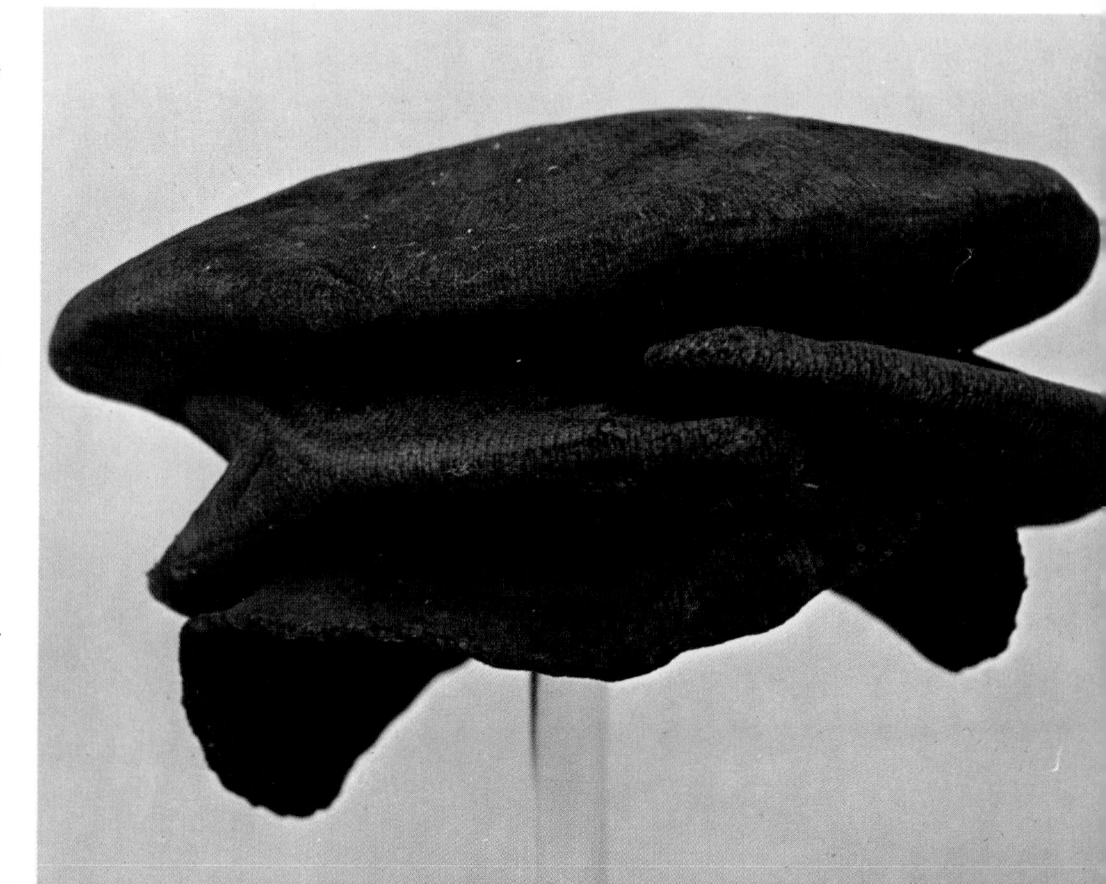

'NAHYAT,' the story of an ancient craft

◀ Continued from P.21

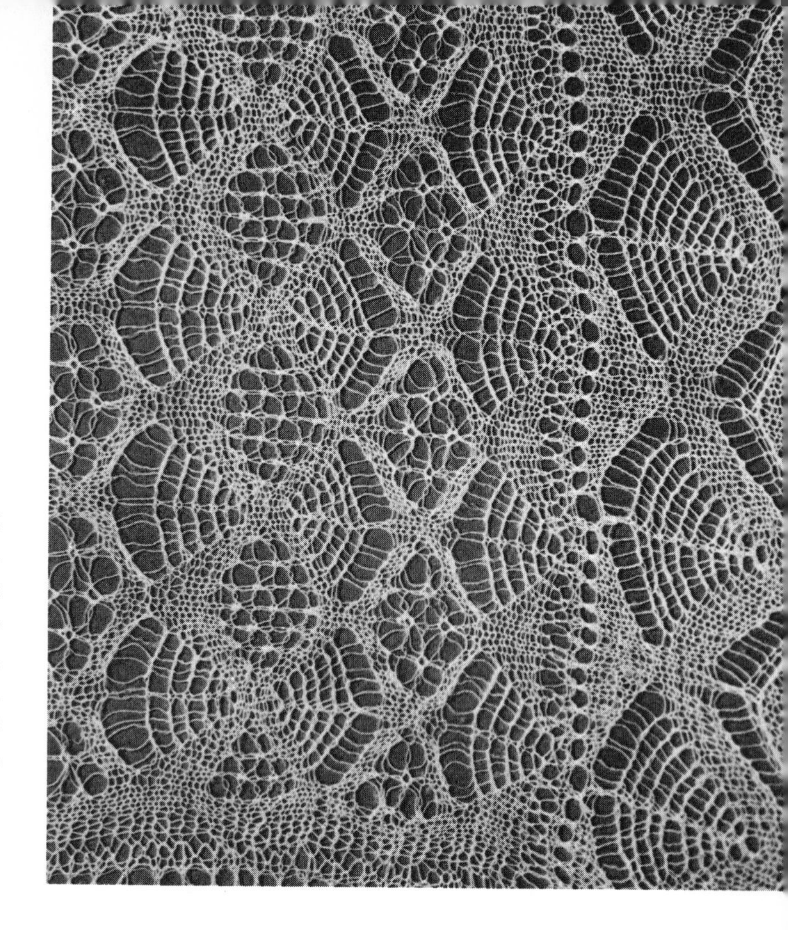

Knitting machines – and the decline of hand knitting

In 1589, when English hand knitting had still not reached its full potential in skill or production, William Lee invented his knitting machine in a small village outside Nottingham. Unlike other European countries, England had not had time to develop its own traditions in knitting design. This, and the rapid development of Lee's machine, meant that within 100 years the English hand knitting trade was to come to an end.

Three or four centres did manage to survive beyond the end of the 17th century. These were in Scotland, Ireland, Yorkshire and North Wales. In these places men and women, both young and old, knitted whenever they were doing things that did not require the use of their hands. There is the story of a woman from the Yorkshire Dales in 1814, "who was accustomed regularly to walk to market at Hawes, a distance of 3 miles, with the weekly knitting of herself and her family packed in a bag on her head, knitting all the way. She continued her knitting, purchasing the little necessities for her family, with the addition of worsted yarn for the work of the ensuing week, all of which she placed on her head, returning, occupied with her needles as before. She was so expeditious and expert, that the produce of the day's labour was probably a pair of men's stockings".

The average knitter could produce two pairs a week which during the 17th century sold for £2 0s. 0d. a pair. Everybody knitted, "even lovers went courting with their knitting and it was well understood that no matter what their shortcomings in housewifery and husbandry, if both were expert knitters, they would do alright and get on in the world". Yorkshire's "Golden Age" in knitting was from 1700 to 1850 but after, demand dwindled and the art died.

In North Wales knitting was centred around Bala in Merionethshire. Knitted gloves, wigs, socks, caps and stockings were produced and the finished goods were taken to Bala market where, around 1750, about £200 worth of knitted goods was handled each week. Sometimes, instead of taking their goods to market, knitters would wait by the side of the stage coach route hoping for a sale. However, in the 19th century the new railway brought machine made goods into the area and the hand knitting trade died.

Although hand knitting as an industry languished in Wales, it fared a good deal better in the coastal areas

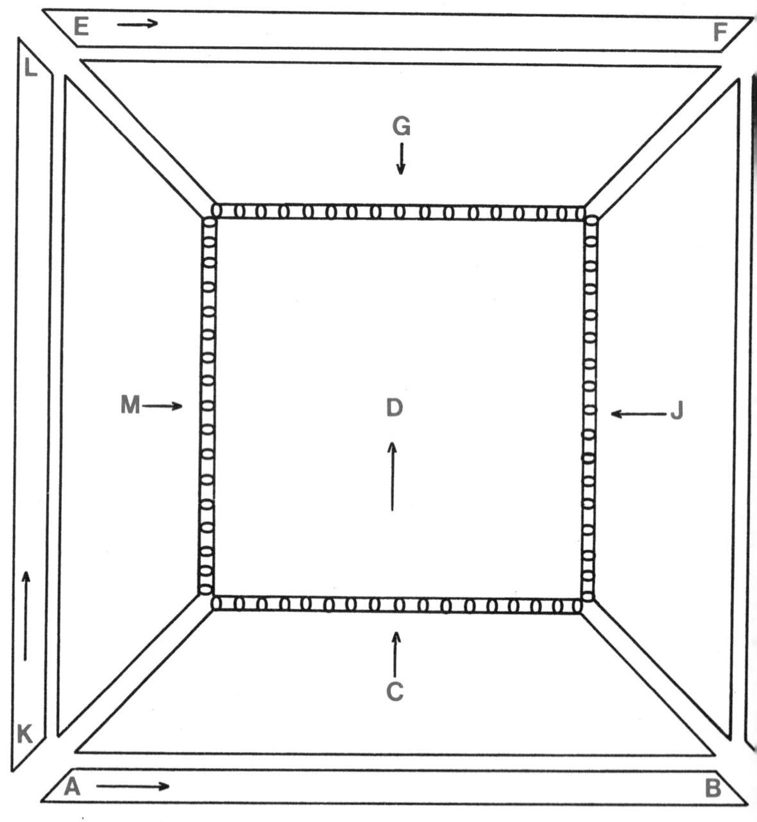

of England, Scotland and Ireland, possibly because over many years the knitters had developed their own specific types of designs and these became part of true folk tradition. In addition to this folk element the skill of hand knitting continued in the home but by the 18th century the great schools and guilds were on the decline. Knitting was to become essentially a domestic matter although encouraged in education for girls.

Commercial hand knitting did not develop in the East as it did in Europe. There was almost certainly

trading in knitted goods by the Arabs throughout the Middle East but there is no evidence that the industry was organized to the degree it was in Europe.

As the craft spread through Afghanistan and Tibet it took on a different structure. It became localized so that different patterns became associated with different regions although they each had a certain similarity in that local yarn was used, home-spun from goats' and sheeps' wool. The products were very practical for the climate – thick, felted, thigh-high socks, woollen

Although hand knitting languished in Wales, it secured a firm foothold in the coastal areas of England, Scotland and Ireland. There is a distinctive and characteristic look about island knitting as the Aran pattern above demonstrates. The corner of a Shetland shawl (top left) shows the variety of stitches used and the diagram indicates the various stages in the knitting of a Shetland shawl (see Page 30).

Continued on P.28. ▶

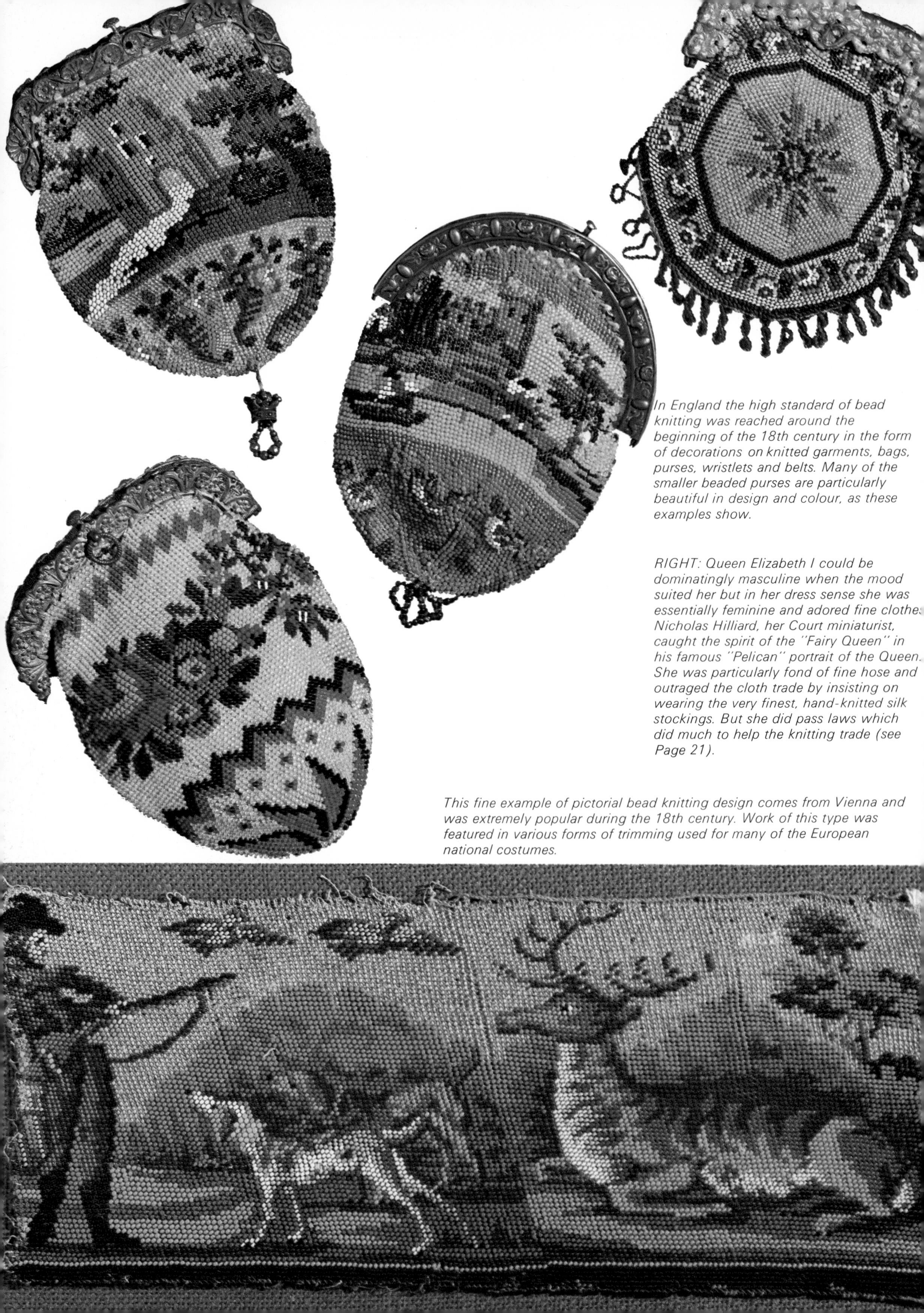

In England the high standard of bead knitting was reached around the beginning of the 18th century in the form of decorations on knitted garments, bags, purses, wristlets and belts. Many of the smaller beaded purses are particularly beautiful in design and colour, as these examples show.

RIGHT: Queen Elizabeth I could be dominatingly masculine when the mood suited her but in her dress sense she was essentially feminine and adored fine clothes. Nicholas Hilliard, her Court miniaturist, caught the spirit of the "Fairy Queen" in his famous "Pelican" portrait of the Queen. She was particularly fond of fine hose and outraged the cloth trade by insisting on wearing the very finest, hand-knitted silk stockings. But she did pass laws which did much to help the knitting trade (see Page 21).

This fine example of pictorial bead knitting design comes from Vienna and was extremely popular during the 18th century. Work of this type was featured in various forms of trimming used for many of the European national costumes.

'NAHYAT,' the story of an ancient craft

◀ Continued from P.25

mittens and warm hoods or hats. These were decorated with various patterns in the same way as the Arab coloured knitting, using natural wool colours, black, grey, brown, cream and white as the basis with some bright colours added. Occasionally garments were made for special celebrations, a wedding or a village feast. These would be very carefully made and lavishly decorated.

Similar garments and patterning also developed in Greece, although the ground colours were often in dark tones and this type of knitting has also been found in various parts of Russia, especially those areas with particularly cold climates. On an archaeological site on the Island of Fadeer in the East Siberian Sea, the remains of a mitten have been found, dating to around the 16th century. Knitting examples of the same period were also found in Latvia, the Komi Republic, the Archangel district, Estonia and the Caucasus.

In Estonia, stockings, gloves, headgear, tunics, shirts and stockings without soles were made using undyed wool with blue patterns. The Caucasians knitted much the same type of thing but also whole costumes and special shoes with heavily felted soles and up-turned toes. A similar type of knitting exists today in Scandinavia. In Finland the patterns are usually in bands with two colours in each, one light, the other dark. Sometimes more than two colours in a row are used as in the illustration of the gauntlet mitten from Inari in Lapland. In this, the balls of different coloured wool have a long knitting needle thrust through them to keep them all in order. The bands of pattern often border areas of birdseye pattern. This is shown in the mitten from East Karelia shown on the opposite page.

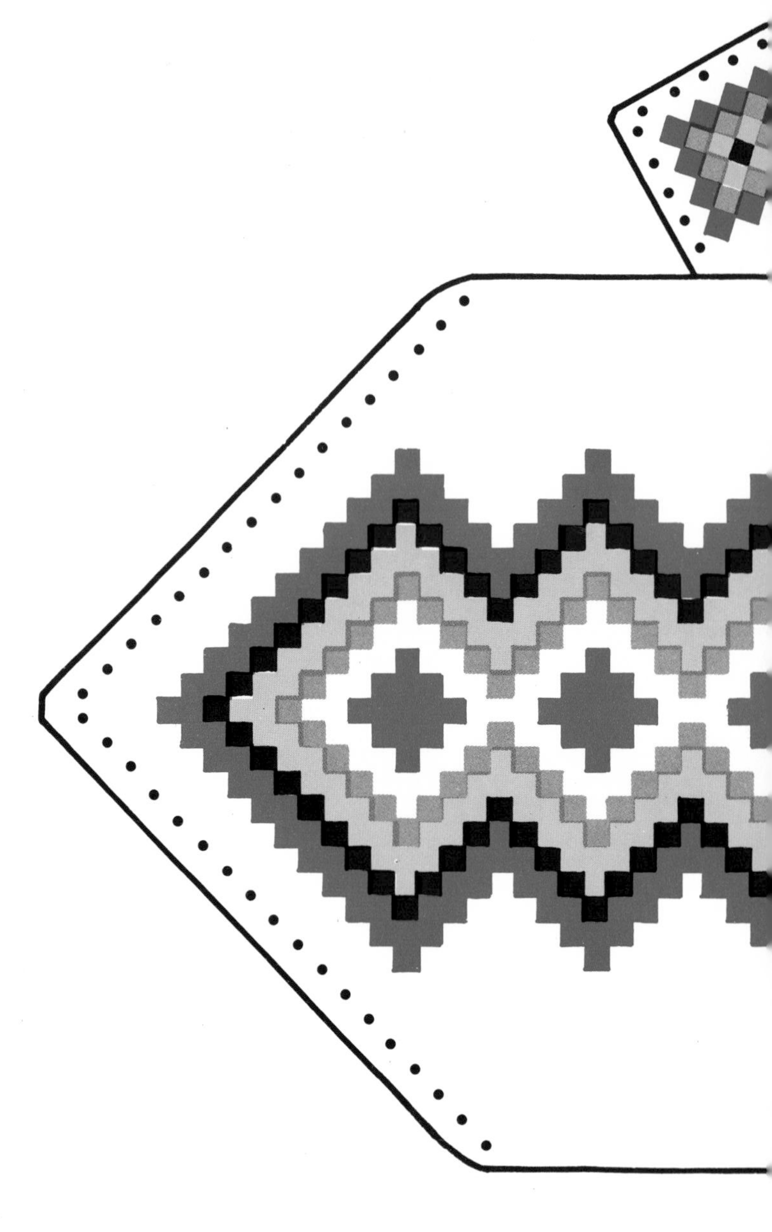

The Story of Fair Isle

How and when knitting reached Karelia are not known but this is not the case with knitting from Fair Isle. It is said that in 1588 one of the Spanish galleons from the defeated Armada fled from the English fleet up the Scottish coast and was wrecked off Fair Isle. The local tradition claims that the islanders copied their knitting patterns from the clothing of the surviving Spanish sailors. The true Fair Isle pattern is based on bands of geometric shapes in two colours to each band. The colours alternate, in one band being the ground, in the next the pattern. There is often a more complicated sequence. For instance:

1st band ground colour 1, pattern colour 2
2nd band ground colour 1, pattern colour 3
3rd band ground colour 4, pattern colour 2
4th band ground colour 4, pattern colour 3
5th band as band No. 1, etc.

The geometric shapes used in Fair Isle patterns show a strong Spanish influence even today and have names such as the Armada Cross, the Star of Life, the Sacred Heart and the Rose of Sharon. This last pattern is formed using four Sacred Hearts.

There is a charming story of a grandmother on Fair Isle knitting a sweater for her grandson, which began at the bottom with patterns called the Water of Life and the Seed of Life, which grew into the Flower of Life; this in turn was followed by the Anchor of Hope and then the Star – to guide him. At the shoulder

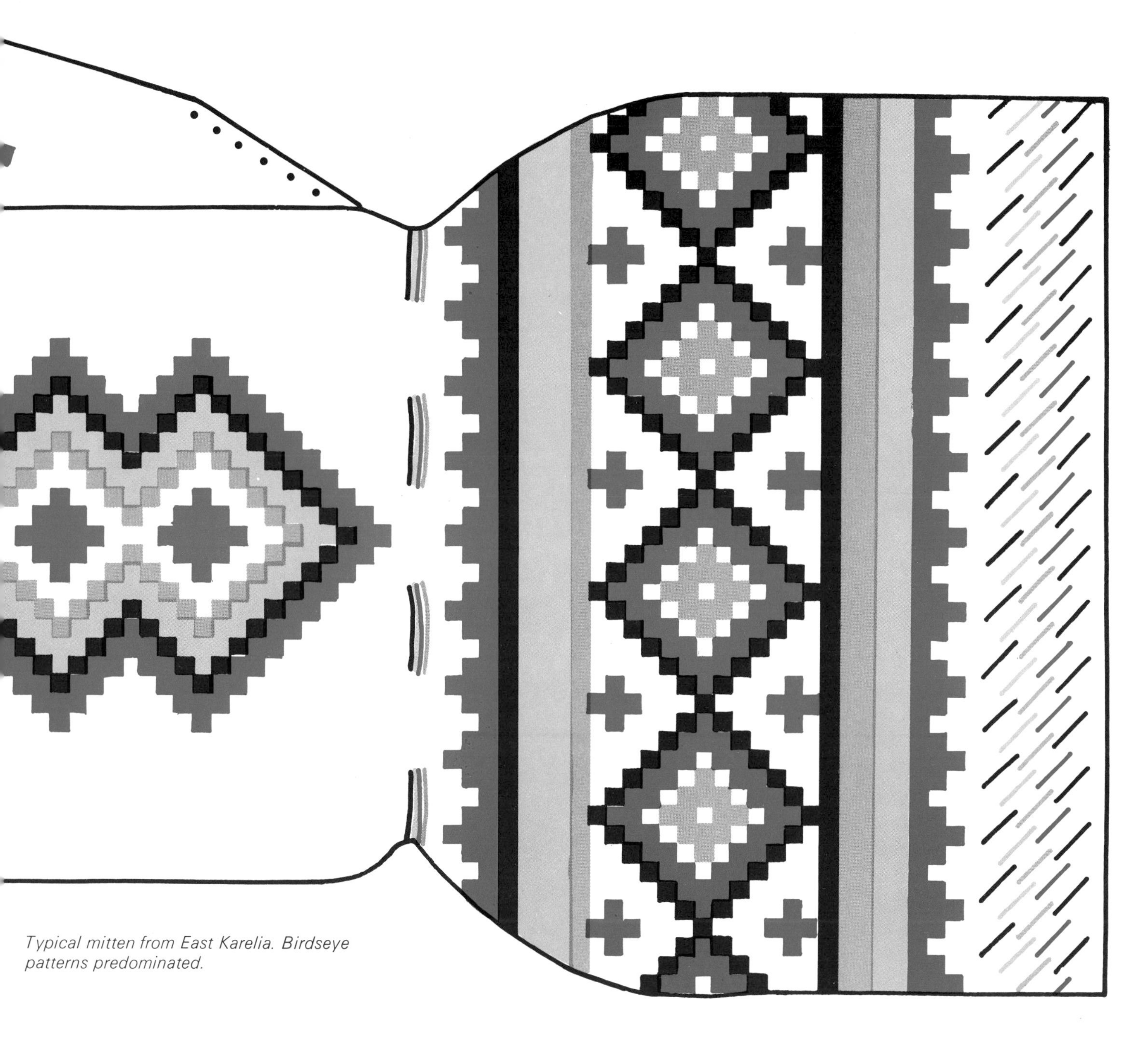

Typical mitten from East Karelia. Birdseye patterns predominated.

she knitted the Crown of Glory, this being the reward for a good life.

Shetland Knitting

In the nearby Shetland Islands the patterns are said to have derived from Scandinavia, for in the 9th and 10th centuries Shetland was settled by immigrants from Norway. Unlike Fair Isle, the traditional Shetland pattern is based on natural colours, undyed white, grey, natural brown and black with the occasional bright colour used to emphasise the design. The traditional Shetland sweater was knitted in the round without side seams, the pattern used only on the yoke, but modern garments often have an all-over pattern. As knitting became more popular it developed from wives producing clothes for their families into an organized commercial production and entire families became involved. Children were given knitting to do for fun from the age of three or four, to help them to build up the rhythm that is so important to a fast knitter. The knitting sheath appears again or, alternatively, an oval pouch stuffed with horse hair was used, tucked into a belt or apron string on the right hip to support the right needle. Sometimes bunches of feathers were worn in the belt and the needle was thrust into them when the knitter had to stop knitting to use his hands for other chores. When the needles were not in use they were wrapped in leather to preserve their smoothness and protect their points.

The genuine Shetland garments were made from Shetland wool, hand carded and spun. This wool was

'NAHYAT,' the story of an ancient craft

unique and the fineness of it was a direct result of the poor grazing on the islands. The Shetlanders "rooed" the wool from their sheep when the fleece was well grown and came away easily at a touch.

Another product from these islands is the fine, spidery Shetland shawl. In the late 18th or early 19th century, when the vogue for lace was growing, fine spidery shawls began to be knitted made of the very finest Shetland wool spun into two ply. The threads are so fine they are scarcely distinguishable and it is said a shawl containing over a million stitches can be drawn through a wedding ring. These "ring shawls" as they came to be known, were knitted on steel wires. In the centre there was usually a square in garter stitch with borders worked in one of a variety of traditional patterns. The best known are: Ears o' Grain, Cat's Paw, Print o' Waves, Bird's Eye, Fern, Fir Cone, Acre or Plough, Old Shale, Horse Shoe, Spout or Ray or Shell. A ring shawl was knitted in a very interesting way (Page 24). Work started at point A and the lacey edging was knitted along to point B. The long edge of this was picked up and border C was knitted, decreasing as it went. A line of holes was knitted before section D was commenced. When this was completed the lace edging for the opposite border was begun at E, and the same sequence as before was followed until the border was complete. The same procedure was followed for the other two borders. All three borders were then attached to the main square making a line of holes as between C and D.

The sides of these borders were then grafted to each other by knitting a stitch from each together. When finished the shawl was washed and dried to shape, pegged out on a board with nails round the edge. This made the scalloped edge.

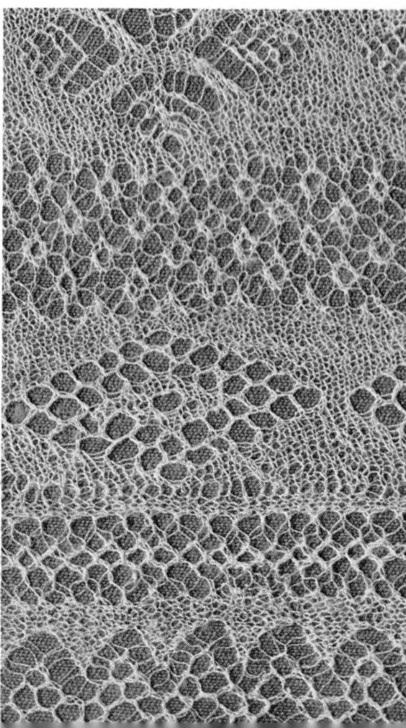

A fine example of a baby's robe knitted in a typical Shetland pattern. Our enlargement shows details of the patterns used. RIGHT: St. Daniel in his winter outfit. It has been suggested that the saint, in this small illumination from the 9th-century Book of Kells, is wearing Aran knitted stockings and a Bainin sweater. Whether this is so or not, there is evidence that Aran knitting originated from the Coptic sect in Egypt. Some scholars believe that these Coptic designs reached Aran via the old sea routes to Western France and the Mediterranean. The Celts became famous for the elegance of their designs.

Jerseys and Guernseys

South of the British Isles, another type of folk knitting developed, completely different from that of Scandinavia or the Scottish islands. This was Guernsey and Jersey knitting, originally produced especially for the local fishermen and sailors. Later, the technique spread to the coastal areas of Devon, Cornwall, Yorkshire and Northumberland. The sweaters produced in the islands were known respectively as Guernseys and Jerseys and the garments are identical in shape, square like a smock, with sleeves knitted in with a gusset under the arm. The sleeves are knitted deliberately short to make them easy to work in.

The Guernsey was knitted in thick, blue worsted

yarn which faded with age to grey-green, while the Jersey was thinner in texture and knitted in various colours. The Jersey became better known since the fishermen from Jersey journeyed farther afield.

Guernseys were originally knitted by wives, mothers and sweethearts to replace sealskin waistcoats. Made on fine needles using thick wool, the texture was extremely tight and therefore almost completely waterproof. The names given to the patterns, like those of Shetland, were taken from everyday life but they were often specific to families, towns or individuals. Two of the more commonly used are the "Tree of Life" and "Marriage Lines". More ambitious knitters worked names, initials, or even the shape of a ship into the front of the sweater before starting the yoke. The yoke patterns provided an extra thickness of fabric over the chest and shoulders. The hard, crisp yarn used made the stitches stand out and Guernsey patterns have a distinctive and attractive texture.

Some of the sweaters were quite plain, the only pattern being round the armhole, both on the body of the garment and the sleeve. Often a Guernsey was not ribbed at the bottom edge but ended in a band of purl stitch.

Aran knitting

Aran knitting has an ancient and fascinating history. Its celebrated and almost sculptured relief patterns are now part of Ireland's heritage and, indeed, the natural creamy coloured and oiled wool is unique to the area. In the 9th century Book of Kells – one of the most famous illuminated manuscripts in the world – there is a small illumination of St Daniel wearing a fashionable winter outfit. The saint is seen sitting on a folding chair and the pillow on the chair bears the holy sign of the Trinity. He is wearing a milk-white Aran, or Bainin, sweater and Aran knitted stockings.

There is evidence that Aran knitting originated from the Coptic sect in Egypt. The Coptic designs most likely reached Aran via the old sea routes to Western France and the Mediterranean. Monks are believed to have brought the Coptic designs to Ireland but these designs themselves have an even longer history since many of the symbols used can be traced back for more than 3000 years.

The Celts were noted for the delicacy and elegance of their designs on metal objects dating from the Iron Age and their sense of design symbolism is carried forward into the Aran patterns – spiral swirls, whirls and curls, zig-zag and twist knots forming a circle. All these designs had meanings. It is believed the diamond sign – a single moss stitch reversed on alternate rows – symbolises wealth, the zig-zag stitch moving diagonally across a purl panel is supposed to represent the twisting cliff paths, cables themselves represent the fishermen's ropes and the tree of life patterns – knit or twist stitches against a purl background – are a sign of long life and a promise of many strong sons. Some experts believe the trellis pattern is a knitted representation of the small, stone-enclosed fields so typical of the west of Ireland.

These Aran patterns have many local variations – indeed, many of the fishing families seem to have developed their own traditional patterns which served the family almost in the sense of a coat-of-arms in more exalted social circles. Tradition has it that a drowned fisherman could always be identified when his body was swept ashore by the pattern on his sweater.

Certainly early Celtic culture is rich in the sort of symbolism which has been incorporated into Aran knitting patterns. The interlacing so typical of Aran knitwear is held to exemplify man's relationship with God and the monkish influence is everywhere apparent.

French Folk Knitting

A similar tradition of knitting plain-coloured textured sweaters for protection from weather is found on the northern coast of France. This is known as "Brioche" knitting. There is a whole range of variations on the basic stitch – brioche rib, brioche honeycomb stitch, half brioche stitch – but all are based on the technique of knitting into the centre of the stitch below that normally knitted, so that the two are knitted together. In the far south of France the main centre of folk tradition was in the district of Landes. Here, as in many other parts of Europe and Asia, knitters displayed a phenomenal skill and speed but in Landes they went one better, managing to knit while walking on stilts and tending flocks of sheep at the same time! These shepherds even did their folk dancing on stilts. The man in the illustration opposite also wears a knitting pouch worn round his neck like a satchel. This was made of layers of sheepskin sewn together with coloured wool and was used to store the raw wool gathered during the day, spun yarn, needles and the finished knitting. These shepherds were one of the few groups of knitters in Europe to use hooked needles.

The patterns of southern France are similar to those of the Basque peasants of Spain who were believed to have introduced knitting into France across the

In the French district of Landes the locals knitted in the most improbable situations. They tended their sheep on stilts and knitted at the same time. The peasants were experts in the use of stilts and even danced on them.

'NAHYAT,' the story of an ancient craft

Pyrenees. Basque patterns were based on religious symbols and natural forms and were knitted in natural wool colours or in bright contrasts much like the folk knitting of Eastern Europe.

Knitting survives as a home craft

By the 18th century, hand knitting as a home craft had become widespread in Europe and America and was a recognized pastime for men as well as for women. Women knitted mostly for their children, and occasionally winter petticoats, sleeves, shawls and caps for themselves and waistcoats for their men. They usually knitted with wool but sometimes silk was used if the knitter was sufficiently skilled. Housewives also knitted pretty things for the home such as the delightful silk pin cushion on page 86.

Between 1770 and 1780 silk knitting was superseded by "white" knitting, so-called because it was worked in linen or cotton thread. This was to become extremely popular.

Trade with India and the East had increased and raw cotton was being imported into Europe in vast quantities. Imitation lace, knitted in natural cotton on wire needles was much admired. A magnificent late example of this skill is the Christening dress entered for the 1851 Exhibition (page 78). Lace knitting became most popular in Germany, Holland, Scandinavia and Britain – all areas without their own lace tradition. All kinds of articles were made – capes, stockings, fichus and caps – but some of the prettiest were the babies' bonnets and jackets, often profusely trimmed with ribbons and beads.

Bead knitting became popular at about the same time. Beads were used in knitting in two ways, either worked in massed designs or interspersed on a background. The first technique was perfected in Vienna, where small bags, bottle and box tops were knitted, using beads in fine delicate colours. Patterns depicted romantic and hunting scenes, figures and flowers and the results looked very like beaded tapestry work.

The second type of bead work was used on dresses, scarves, bonnets, mittens and accessories such as bags, purses and belts and became very popular with the ladies of Victorian England. A favourite accessory was the stocking purse knitted in silk, with a spot design in gold beads at one end for gold coins, and steel beads at the other for silver coins.

The Victorian period in England – as in many other matters – was a period of paradox so far as the textile handcrafts are concerned. During the 70 years of Queen Victoria's reign there was great activity in these crafts at a domestic level and a good deal of literature was printed. But despite this the actual standard of skill declined in many of the crafts concerned.

In England and America – and to a lesser extent in western Europe – this period was one of rapid economic expansion and society could not always keep pace. A whole new group of people joined the ranks of the middle and upper classes, who almost exclusively owed their shift of fortunes to trade or manufacturing. However, society was not quite prepared to accept these two spheres as "gentlemanly" (and they certainly were not "ladylike") but the efforts by the dedicated to prove that they were produced a whole new language of snobbery.

Part of the vocabulary of this language consisted of a style of living where a self-respecting man cocooned his wife and daughters in a life of idleness. They were allowed to do little more than the occasional light dusting of the many "knick-knacks" and "whatnots" that cluttered their lives. This meant that there was ample time for the ladies of the household to devote their talents to making the innumerable objects which swamped the average middle-class Victorian home.

This, in turn, helped to contribute to another part of the vocabulary of snobbery which consisted of the acquisition of material objects. As James Laver wrote, "Never before in human history had so many objects come into being." This insatiable desire for objects, combined with incomparable ingenuity, had its effects on the humblest of the arts – knitting.

About 1840 there appeared a new delight – the woman's magazine. These early magazines were filled with all kinds of information such as etiquette, advice to the love-lorn, stories, articles on the Royal family, the latest Paris fashions, advice on household problems and hundreds of items for the idle Victorian lady to make. The magazines were essentially aimed at the genteel middle class. The lower classes were partially illiterate and had little time to spare from the battle against poverty for such indulgences. The very rich tended to stick to the thoroughbred of the textile crafts – embroidery. This accomplishment could then

Continued on P.38 ▶

Some of the prettiest knitwear in the late 18th century was produced for babies' bonnets and jackets. This was particularly so in the case of France as this picture of the Duc de Bordeaux and his sister by Louis Hersent shows.

The incredible Victorians~they knitted

Let us speak for a moment of the unspeakable – knitted drawers for ladies, with a crochet border. The ribbon was run through the first row of crochet and tied in a bow at the side. There was a linen band at the top. Made of "Peacock fingering wool", these drawers were a star item in the Young Ladies Journal of 1878.

Not, be it noted, a sock – or a stocking – but a half-hose. And for a gentleman, to boot. Worked in basket pattern.

For baby no trouble was too great as this splendidly worked bootee demonstrates.

Not a chastity girdle in chain mail but a child's necktie in looped knitting.

ust about everything...

Even foot cushions were covered with knitting. These were the years of leisure for the middle classes. There was plenty of time to knit just about everything. Slippers, braces, smoking caps, bottle covers. Here we show just a few examples of the Victorian lady's indefatigable zeal.

Anything that could possibly be covered was covered in the high noon of Victorianism. This lamp is a fine example of the scores of useless articles produced by middle-class ladies of the period. This lamp cover was in seven shades of green wool and four shades of scarlet.

'NAHYAT,' the story of an ancient craft

◀ Continued from P.35

be added to those of drawing, piano-playing, singing, dancing and speaking French and Italian, essential to any girl who wished to find a husband.

The items contained in these magazines cover all types of skills besides embroidery (in all its forms). They describe how to make shell flowers, tat, make curl-work feathers, do rice work, make lace and do bead work besides constructing all manner of things from card and fabric. They also provided knitting and crochet patterns for making a wide variety of items.

It is difficult to distinguish the good from the bad since many of the items are so bizarre that they are today a source of amusement. The names given to some of them are also entertaining. Shawls appear under the name "fascinators", "clouds" and "comforters"; the short bolero-type jacket was called "zuave" or a "hug-me-tight" and a chest warmer was called a "bosom-friend".

Ladies were encouraged to knit anything from a hearthrug, curtains and bell-pulls, to pin cushions and pen-wipers. For men, they knitted belts, scarves, gloves, ties, suspenders and all manner of caps. Among the usual plethora of children's clothes can be found instructions for reins, balls, a variety of dolls, such as sambos, harlequins and soldiers. On the domestic scene they were given ideas for nightdress cases, twine ball cases, coffee strainers, blue-bags, bath mittens, floor cloths and the most elaborate holder for keeping four boiled eggs warm, bedecked with bows and rosettes of ribbon. Edges and borders were knitted to decorate anything from combinations to place-mats.

To illustrate fully the delights of knitting there follows a list of items from Mrs Owen's *Illuminated Book of Needlework* published in 1847: Shawl fringe, Gentleman's Bosom Friend, Spencer Sleeves, Deep Cuffs (to wear over the dress when walking out), Bustle, Berlin Boa, Ruff for the Neck, Comforter, Siberian Bodice, Knee Caps, Baby's Boots (to look like slipper and sock), Baby's Shoe, Border of Escallops (for the ends of a scarf), Broad Vandyke Border, Shawl, Gent's Travelling Cap, Baby's Hat, Fancy Cuff, Dessert D'oyleys, Fancy or Nervous D'oyleys, Sofa Pillow Tidy, Antimacassar, Netting Stirrup (band to hold curtains), Neck Tie, Opera Hood, Opera Cap, Scarf, Shetland Square Shawl, Sable Muff, Hat, Bead Purse, Cradle Quilt.

Another favourite of the Victorians was woven knitting. This was done with two or more coloured threads. One was thicker than the other and this was worked above and below the needles as the thinner one actually knitted. The fabric was often embroidered in cross stitch which linked two weave threads together. This was used to make brightly coloured waistcoats which were worn with the woven side outwards and ornamented with wooden buttons. These were particularly favoured by the railway construction gangs. Besides these waistcoats, the knitted jersey itself became more common dress for the working man of the 1850s.

All types of yarn were used: silk, wool, cotton, linen, cashmere, string, sewing cotton, angora, rope and every technique or combination of techniques. Even their knitting implements did not escape the Victorian passion for ornamentation. They made needle-guards, carved in the form of Dutch dolls, Punch and Judy and Darby and Joan, to protect the points of the needles. Often they kept their needles in elaborately carved cases of ivory, tortoiseshell and similar materials.

Knitting books also gave advice on the care of the items once made. This was quite an art in itself before the industrial chemist concocted soap powders, detergents and softeners. For instance an instruction for washing silk starts with a wash in a mixture of oxgall and white castile, followed by a cold rinse with a mixture of cream of tartar, tartaric acid, alum or vinegar added to the water, with the provision that if black silk was being washed then it should be rinsed with ammonia in the water.

This type of magazine was not restricted to Britain. For instance, the first American women's magazine was published in 1838 – *Godeys Lady's Book*. Over the next few decades it gave instructions for articles very similar to those in Mrs Owen's book.

The first revolt against the stuffy, cluttered image of Victorian homes, clothes, life style and values came about in 1870 after the formation of the Pre-Raphaelite Brotherhood by a group of writers and painters which included Dante Gabriel Rossetti, Collins and Holman Hunt. These men rejected the formal, technically correct, scientific approach to art of the academic establishment and wished to return to the standards of medieval times. Among these they particularly believed in craftsmanship and truth to nature. They deplored mass production and, as a reaction to the growing dominance of science, they took a great interest in religion, myths and legends. Over the following 30 years this movement gradually altered not only painting and literature but architecture,

Continued on P.42 ▶

ʼfine example of 19th-century domestic ʌvotion – a "gentleman's cycling jersey ɗ necktie". Soon the New Woman was to be too busy cycling herself to find time for this sort of labour of love.

Those Victorians again...both sides of th

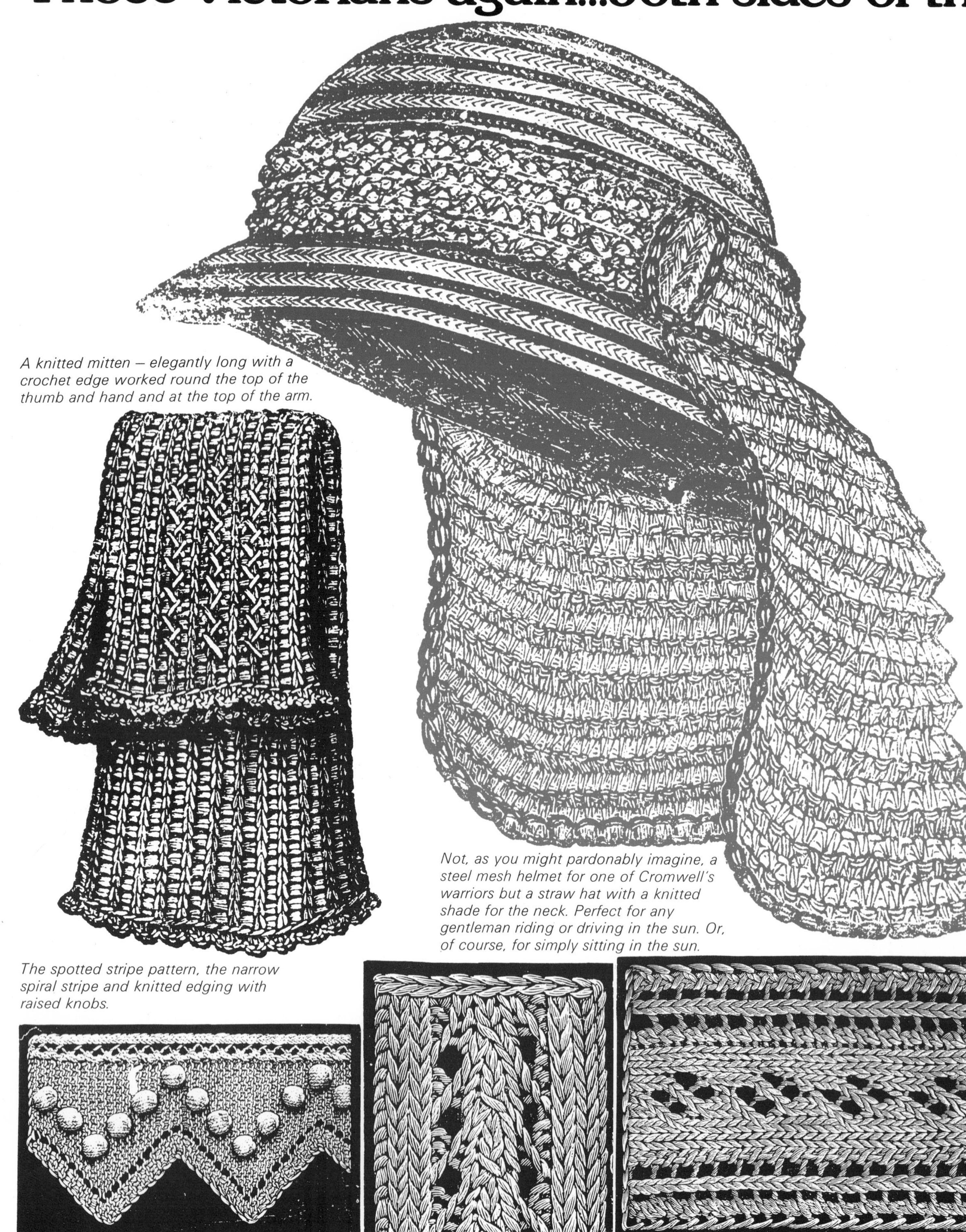

A knitted mitten – elegantly long with a crochet edge worked round the top of the thumb and hand and at the top of the arm.

Not, as you might pardonably imagine, a steel mesh helmet for one of Cromwell's warriors but a straw hat with a knitted shade for the neck. Perfect for any gentleman riding or driving in the sun. Or, of course, for simply sitting in the sun.

The spotted stripe pattern, the narrow spiral stripe and knitted edging with raised knobs.

Channel

The year is 1876 and this manteau-pèlerine avec capuchon *is a particularly painstaking example of the French knitwear of those days. Note the exquisitely worked lace-edging structure.*

'NAHYAT,' the story of an ancient craft

◀ Continued from P.38

textiles, furniture, ceramics, dress and social attitudes.

One of the offspring of the Pre-Raphaelite Brotherhood was the arts and crafts movement whose leading protagonist was William Morris. This movement, however, tended to concentrate on slightly more romantic crafts, such as beautiful embroidery, silversmithing, ceramics, glass and fabric printing.

The second and more violent attack on Victorian life was the emergence of "the new woman". She was not content to sit in the splendour of her cluttered drawing room, playing the piano, painting watercolours, embroidering footstools, crocheting clouds, knitting pen wipers and reading novelettes. Ultimately she was to insist on having the opportunity of a job in the working community and the vote. But her first step along the stony path to these goals was to get out and about. This she did with a vengeance. She played tennis, she began to play cricket and golf, she cycled, she walked all over the countryside, she joined societies of various types and because of all these activities she had little time for the domestic joys of knitting, crochet and the rest.

Partly because of these two phenomena the deluge of instructive literature began to peter out. Hand knitting as an art had already started a decline of its own volition, to such an extent that a law was passed in Britain in 1872 enforcing the teaching of the skill in schools. This was the period of the expansion of the state schools and many were built to improve the educational standards of those who could not afford expensive private education.

This is the type of state school in which knitting would have been taught but probably at a very utilitarian level. Having left school these children would have had little time or spare money to pursue the skill for other than providing the most practical of garments. This, therefore, had little effect on the standard or type of article produced.

The women's magazines – although much reduced in number – continued to keep middle-class women well versed in domestic arts. The results, however, were a far cry from the delicate work of the late 18th and early 19th centuries. There is a noticeable change in the content of these magazines in the early 20th century. By 1915, largely as a result of the war conditions, most of the items are emphasized for their usefulness. The usual types of garments are included, the vest, babyclothes, socks, gloves and hats but a new addition is the sports sweater, masquerading under the title of "a butterfly tennis jumper", or there are "Patterns for Youthful Housekeepers". Gone is the romance of the rabbit pen wiper, the cardinal cape and the knitted opera hood, now replaced by the ubiquitous jumper, although some light relief was provided by the addition of knitted toys such as Robert the Terrier.

Between the two world wars the role of the knitting book was assumed by the early versions of the women's magazines as they are known today. These often included instructions for making household articles, underwear, men's socks, hats and of course children's clothes, but the most popular item of all was undoubtedly the "jumper" or sweater. These took many forms. In the Twenties they were long, slim and shapeless, while in the Thirties they went in for short sleeves with lacy yokes, Peter Pan collars, clever little neck trims, all of which to the end of the Thirties, and early Forties, would have padded square shoulders "a la Crawford".

During the Second World War this type of knitting continued as much out of necessity as for pleasure. The Forties "jumper" had much in common with those of the Thirties. It was not until almost the mid-Fifties that the jumper changed its shape to become the enormous chunky "Sloppy Joe" much favoured by the fashionable beatniks of the period.

Since the early Sixties there has been a veritable bonanza of knitwear on the market. The knitted garment has become an integral part of both high fashion and everyday life. The introduction of excellent domestic knitting machinery has brought good workmanship and design scope within the range of the busiest woman. Even for those without a machine there has never been as wide a range of yarn and colours and types of clothes to make.

The one thing that the life of the Sixties did not have was time. Without this precious commodity the skills of the past cannot hope to be revived. One of the most publicized characteristics of the Seventies is the interest, especially by the young, in the past; its pace, its sense of style, sense of quality and above all its human scale. Buildings are related to the human height, instead of soaring away into the skies. Food is to be grown in the garden, or the neighbour's garden, on the farm up the lane, or on the land round the city or town, instead of being flown in from some exotic clime. Food is then prepared in the kitchen instead of miles away in some vast modern factory producing the lowest common denominator in shape, size, colour and flavour in carefully designed packages to fit into the ice box.

A place for everything...

Everything in its place and a place for everything, especially knitting needles. Three views – open, shut and needle support strut – of a knitting needle case in the high noon of Victorianism.

The nostalgia of fashion

In clothes more than any other commodity, there is a tremendous nostalgia. This is not just a whim dictated by fashion's trendies. The scavenging of old clothes markets by the young is no new craze. It has been going on now for almost ten years. There is a genuine admiration not only for the styles but for the quality of fabric, of printing, of making and the tremendous attention to detail. How many clothes from the swinging Sixties will survive to tell the tale in the 1980s?

When every second shop has the same goods as the shop before, then the adventure of finding something unique has great appeal. The traditional garment also has its charisma. The farmer's smock, the fisherman's shirt, the poncho and the caftan all in their many forms are very popular. We hope we have captured all these elements and have given the reader the opportunity to produce something with patience and skill which will bring great delight to both the knitter and the wearer.

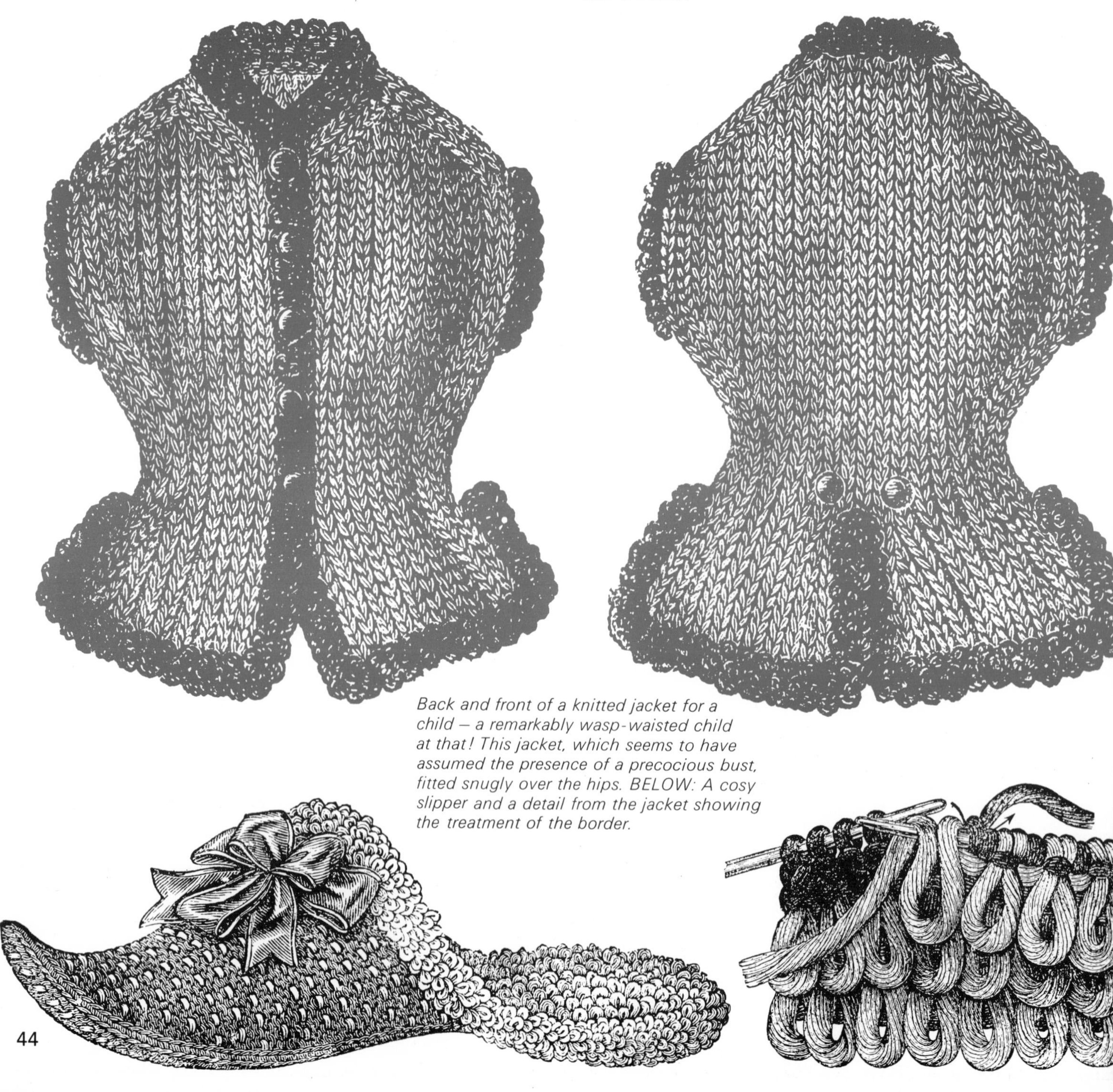

Back and front of a knitted jacket for a child – a remarkably wasp-waisted child at that! This jacket, which seems to have assumed the presence of a precocious bust, fitted snugly over the hips. BELOW: A cosy slipper and a detail from the jacket showing the treatment of the border.

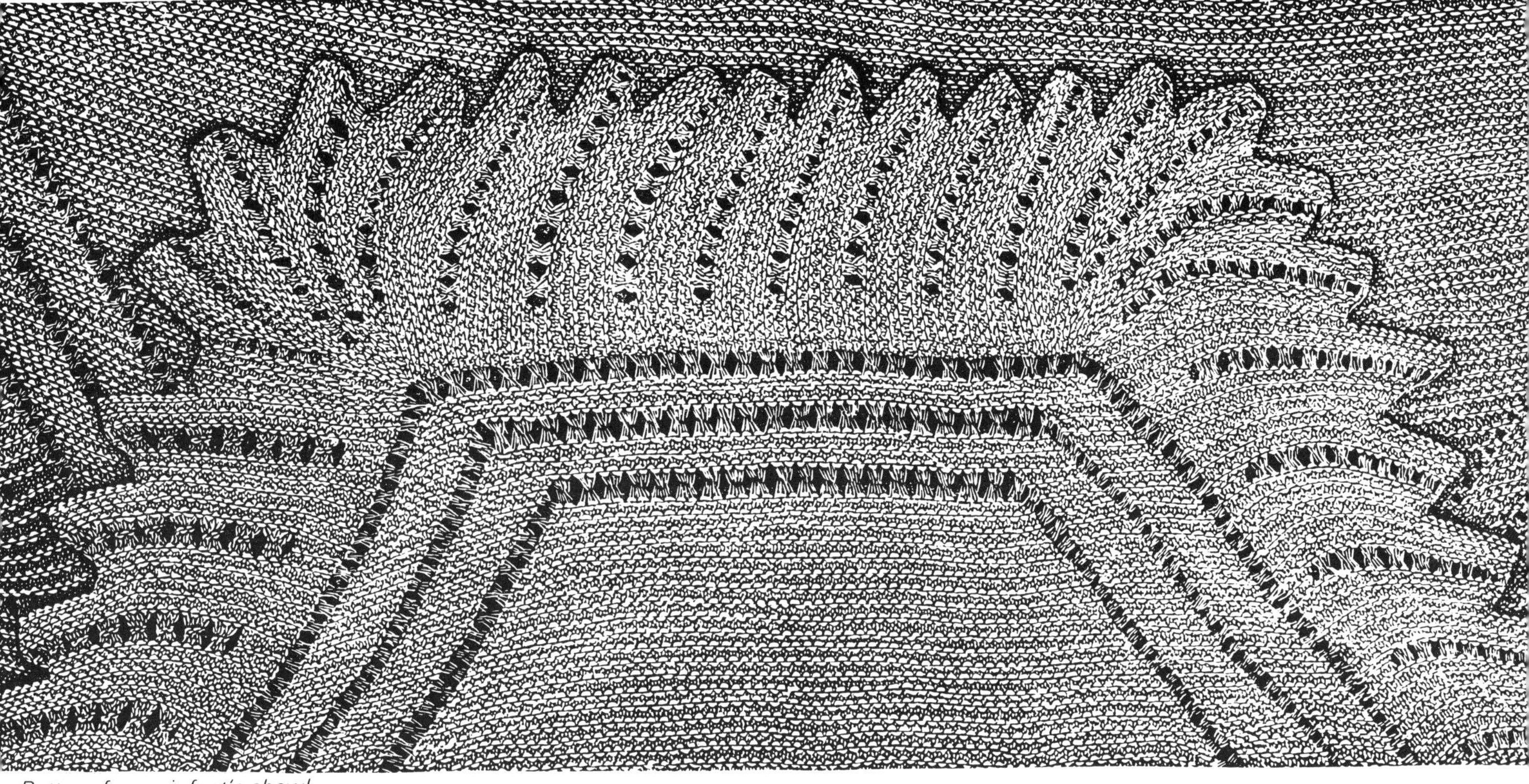

Pattern for an infant's shawl.

A beautifully worked chestnut leaf pattern for a quilt square – and the Brompton quilt square. Both these patterns are highpoints in Victorian knitted quilt work.

The landscape of knitting~a child c

As with all art forms – and knitting at its high points of development touches art – physical environment and social mood played an important part in the evolution of knitting. The knitters were influenced by contemporary taste in their epochs and in their regions and the regions in turn were constantly exposed to waves of influence reaching out to them from the constantly shifting and evolving civilisations.

Since knitting was, of course, essentially utilitarian in purpose, the knitters were not themselves the originators of design motifs any more than a modern manufacturer of, say, kitchen plates, who chooses a Picasso-style design, can be called an artistic originator.

For the influences behind the great schools of knitting we must take a deeper look at the whole culture of the period and even at the physical geography of a place.

The hard, firm outlines of the Grecian landscape, with its clarity and sharp contrasts is reflected in the Greek school of knitting. There is a vividness and a directness.

The formal patterns of North Africa – again a mutation from the angular geometry of the Egyptian art forms – is reflected in the knitting patterns of Spain. And something of the floral softness and voluptuousness of Renaissance Italy not unnaturally creeps through into the early Italian knitwear patterns.

In the same way the Early English School was deeply influenced by the abundance of Italian Renaissance fantasy. Court stockings were intricately woven. The designs of the period followed the exuberance of the Elizabethan attitude. Queen Elizabeth herself – the Fairy Queen of the courtier poets – set the tone and the gorgeously ornate clothes she is wearing in

Western Europe
The geometry of colour

The historical knitting examples produced by the countries of Western Europe cover a wide variety of styles, from the rich and sophisticated silk-brocade patterns produced by the knitters of Spain and Italy to the complex wool carpets which were knitted in Germany.

Most of the earlier examples of knitting were patterned by the use of coloured silks and metal threads, worked into Jacquards, the patterns being very much influenced by the geometric patterning of North Africa. Later, the designs became freer in concept and inspiration was drawn from flowers and plants.

As the art of knitting moved northwards across Europe, more use was made of stitches to create decorative effects.

This magnificent knitted carpet from Poland is typical of the large and beautiful carpets produced in the 17th century. Many of these carpets were used as wall hangings. These carpets were often produced under the aegis of the knitting guilds and were produced as evidence of the guilds' competence in their craft. Most of them were produced for patrons.

many cultures

Nicholas Hilliard's famous miniature provide an admirable clue to current tastes.

The very versatility of knitting, which could be carried out in silk threads with gold and silver overlays, helped to popularise the craft.

So to bring these designs from the past to life we must linger for a moment in the times they were created. We must get the feel of the landscape and enter into the mood of the very buildings of the period. Knitting, highly personalised and in its early manifestations highly functional, was the product of simple craftsmen thoroughly involved in all the influences that surrounded them.

Many races and many cultures have gone to the making of our modern virtuosity in the craft. Today, in a rapidly shrinking world, influences tend to be confused. In earlier times there were sharper distinctions of mood and manner.

Probably only in the true folk knitting of Aran, the Shetlands and the "island" groups does the true lineage of ancient design forms linger on. Here the line of descent seems unbroken.

The advent of the machine, of course, enlarged the limits of the possible but it also removed a certain individuality.

Nevertheless, this mixture of races and of cultures is a vital part of the sheer charm of knitting. Here is an art form which grew from a need. And like all such art forms the great knitting schools demonstrate that creative and restless element in the human race: the desire to embellish, to work out a fantasy from a fact, in short to produce a combination of colour and of pattern arrangement which is at the centre of all good art.

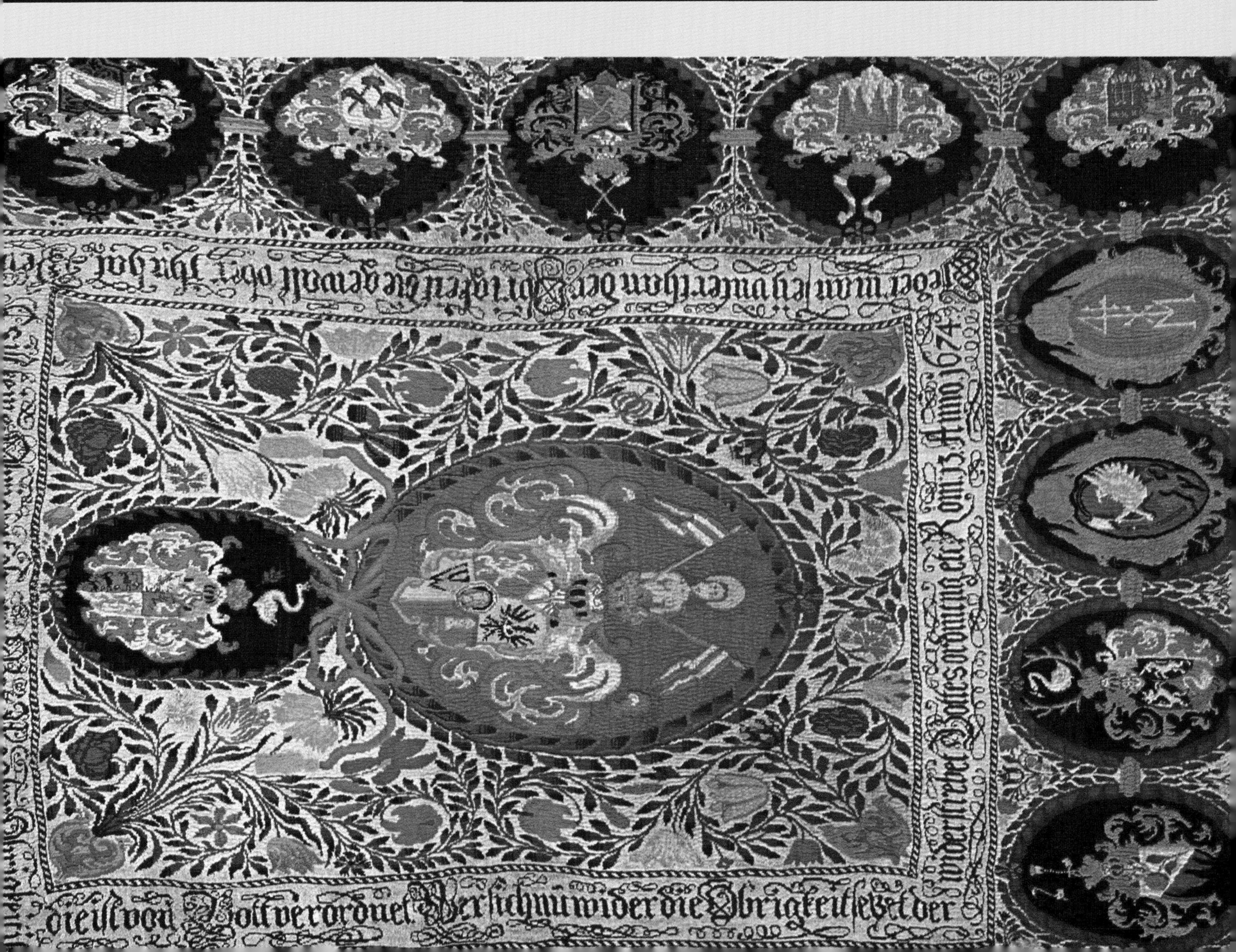

Western Europe

continued

This finely patterned mosaic flooring in the Alcazar, Seville, is typical of the geometric patterning of North Africa which influenced the knitters of Spain in the early years of the craft.

Examples of the use of stitches can be seen on the superb embossed petticoat on page 150 and the Italian silk cap on page 142.

In the wide variety of knitting examples which have survived from Western Europe, every type of stitch and most kinds of yarn are represented. All kinds of accessories and garments were knitted, from tiny boxes with beaded knitting tops to large and colourful carpets, from richly-decorated religious regalia to thick, woolly work-socks.

In Italy, Spain, France, Germany, Holland, Scandinavia and in European Russia, knitting was eventually organised either into a trade or Guilds were set up with prescribed levels of skill. The Guilds of Spain, Italy, France and Germany developed most strongly and the results of their training produced some of the most beautiful and impressive pieces of knitting that exist in the world today.

The Middle East

The Christian sect that founded a tradition

The Middle East is said to be the "cradle of knitting", since the origins of the craft are supposed to have been in Egypt. Certainly the earliest fragments and examples of knitting in existence were found at Bahnasa, in Egypt, and have been dated at around the 4th and 5th centuries A.D.

Most of these early examples are sandal socks, knitted in a single colour yarn but a child's sock, striped in blue and white was also found.

Later, Egyptian knitters introduced more colour into their knitting and examples discovered at Fostad, which were dated at between the 10th and 12th centuries, show the use of two or more colours, worked in broad bands of geometric patterning. In Egypt, knitting was strongly associated with the Copts, a Christian sect, and, as the Christian faith became more strongly established in Europe, so too did knitting. The type of coloured patterning found at Fostad obviously influenced early European knitting and this influence is still evident in folk knitting traditions.

As knitting spread across Europe, so it appears to have waned in the Middle East. In the 20th century, very little hand-knitting survives.

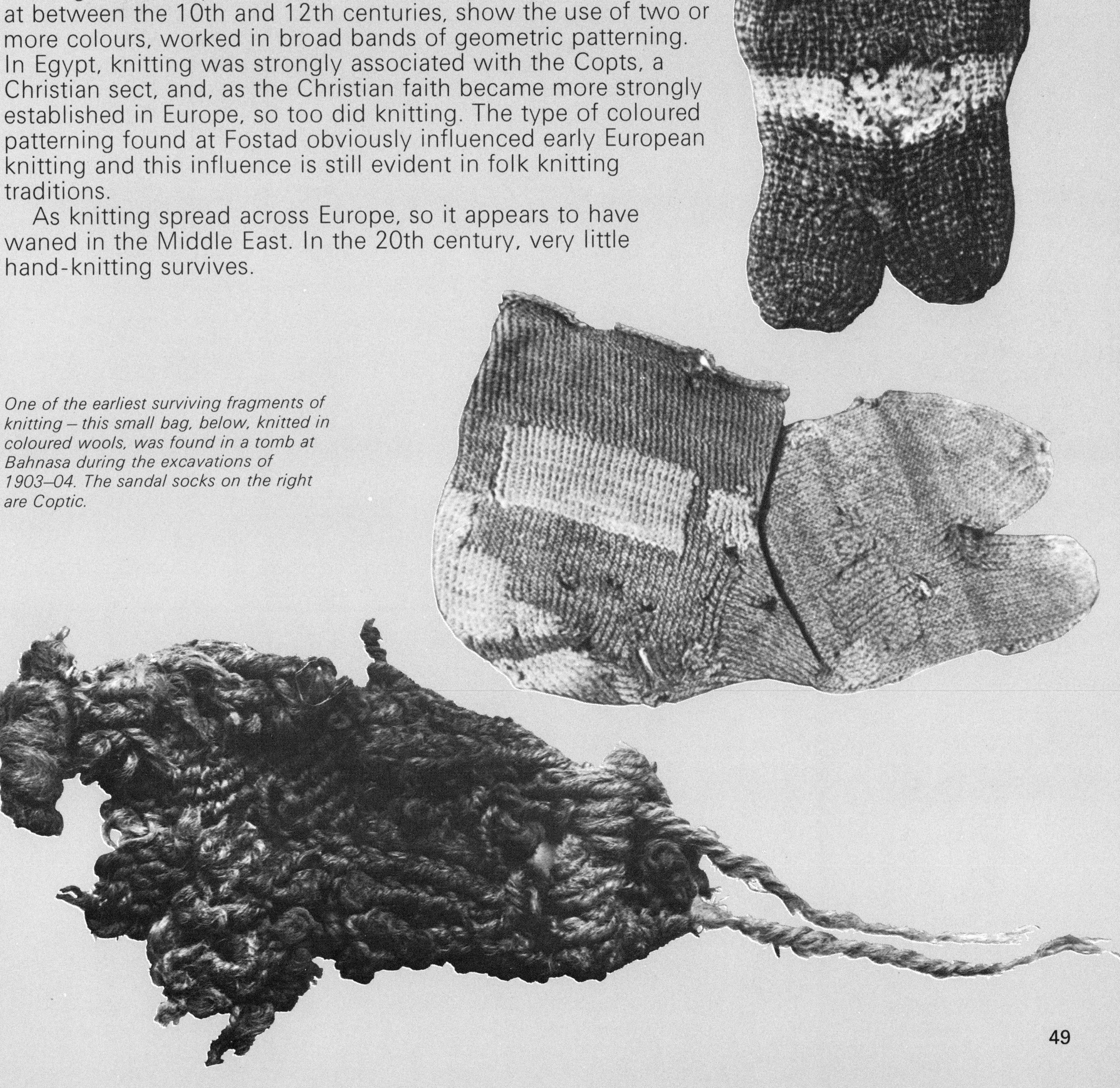

One of the earliest surviving fragments of knitting – this small bag, below, knitted in coloured wools, was found in a tomb at Bahnasa during the excavations of 1903–04. The sandal socks on the right are Coptic.

Asia
Patterns from the mountains

It is generally supposed that knitting first spread eastwards, from the Middle East towards India, Afghanistan and Tibet, carried with the caravans of the Arab traders. However, some historians contend that the craft travelled in the opposite direction, from Asia to North Africa.

Whichever is true, a tradition of folk knitting developed in Northern India and the surrounding countries and the patterns show similarities to the folk patterning of other parts of the world.

Curiously, although cotton was grown in Asia, the knitting which was produced uses wool. This may have been because weaving was strongly established as a craft in the cotton-growing areas and there was therefore little interest in a new craft.

Knitting appears to have developed only in the northern regions, where cotton was not grown, and specifically in the mountainous regions, where sheep and goats were grazed. In these climes, there would also have been a need for warmer, heavier clothing as a protection against the cold.

Both of the knitted examples illustrated on pages 94 and 98 were found in Kashmir, in Northern India. They show a different interpretation of the banded patterning seen in European folk knitting. Although the grounds are still coloured, the patterns themselves use natural forms such as flowers, rather than the geometric designs typical of folk knitting.

The lovely land of Kashmir in northern India where a strong tradition of folk knitting developed and goats, of course, were grazed in these mountain regions.

Greece and Albania
Bright colours~and strong contrasts

Greek and Albanian knitting follows many of the traditions of the folk knitting of Europe and Asia in that it was produced by domestic knitters for the practical purpose of making hard-wearing clothing.

In some areas of the Balkan states knitted garments may also have been produced for festive occasions and these would have been embroidered in the same way as woven garments. However, this type of garment was rare and the majority of the items knitted were such things as socks, oversocks with felted undersoles, gloves, caps and small accessories such as bags and belts.

Gradually the basic knitted garment became a simple, plain-coloured cotton stocking worn by the women throughout the Balkan area but these stockings were not common much before the 19th century.

In the two examples of knitting illustrated in this chapter, the bag from Greece (Page 122) and the sock from Albania (Page 118), the yarn appears to be of a much harder twist and fibre than the kinds of yarns used in, say Shetland knitting.

Unlike northern Europe but similar to the knitting of parts of Asia and southern European Russia, the grounds for the patterns are strong in colour, mainly black with bright colours making the patterns. This creates a very rich effect which is similar to weaving and embroidery of these areas.

This type of patterning and yarn also appears in Peruvian knitting. The colourings are either bright on a white or black ground or in toned shades of brown, black, cream and white.

Land of sharp contrasts – as this rough-hewn Greek village shows. The knitting from these areas has a practical and down-to-earth quality about it but also a fine sense of colour.
Gay colours and the blue skies of Greece seem synonymous and, indeed, there is a "folksy" quality about Greek and Albanian knitting.

The Island Schools

How knitting became a part of folklore

The term "Folk Knitting" conjures up a picture of multi-coloured geometric patterns, knitted into sweaters, socks, mittens, gloves and hats and similar warm garments. This type of knitting has existed in many places throughout the world at different times.

Folk knitting is the effect produced by the use of a series of patterns on articles of practical clothing produced by home knitters. The yarn used is usually spun in the home from the fleece or hair of domestic livestock. The patterns which are now typical of folk knitting were used over and over again by the knitters of the different communities and, over hundreds of years, the patterns were altered and adapted until each area evolved a distinctive style of patterning of its own.

As European society became more sophisticated, only the more isolated areas of the world retained their traditions of folk knitting, forming a kind of "fringe" around Europe. These areas include Scandinavia, the northern islands, Shetland, Faroes and Fair Isle, isolated parts of Russia and Lapland, the Landes area of France and parts of the Pyrenees districts in Spain.

A different type of folk knitting developed around the fishing areas of Britain and in Brittany as well as on the islands of Jersey, Guernsey and Aran. In this type of knitting, textures are formed by the use of stitches, using a single-colour yarn rather than patterning in coloured yarns.

Island knitting reaches its high point in the great Aran tradition. This in turn descends from Celtic influences – the Celtic crosses shown here are typical of the region. Island folk knitting has a "family" similarity.

The English School

That practical touch

Hand-knitting came to England much later than to other European countries and did not become established as a trade until quite later in the 16th century. But unlike France, Spain, and Italy, where phenomenal skills in knitting were developed to service a highly fashionable élite, the English trade was based mainly on the production of worsted stockings, caps and similar commonplace garments.

Unfortunately, the invention of the knitting machine at the end of the 16th century all but destroyed the English hand-knitting industry. Knitting machines were first operated in London to satisfy the demands of the high fashion market but by 1650 machines were in use in Nottingham, Derby, Leicester and other areas of Britain. After only 50 years, hand-knitting as a trade had virtually disappeared and only isolated areas in North Wales and the Yorkshire Dales were still producing hand-made goods.

During the 18th century, hand-knitting began to be revived as a fashionable pastime and fine, silk knitting began to appear. With the introduction of Indian cotton around 1730 and the advances being made in the spinning industry, "white knitting" became the craze. Fine white cotton was used to knit intricate lace patterns on the thinnest of wire needles and English domestic knitting reached heights of skill and beauty. Tne English gentlewoman of the late 19th century was overwhelmed by the variety of arts and crafts which she was urged to pursue and knitting was still one of the most popular pastimes. The miscellany of useful, useless and purely decorative objects which a determined knitter could make on her needles from the patterns provided in her magazines, was astonishing, ranging from hearth rugs, curtains, bell-pulls and pen wipers to suspenders, coffee strainers and egg cosies.

From 1900, English knitting was largely directed in style by the women's magazines and has little to distinguish it from the knitting of other European countries. The most distinctive patterns produced by home knitters are derived from the folk traditions, the Aran and Fair Isle patterns.

The skills that produced the fine, intricate work of the 18th and 19th centuries have gone, together with the social structure and the gentle tempo of living which allowed their development.

The first knitting machine

In 1589, a Nottinghamshire clergyman, William Lee, devised the first knitting machine, a knitting frame on which the knitter manipulated a series of movable hooks so as to draw the stitches over a series of fixed hooks. The knitting produced by the machine was coarse and unattractive – but it did speed up the production of knitted stockings.

Together with his brother James and four or five other men, Lee practised machine knitting in the village of Calverton, Nottinghamshire. After two years, a patron, Lord Hunsdon,

Yorkshire was a recognised centre of knitting and this celebrated picture of some of the knitters of Wensleydale in action proves the point. People knitted everywhere – driving sheep to market, gossiping in the village square, sitting on their cottage steps. There is a famous story of one woman from the Dales knitting all the way on her three mile walk to the local market. The average knitter could produce at least two pairs of stockings a week. It is said, in fact, that even lovers knitted during their evening courtship strolls.

encouraged the young clergyman to go to London and, after setting up a knitting factory at Bunhill Fields, Lee decided to apply to Queen Elizabeth for a patent of monopoly. The Queen graciously consented to visit the factory but upon being presented with a pair of the thick, coarse hose which Lee's new invention produced declared her disappointment in no uncertain terms and refused the patent.

For seven more years Lee worked on his invention and eventually, in 1598, produced a pair of knitted silk stockings, literally fit for a queen. That perverse lady accepted the stockings graciously – but feared the new invention would put hundreds of home knitters out of work! Queen Elizabeth again refused her patronage and the patent.

By this time, news of the invention had reached France. The king, Henry IV, invited Lee to settle in France, with his workmen, promising great rewards and privileges. William Lee, his brother James and nine workmen with eleven knitting frames emigrated to France and settled in Rouen.

Under the king's patronage, they enjoyed great success and some prosperity. But Lee's luck was not to hold. With the assassination of Henry IV and the subsequent troubles in France, the royal protection was withdrawn.

Disappointed, William Lee died of grief in Paris in 1610. On his death, seven remaining workmen returned to England and with Aston, a previous apprentice of Lee's, again set up machine knitting in Nottinghamshire.

By the 18th century, Lee's frame knitting machine had become the basis of an important new industry in England, and, in particular, the East Midlands.

LEFT: *A manual stocking frame of around 1770. This machine for producing a flat web is similar to the original frame invented by Parson Lee in 1589.*

BOTTOM LEFT: *A Victorian stocking knitting factory in full swing at Tewkesbury in 1860. By contemporary standards this factory owned by Owen and Uglow was something of a model. It was large, relatively airy and as well-lit as the technology of the period could make it. But hours were long and rules were strict – notice the reminder placards on the walls.*

RIGHT: *The Rev. W. Lee in the moment of inspiration that was to produce his famous knitting machine of 1589. Legend has it that he was watching his wife knitting when the idea of a machine to do the job first formed. But Lee was to die a disappointed man.*

BOTTOM RIGHT: *18th century stocking frame knitters at work, from an early print. The two "handmaidens" are vigorously spinning while early industrial man works away at the machine. Beer mugs and dog make the scene almost domestic.*

And now, the garments and patterns

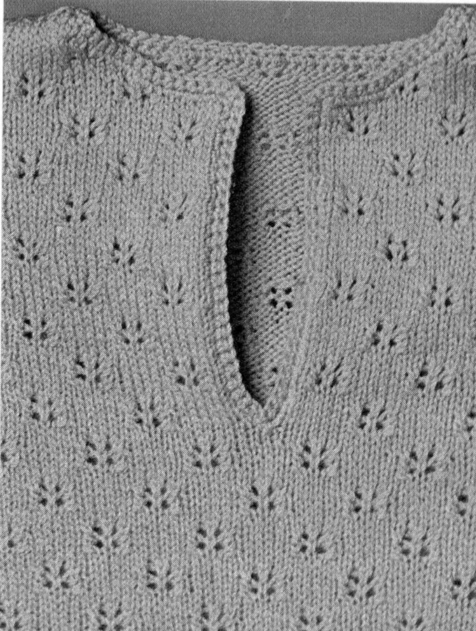

Caftan from a mystery...

Cotton sampler

This lace sampler is a rather puzzling piece of knitting. Shaped into a rectangle, it appears to have been knitted on fine, wire needles using white cotton yarn. The area is divided roughly into six sections and four different lace patterns are featured on the sampler.

The purpose of this piece is not known for certain. It might have been intended for some practical use, such as a table centre or a chair back cover or perhaps, as a "fall", which was a kind of scarf worn under a bonnet. However, the arrangement of the lace patterns seems too random for any of these. It is more likely that the piece was knitted by a professional knitter as an example of his skill at lace knitting, to gain commissions. More simply, it may have been knitted entirely for pleasure, in much the same way that 19th-century children stitched cross-stitch samplers.

This type of knitted lace became very popular in England from the 18th-century onwards. Lace was an extremely important part of dress for both men and women but it was very expensive. When white and natural-coloured cotton yarn began to be imported into Britain during the middle 18th century, knitted cotton lace became a substitute for the not-so-wealthy. The patterns were used for all kinds of clothing, accessories and for household articles. The subsequent invention of lace-making machinery gradually removed the incentive for lace knitting and by the middle of the 19th century the skill had practically disappeared.

This fabulous caftan is like a modern sampler of lace stitches! Basically a very simple shape, the caftan is made up of squares and rectangles of lace stitches which are afterwards joined with strips of open-work knitting. Candle stitch is used for the chestnut-coloured panels, butterfly stitch for the gold panels and a chevron stitch for the brown. A knitted rouleau tie is threaded through the holes of the open-work strip under the bust, to tie in front.

The caftan illustrated was knitted in Sirdar Fontein 4-ply crêpe yarn in Pebble Beige, Horse Chestnut, Turf Brown and Mellow Gold.

Gorgeously patterned panels give this caftan an unusually rich and attractive look. The flowing line adds grace to any figure.

Materials
4-ply crepe yarn, 14 25gr. [13 1oz.] balls in chestnut brown, 16 [14 1oz.] balls in turf brown, 12 [11 1oz.] balls in beige and 3 [3 1oz.] balls in gold.
One pair each of Nos. 9, 10 and 11 [US Nos. 4, 3 and 2] needles.
Crochet hook ISR No. 3.00 [US No. F Bernat].

Special abbreviations for this design:
yf yarn forward
yb yarn back
yrn yarn round needle

Size
One size only.
Total length, 57in. [144cm.].
Note: The caftan is worked in six panels, back and front, see diagram.

Candle pattern
(Make 2 for lower centre panels)
Tension or Gauge: 14 sts to 2in. [5cm.].
Using No. 9 [US No. 4] needles and chestnut brown, cast on 61 sts and work in pattern as follows:
1st row K1, *yf, sl 1, K1, psso, K7, K2 tog, yf, K1, repeat from * to end.
2nd and subsequent even-number rows P.
3rd row K1, *yf, K1, sl 1, K1, psso, K5, K2 together, K1, yf, K1; repeat from * to end.
5th row K1, *yf, K2, sl 1, K1, psso, K3, K2 together, K2, yf, K1; repeat from * to end.
7th row K1, *yf, K3, sl 1, K1, psso, K1, K2 tog, K3, yf, K1; repeat from * to end.
9th row K1, *yf, K4, sl 1, K2 tog, psso, K4, yf, K1; repeat from * to end.
11th row K4 *K2 tog, yf, K1, yf, sl 1, K1, psso, K7; repeat from * ending last repeat with K4.
13th row K3, *K2 tog, K1, yf, K1, yf, K1, sl 1, K1, psso, K5; repeat from * ending last repeat with K3.
15th row K2, *K2 tog, K2, yf, K1, yf, K2, sl 1, K1, psso, K3; repeat from * ending last repeat with K2.
17th row K1, *K2 tog, K3, yf, K1, yf, K3, sl 1, K1, psso, K1; repeat from * to end.
19th row Sl 1, K1, psso, *K4, yf, K1, yf, K4, sl 1, K2 tog, psso; repeat from * ending last repeat with sl 1, K1, psso.
20th row P.
These 20 rows form the pattern.
Continue in pattern until work measures 41in. [104cm.] ending with a 10th or 20th pattern row.
Cast off.

Top side panels
(Make 4)
Using No. 9 [US No. 4] needles and chestnut brown yarn, cast on 73 sts and work 100 rows in Candle pattern. Cast off.

Chevron lace stitch
(Make 4 for lower side panels)
Tension or Gauge: 12 sts to 2in. [5cm.].
Using No. 9 [US No. 4] needles and turf brown yarn, cast on 56 sts and P 1 row.
Work in pattern as follows:
1st row *Sl 1, K1, psso, K2, yf, K2; repeat from * until 2 remain, K2.
2nd and 4th rows P.
3rd row K1, *K2, yf, K2, K2 tog; repeat from * until 1 st remains, K1.
These 4 rows form the pattern.
Continue in pattern until work measures 41in. [104cm.], ending with a 2nd or 4th pattern row, then cast off.

Butterfly stitch
(Centre top front panel)
Tension or Gauge: 14 sts to 2in. [5cm.].
Using No. 10 [US No. 3] needles and gold, cast on 65 sts and work in pattern as follows:
1st row K5, *K2 tog, yf, K1, yf, sl 1, K1, psso, K5; repeat from * to end.
2nd row P7, *yf, sl 1 purlwise, yf, P9; repeat from * ending last repeat with P7.
3rd and 4th rows Repeat 1st and 2nd rows.
5th row K.
6th row P.
7th row *K2 tog, yf, K1, yf, sl 1, K1, psso, K5; repeat from * until 5 sts remain, K2 tog, yf, K1, yf, sl 1, K1, psso.
8th row P2, *yb, sl 1-purlwise, yf, P9; repeat from * until 3 sts remain, yb, sl 1-purlwise, yf, P2.
9th and 10th rows Repeat 7th and 8th rows.
11th and 12th rows Repeat 5th and 6th rows.
These 12 rows form the pattern.
Continue in pattern until work measures 6in. [15cm.] ending with a right side row.
Divide sts for neck and shoulders and front opening.
Next row Pattern 32 sts and leave on holder until required, cast off 1, pattern to end and work on the last set of 32 sts.
Continue in pattern until work measures 10½in. [27cm.] ending at neck edge.

Shape neck
Cast off 6 sts at beg of next row, then dec 1 st at neck edge on the 6 following rows and then on the next 4 alternate rows.

Shape shoulder
Cast off 5 sts at beg, still dec 1 st at neck edge of next row.
Cast off 5 sts at beg of next 2 alternate rows and fasten yarn off.
Rejoin yarn to neck edge, 32 sts, and complete as 1st side.

Centre top back panel
Work in pattern as for centre top front panel, until work measures same as front to shoulders.

Shape shoulder and back neck
Next row Cast off 5 sts, pattern next 12 sts; cast off 29 sts, pattern to end and work on the last set of 18 sts.
1st row Cast off 5 sts, pattern until 2 sts remain, K2 tog.
2nd row K2 tog, pattern to end.
3rd row Repeat 1st row.
Work 1 row then cast off remaining 5 sts.
Rejoin yarn to remaining 13 sts.
1st row K2 tog, pattern to end.
2nd row Cast off 5 sts, pattern until 2 sts remain, K2 tog.
3rd row Repeat 1 row.
Cast off 5 remaining sts.

Ribbon stitch vertical panels
(Left front and right back)
Tension or Gauge: 15 sts to 2in. [5cm.].
Using No. 11 [US No. 2] needles and beige yarn, cast on 23 sts and work in pattern as follows:
1st row K.
2nd row P.
3rd to 8th row Repeat 1st and 2nd rows 3 times.
9th and 10th rows K.
11th row P1, *yrn, P2 tog; repeat from * to end.
12th row K.
Repeat these 12 rows 50 times – for right front and left back vertical panels work the 1st row again.

Shape shoulder
Cast off 5 sts at beg of next row; 6 sts at beg of 3 following alternate rows and fasten off yarn.

Right front and left back
Work as for left front and right back, working the extra row where indicated.

Ribbon stitch insertion
(Make 6 for waistline)
Using No. 11 [US No. 2] needles cast on 67 sts.
Work the 20 rows of ribbon stitch. Cast off.

The crocheted tie
Using gold yarn and crochet hook, make a chain 100in. [254cm.] long.
Next row 1dc [US, single crochet, 1sc] into 2nd ch from hook, 1dc [1sc] into each remaining ch and fasten off.

To make up
Press each piece on the wrong side with a warm iron over a damp cloth.
Join back and front panels together as shown in diagram, carefully matching holes on the ribbon stitches at waist and on each top Candle pattern panel and leave 12 cast-on stitches free at side seam as shown. Fold cast-on edge of these stitches inside and catch down, tapering off at sleeve edge. This forms the underarm seam. Join shoulder and side seams. Press seams.

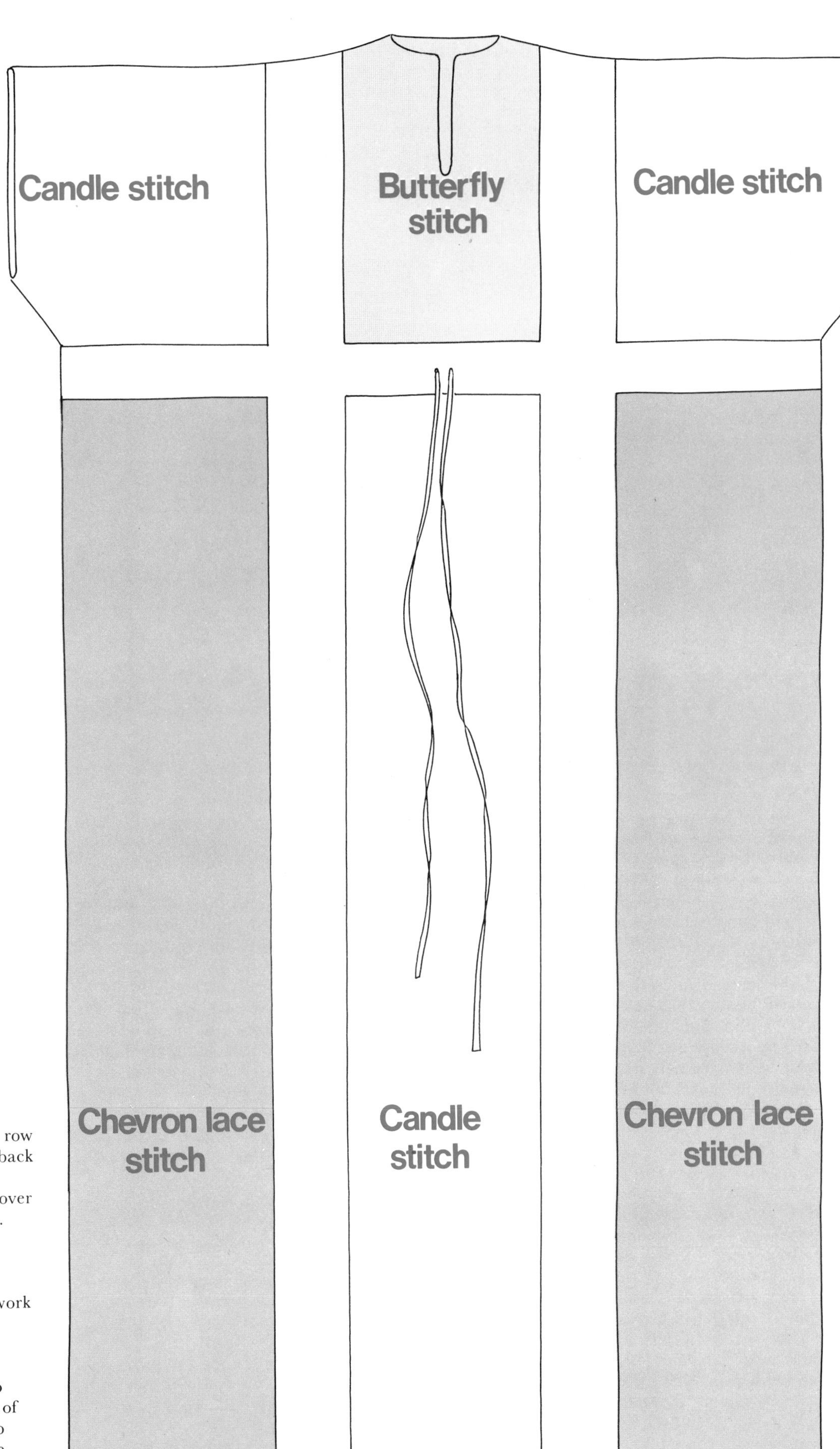

Neck edging
Using gold yarn and crochet hook, work a row of dc [sc] up right front neck edge, round back neck and down left front.
Turn with 1 ch and work 1 row of dc [sc] over dc [sc], working 2 dc [2 sc] in each corner.

Sleeve edgings
(Two alike)
Using chestnut brown and crochet hook, work 2 rows of dc [sc] along armhole edge.
Beg at centre front, thread the tie through ribbon stitches at waist to outside edge of vertical panel, pass tie through garment to back, and thread through waist to outside of vertical panel; pass tie through garment to front and thread through to meet at centre front.

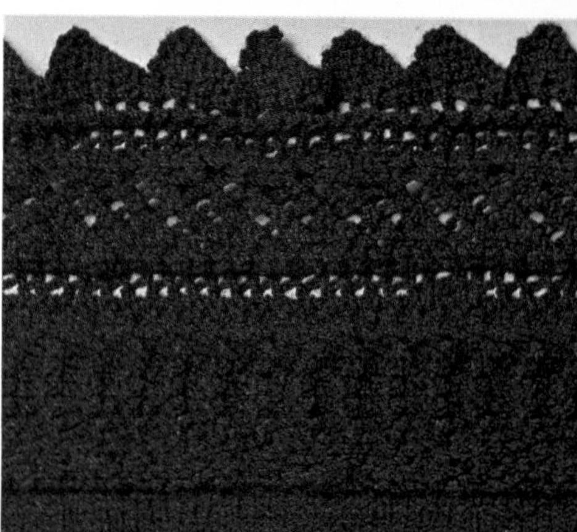

'Parliament' party dress

Prayer panel from the Great Exhibition

This knitted prayer panel is assumed to be an exhibit from the Great Exhibition held in London in 1851, as it seems to match the description of entry no. 214, "Knitting by a blind person, Prayer for the Houses of Parliament". The class into which this panel of knitting was entered was for Tapestry, Carpets, Floor-cloths, Lace and Embroidery.

The panel is knitted in two-ply cotton yarn to a tension or gauge of 13 stitches and 17 rows over one inch (25mm.). Overall, it measures 32ins. long by 15ins. wide (approximately 81cm. long by 38cm. wide). The letters are knitted on a plain ground in purl stitches and the panel is edged with a border of lace knitting, including the shell or wave stitch which is sometimes used on Shetland shawls.

The panel is an extremely beautiful piece of knitting but its chief attraction lies in its curiosity value as an example of the white cotton knitting which was still popular in Britain in the early 19th century. At the time of the Great Exhibition, however, the skill for fine knitting on wire needles had passed its zenith. The Great Exhibition, at best, provided a temporary remission for the decline of such beautiful work.

The prayer on the panel is the Prayer for the High Court of Parliament and reads as follows:

Most Gracious God, We humbly beseech thee, as for this Kingdom in general and especially for the High Court of Parliament under our most religious and Gracious Queen at this time assembled that thou wouldst be pleased to direct and prosper all their consultations to the advancement of thy glory, the good of thy church, the safety, honour and welfare of our sovereign and her Dominions, that all these things may be so ordered and settled by their endeavours, upon the best and surest foundations, that peace and happiness, truth and justice, religion and piety may be established among us for all generations. These and all other necessaries for them, for us and thy whole church, we humbly beg in the name and mediation of Jesus Christ our most blessed Lord and Saviour. Amen.
God Save the Queen.

Designed with absolute simplicity of shape, this low-backed sheath dress is lifted into the "designer" class with its knitted lace detail. The lace is an exact replica of the lace bordering the prayer panel above and provides the knitter with an opportunity of reproducing a truly historical pattern.

The dress illustrated is knitted in Wendy Tricel-Nylon 4-ply crêpe yarn in black.

Simple and strikingly plain, this evening dress derives from a prayer panel. The edging follows the panel's border and is delicately and beautifully worked. The result is an evening dress of real distinction.

Materials
29(31:33:35) 20gr. [21(22:24:25)oz.] balls of Black Tricel/Nylon 4-ply crepe yarn.
One pair of No. 10 [US No. 3] needles.
12in. [30cm.] zip fastener.

Tension or Gauge: 14 sts and 19 rows to 2in. [5cm.].

Special abbreviation for this design:
yf yarn forward.

Sizes
To fit bust sizes 32(34:36:38)in. [81(86:91:96)cm.].
Side seam including lace edging, 44(45:46:47)in. [111·5(114:116·5:119)cm.].
Length to shoulder seam, 51 (52:53½:54½)in. [129·5(132:135·5:138)cm.].
Note: Figures in parentheses ( ) refer to the larger sizes. Where there is only one figure this refers to all sizes.

Back and Front centre panels
(Both alike)
Using No. 10 [US No. 3] needles cast on 82(86:90:94) sts and beg with a K row, work in st st (stockinette stitch) for 6½(7:7½:8)in. [16·5(18:19:20·5)cm.], ending with a P row. (If longer or shorter dress is required adjust length here.*)
Dec 1 st at each end of next row and every following 16th row until the 7th dec row has been worked, then every 10th row for a further 13 dec rows.
On 42(46:50:54) sts st st (stockinette stitch) 15(19:23:27) rows.
Inc 1 st at each end of next row and every following 6th row until 9 inc rows have been worked.
On 60(64:68:72) sts st st (stockinette stitch) 8(10:12:14) rows ending with a K row. Now divide sts for neck.
Next row P11(12:13:14) sts. Cast off 38(40:42:44) sts, P to end and work on the last set of sts and K 1 row.

First side
Shape neck
1st row Cast off 3 sts, work to end.
2nd row Work to end.
Repeat last 2 rows twice (2:2:3 times).
Cast off the remaining 2(3:4:2) sts.
Rejoin yarn to right side of the 11(12:13:14) sts and work as First side.

Left Front and Back Right side panels
(Both alike)
Using No. 10 [US No. 3] needles, cast on 44(46:48:50) sts and work as for front panel until * is reached.

Shaping side seam edge
Dec 1 st at beg and end on right front and back left panels of next row and every following 16th row until the 7th dec row has been worked, then every following 10th row for a further 13 dec rows.
On 24(26:28:30) sts st st (stockinette stitch) 15(19:23:27) rows.
Inc 1 st at side seam edge of the next row and 3 following 6th rows.
On 28(30:32:34) sts st st (stockinette stitch) 49(51:53:55) rows – work 1 row more here on the right front and back left panel – ending at side seam edge.

Shape armhole
Cast off 4 sts at beg of next row and following alternate row.
Dec 1 st at armhole end of every alternate row until 10(12:12:12) sts remain.
Cont on these sts until armhole measures 7(7:7½:7½)in. [18(18:19:19)cm.] then cast off.

Right Front and Back Left side panels
(Both alike)
Work as given for Left Front panel but working the decreasing and increasing at end of rows and working the extra row where indicated, before shaping armhole.

To make up
Press on wrong side with a warm iron over a dry cloth. Join tog side seam edge of left front and left back side panels, leaving 12in. [30cm.] free for zip fastener, then right front and right back side panels. Now sew centre panels in position. Join shoulder seams. On wrong side catch together the row ends on shoulders for about 3in. [8cm.] on each side of shoulder seam, then turn under ¼in. [6mm.] all round neck edge and armholes and sew in position.

Lace edging for lower edge
Using No. 10 [US No. 3] needles, cast on 31 sts.
Foundation row K6, P7, K5, P12, K1.
1st row K13, *sl 1, K2, yf, K2 tog, K2, K2 tog, yf, K5, yf, K2 tog, yf, K1, yf, K1.
2nd row K6, yf, K2 tog, P7, K2, yf, K2 tog, K1*, P12, K1.
3rd row K1, inc 1, inc 1, ** P2 tog; rep from ** 3 times, inc 1, inc 1, *sl 1, K2, yf, K2 tog, K1, K2 tog, yf, K2 tog, yf, K4, yf, K2 tog, yf, K1, yf, K3.
4th row K8, yf, K2 tog, P7, K2, yf, K2 tog, K1*, P12, K1.
5th row K13, *sl 1, K2, yf, K2 tog, **K2 tog, yf; rep from ** twice, K3, yf, K2 tog, yf, K1, yf, K5.
6th row K10, yf, K2 tog, P7, K2, yf, K2 tog, K1*, P12, K1.
7th row K1, inc 1, inc 1, **P2 tog; repeat from ** 3 times, inc 1, inc 1, *sl 1, K2, yf, K2 tog, K1, K2 tog, yf, K2 tog, yf, K4, yf, K2 tog, yf, K1, yf, K7.
8th row Cast off 8, K next 3 sts, yf, K2 tog, P7, K2, yf, K2 tog, K1*, P12, K1.
These 8 rows form the lace edging; repeat these 8 rows until edging is long enough to go round lower edge of dress. Do not cast off. Sew edging in position casting off when all but 1in. [25mm.] has been sewn on and the correct length is assured.

Armhole edgings
(Both alike)
Using No. 10 [US No. 3] needles, cast on 3 sts, then K 1 row.
1st row K1, yf, K1, yf, K1.
2nd, 4th and 6th rows K.
3rd row K1, yf, K1, yf, K3.
5th row K1, yf, K1, yf, K5.
7th row K1, yf, K1, yf, K7.
8th row Cast off 8, K to end.
These 8 rows form the edging.
Continue in pattern until edging is long enough to go round one armhole. Sew in position as given for lace edging.

Front inset and neck edging
Using No. 10 [US No. 3] needles, cast on 15 sts.
Foundation row K6, P7, K2.
1st row Inc, K3, K2 tog, yf, K5, yf, K2 tog, yf, K1, yf, K1.
2nd row K6, yf, K2 tog, P7, K2, inc.
3rd row Inc, K4, K2 tog, yf, K2 tog, yf, K4, yf, K2 tog, yf, K1, yf, K3.

4th row K8, yf, K2 tog, P7, K2, yf, K2 tog, inc.
5th row Inc, then work from * to end of 5th row in instructions for lace edging.
6th row As 6th pattern row of lace edging to *, P1, inc 1.
7th row Inc, K2, work from * to end as 7th lace edging pattern row.
8th row As 8th lace edging pattern row to *, P3, inc.
9th row Inc 1, K4, work from * to end as 1st lace edging pattern row.
10th row As 2nd pattern row to *, P5, inc 1.
11th row Inc 1, K6, rep from * to end as 3rd pattern row.
12th row As 4th pattern row to *, P7, inc 1.
13th row Inc 1, K8, work from * to end as 5th pattern row.
14th row As 6th row to *, P9, inc 1.
15th row Inc 1, P4, P2 tog, P2 tog, inc 1 in each of next 2 sts, repeat from * to end as on 7th pattern row.
16th row As 8th row to *, P11, inc 1. 31 sts.
Now repeat the 8 rows of lace edging 8(9:9:10) times. Pattern 16 rows, decrease 1 st at beginning of next row and end of following row. 15 sts remain.
Next row Cast off 12, yf, K1, yf, K1. 5 sts.
Sew inset in position.
Beg with 2nd row of armhole edging on these 5 sts, cont in pattern until edging is long enough to go all round neck, ending at beg of inset.
Do not cast off. Sew edging in position, casting off when correct length is assured. Press all seams. Sew in zip fastener.

A detail from the prayer panel which it is thought was shown in the Great Exhibition in London in 1851.

Say it with flowers

19th-century knitted apron

This knitted apron may have been inspired by the Victorian pattern books that encouraged middle class English ladies to knit all kinds of decorative but impractical accessories and garments. Similar aprons were usually worn by ladies during the day, around the house, but they were usually made of woven fabric with a lace trimming or embroidered with floral patterns in silk threads and beads. This knitted apron is unique and was probably made by an enthusiastic and accomplished knitter to simulate a woven fabric.

The apron is knitted on fairly fine needles, using wool yarn in bright, cheerful colours, and the effect has all the zest of the folk knitting colour schemes of eastern Europe. Three different flower motifs are used in the design. A large, pink rose on a black ground is used for a wide border round the central panel. On this, a different flower motif is worked in stripes on a white ground. Strips of lace knitting divide the flower stripes. A third, smaller flower motif is repeated along the length of the waist band.

The apron is edged on three sides with a purl stitch border in white which produces a serrated pattern where it joins the black of the border. This pattern is repeated where the border meets the central panel and is also used around the edges of the pockets.

The skirt is gathered onto the separate waistband and the shaped pockets are also sewn on separately. As the entire skirt of the apron was knitted in one piece, this must have been a very complicated pattern to follow, particularly when the central panel was being knitted.

The charming rose motif on the border of the Victorian apron has inspired the rose which decorates this simply-designed sweater and skirt set. Brilliantly contrasting with the black ground, the rose is worked in two tones of pink with green leaves.

The skirt has an elasticated waistline and is made in four shaped panels. Three rose motifs are placed on the front of the skirt and three on the back.

The matching v-necked sweater picks up the crimson of the rose motif on the neckband, cuffs and ribbed welt and has a single motif on the left shoulder.

The sweater set illustrated was knitted in Hayfields "Gaylon" Double Knitting yarn.

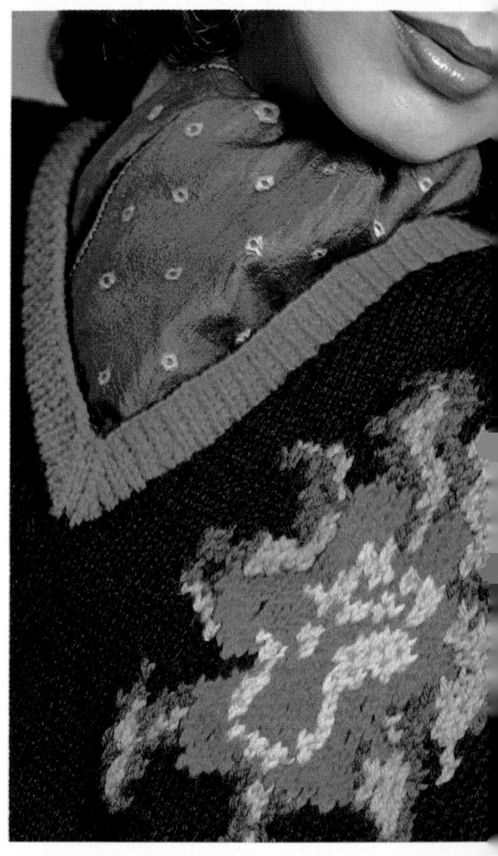

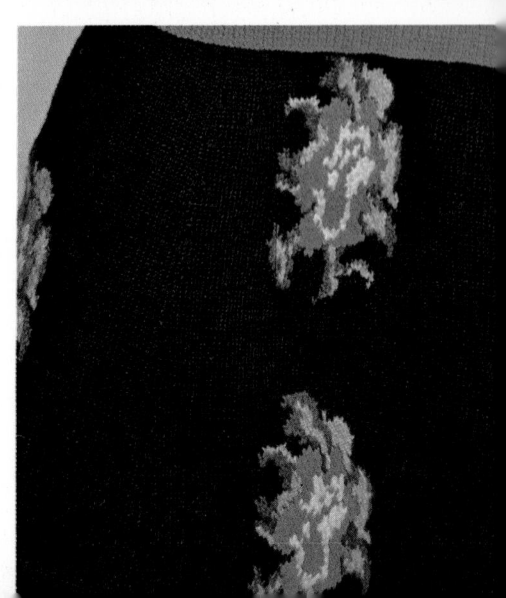

Splashed with stylised roses, this skirt and sweater has a touch of drama and boldness about it.

Materials
Sweater: 15(15:16) 25gr. [14(14:14)oz.] balls of Double Knitting [knitting worsted] yarn in black (B), 5 [5] balls in cherry (C), 1 [1] ball each in emerald (E), jade green (J) and pink (P).
Skirt: 16(17:18) 25gr. [14(15:16)oz.] balls in black and 1 [1] ball each in cherry, emerald, jade green and pink.
1in. [2·5cm.] wide elastic to waist measurement.
For both garments: One pair each of Nos. 9 and 11 [US Nos. 4 and 2] needles and one pair of No. 10 [US No. 3] needles for the skirt.

Tension or Gauge: 12 sts and 16 rows to 2in. [5cm.] using No. 9 [US No. 4] needles.

Sizes
Sweater
To fit bust sizes 32(34:36)in. [81(86:91)cm.].
Length from shoulder, 23½(23½:24)in. [60(60:61)cm.].
Sleeve seam, 18(18:18)in. [46(46:46)cm.].
Skirt
Suitable for hip sizes 34(36:38)in. [86(91:96)cm.].
Length, 26(26:26)in. [66(66:66)cm.].
Note: Figures in parentheses ( ) refer to the larger sizes. Where there is only one figure this refers to all sizes.

Sweater front
Using No. 11 [US No. 2] needles and C, cast on 119(127:133) sts and work in rib as follows:
1st row K2, *P1, K1; repeat from * ending K2.
2nd row K1, *P1, K1; repeat from * to end.
Repeat these 2 rows for 4in. [10cm.] ending with a 1st row.
Break off C and join in B and P 1 row.
Dec row K6(3:6), K2 tog, *K5, K2 tog; repeat from * until 6(3:6) remain, K6(3:6). 103(109:115) sts*.
Change to No. 9 [US No. 4] needles and beginning with a P row work in st st (stockinette stitch) until work measures 12¼in. [31cm.] ending with a K row.
Next row P60(64:68) sts and place a marker after last st, P31 for motif, place a marker after last st, P to end.
The markers denote beginning and end of motif sts.
Continue in st st (stockinette stitch) and work motif.
1st row of motif K12(14:16) B, for 31 st motif, K16 B, 1 E, 14 B, then K to end with B. This row sets the sts for the motif.
Now work from the 2nd to 24th row on chart.
Continue working motif and divide sts for neck and shoulders.
Next row Pattern 51(54:57) sts, turn, leaving the remaining sts on a spare needle.
Left front
Shape neck
Pattern 2 rows.
Next row P1, P2 tog. Pattern to end.
Pattern 2 rows.
Shape armhole and continue to shape neck.
1st row Cast off 4(5:6) sts, pattern until 3 remain, K2 tog, K1.
Pattern 11 rows, dec 1 st at armhole end on first 3 rows, then 4 following alternate rows; at *the same time* dec 1 st at neck edge on every 3rd row following previous dec. This completes the armhole shaping.
Continue to dec at neck edge on every 3rd row until 23(25:27) sts remain, but when the 49th row of motif has been completed, continue with B only.
On 23(25:27) sts, continue in st st (stockinette stitch) until armhole measures 7(7:7½)in. [18(18:19)cm.] ending at armhole end.

Shape shoulder
Cast off 4(5:6) sts at beg of next row, 5 sts at beg of 3 following alternate rows. Work 1 row then cast off remaining 4(5:6) sts.
With right side of work facing you, slip the first stitch onto a stitch holder and leave for neck band.

Right front shoulder
Rejoin B to remaining sts and st st (stockinette stitch) 3 rows.

Shape neck
P until 3 remain, P2 tog through back of loops, P1. St st (stockinette stitch) 2 rows.
Next row K1, sl 1, K1, psso, K to end.
Shape armhole and continue to shape neck.
Next row Cast off 4(5:6) sts, P to end.
Complete as left front shoulder, reversing all shapings.

Back
Work as given for front until * is reached.
Change to No. 9 [US No. 4] needles and using B only, beginning with a P row, work in st st (stockinette stitch) until back measures same as front to armholes, ending with a P row.

Shape armholes
Cast off 4(5:6) sts at beg of next 2 rows.
Dec 1 st at each end of next 3 rows, then 4 following alternate rows.
On 81(85:89) sts, cont in st st (stockinette stitch) until armhole measures same as front to shoulder ending with a P row.

Shape shoulders
Cast off 4(5:6) sts at beg of next 2 rows; 5 sts at beg of 2 following rows.
Shape back neck and continue shaping shoulders.
Next row Cast off 5 sts, K next 11(12:13) sts and work on these 12(13:14) sts, turn, leaving remaining sts on a spare needle.
1st row P2 tog, P to end.
2nd row Cast off 5, K until 2 remain, K2 tog.
3rd row As 1st row.
Cast off remaining 4(5:6) sts.
With right side of work facing you, slip the first 29 sts onto a stitch holder, rejoin yarn to remaining sts and K to end of row.
Continue as follows:
1st row Cast off 5, P until 2 remain, P2 tog.
2nd row K2 tog, K to end.
3rd row As 1st row.
Work 1 row then cast off remaining 4(5:6) sts.

Sleeves
Using No. 11 [US No. 2] needles and C, cast on 47(49:49) sts and work 4in. [10cm.] in rib as given on front ending with a first row.
Break off C, join in B and P 1 row.
Inc row K2, inc 1, *K5, inc 1; repeat from * until 2(4:4) sts remain, K to end. 55(57:57) sts.
Change to No. 9 [US No. 4] needles.
Beginning with a P row, st st (stockinette stitch) 7 rows.
Continue in st st (stockinette stitch) and inc 1 st at each end of the next row and every following 10th (10th:8th) row until there are 75(77:81) sts on the needle.
Continue on these sts until sleeve measures 18in. [46cm.] (or to length required) ending with a P row.

Shape top
Cast off 4(5:6) sts at beg of next 2 rows, then dec 1 st at each end of every row until 57(57:59) sts remain.
Now dec 1 st at each end of every alternate row until 31 sts remain, then 1 st at each end of every row until 17 sts remain. Cast off.

Neck band
Join right shoulder seam. Using No. 11 [US No. 2] needles and C, pick up and K 68(68:72) sts from left front neck edge, K 1 st from holder and mark this stitch with a coloured thread, pick up and K 68(68:72) sts from right front neck edge, 5 sts from right back neck edge. K across the 29 sts of back, inc 4 sts evenly, pick up and K 6 sts from left back neck edge. 181(181:189) sts.
1st row *P1, K1; repeat from * to within 2 sts of marked st, P2 tog, P marked st, P2 tog through back of loops, rib to end.
2nd row Rib to within 2 sts of marked st, sl 1, K1, psso, K marked st, K2 tog, rib to end.
Repeat these 2 rows 3 times more.
Cast off in rib and at the same time dec 1 st each side of marked st.

To make up
Press all parts except the ribbing lightly on the wrong side with a warm iron over a damp cloth.
Join left shoulder seam, cont seam across neck band. Set in sleeves. Join sleeve and side seams. Press seam.

Skirt, Panel 1
(Make two)

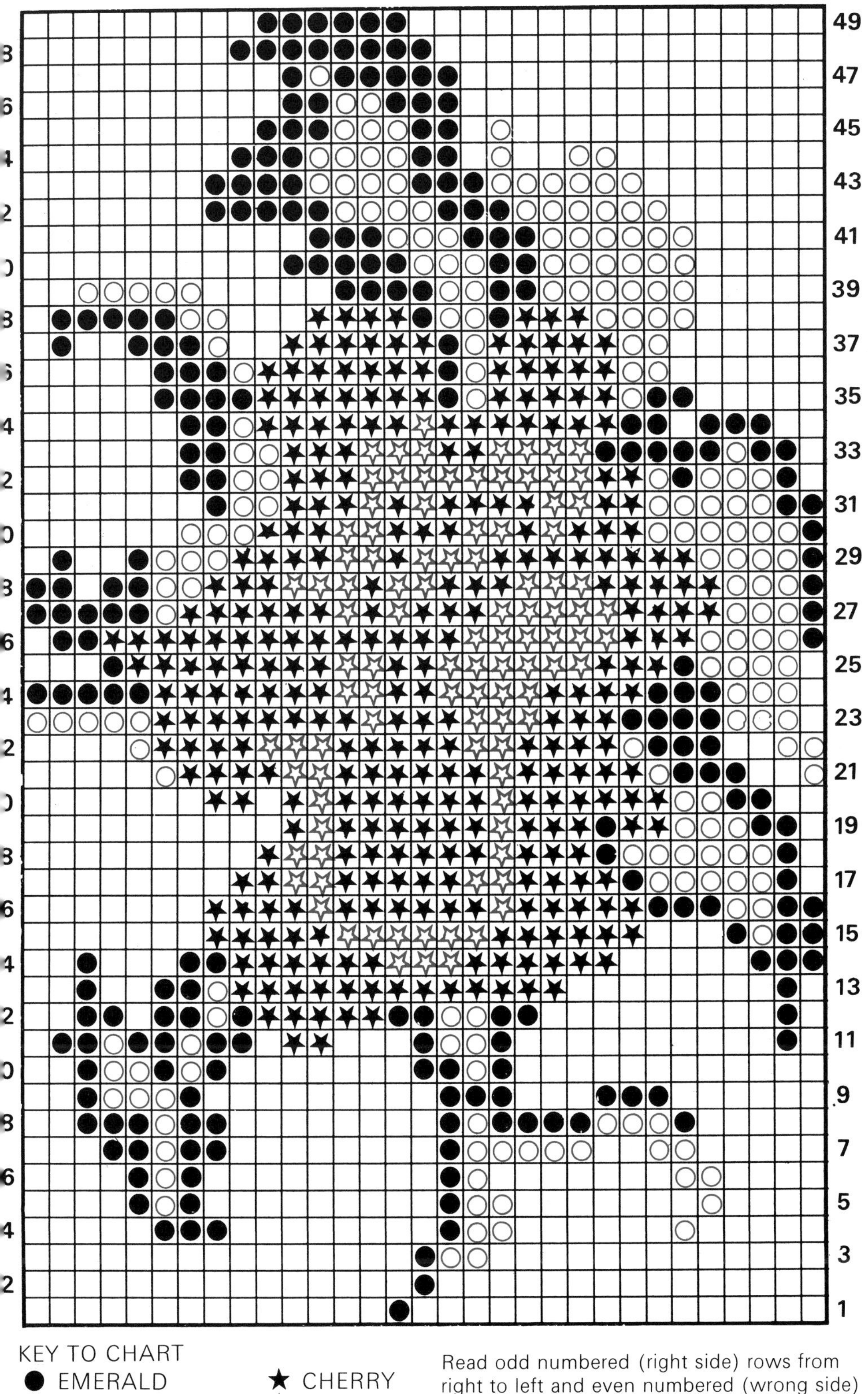

KEY TO CHART
● EMERALD
○ JADE GREEN
★ CHERRY
☆ PINK

Read odd numbered (right side) rows from right to left and even numbered (wrong side) rows from left to right.

Using No. 10 [US No. 3] needles and B, cast on 89(91:93) sts and st st (stockinette stitch) 9 rows.
K 1 row on the wrong side to mark hem line*.
Change to No. 9 [US No. 4] needles and K 1 row.
Next row P29(30:31) sts and place a marker after last st, for motif P31 sts and place a marker after last st, P29(30:31).
1st row of motif With B, K29(30:31), for 31 st motif, K16 with B, 1 with E, 14 with B, K to end with B.
This row sets the sts for the motif.
Now work from 2nd to 8th row of chart.
Continue to work the motif on the 31 sts, and shape panel as follows:
Dec row K1, sl 1, K1, psso, pattern until 3 remain, K2 tog, K1.
Cont to dec in this way on every 8th row until 77(79:81) sts remain and the motif is completed.
Cont with B only, still dec on every 8th row until 71(73:75) sts remain.
St st (stockinette stitch) 2 rows.
Next row P20(21:22) sts, place a marker after last st; for motif P 31 sts, place marker after last st, P to end.
1st row of 2nd motif With B K20(21:22) sts for 31 st motif, K16 B, 1 E, 14 B, K to end with B.
Now work from 2nd to 4th rows on chart.
Continuing to work the 31 sts as on chart, dec 1 st at each end of the next row and every following 8th row until 43(45:47) sts remain, but when the 2nd motif is complete, continue with B only.
On 43(45:47) sts cont in st st (stockinette stitch) until panel measures 26in [66cm.] from hem line, ending with a P row, then cast off.

Panel 2
(Make two)
Work as for panel 1 until * is reached.
Change to No. 9 [US No. 4] needles and st st (stockinette stitch) 10 rows.
Now dec as shown on panel 1, on next row and every following 8th row until 79(81:83) sts remain.
St st (stockinette stitch) 4 rows.
Next row P24(25:26) sts, place marker after last st; for motif P31, place marker after last st, P24(25:26).
1st row of motif With B B24(25:26) sts, for the 31 st motif, K16 B, 1 E, 14 B, K24(25:26) B.
This row sets the sts for the motif.
Work 2nd row of motif.
Continue to work the 31 sts as on chart, dec 1 st at each end of next row and every following 8th row until 43(45:47) sts remain, but when the motif is complete, continue with B only.
On 43(45:47) sts, cont in st st (stockinette stitch) until panel measures same as panel 1, then cast off.

To make up
Press as for sweater. Join panels together alternating panels 1 and 2. Turn up all round at marked hem line and sew cast-on edge in position. Make waist length of elastic into a ring, place on wrong side of skirt at waist and work a casing over elastic to hold in position. Press seams.

A classic twinset

Seamless cotton jacket, English 17th century

Cotton was introduced into Britain in the 17th century and this jacket in London's Victoria and Albert Museum is an excellent example of the way in which the new yarn was knitted into garments.

The patterning is based on crosses and diamonds, knitted in purl stitch. Bands of pattern run round the cuffs and hem and down the front and back of the sleeves. The same pattern bands either side of the front opening and runs down the centre of the back.

The jacket is knitted in stocking or stockinette stitch on two needles and was worked from the hem upwards. The two fronts and the back are knitted in one piece without seams, even the underarm gusset being shaped during knitting. Curiously, although the garment is entirely constructed without seams, a traditional technique in folk knitting in the British Isles, imitation seams have been knitted round the gussets and up the jacket sides.

This type of edge-to-edge jacket, carefully constructed in a yarn and colour that would require careful and frequent laundering, was probably worn by ladies of some social standing in the privacy of their homes. Children are known to have worn similar jackets.

Inspired by the 300-year-old cotton jacket, a similar patterning, in purl and plain knitting, runs round the cardigan cuffs and hem, on the patch pockets and down the fronts. The long-sleeved matching sweater has a square neckline and bands of pattern running down the front and back, from the shoulder seam. The set-in sleeves of both garments have an unusual square raglan design, similar to the cotton jacket, thus giving a softer-looking shoulder line. This sweater set is knitted in Emu Scotch Superwash 4-ply yarn in "Everglades" green.

Classically simple, this sweater and cardigan set brings out the crosses and diamond edging and pockets in bold relief.

Materials
Sweater: 10(11:12:14) 25gr. [8(9:9:11)oz.] balls 4-ply medium-weight yarn.
Cardigan: 14(15:17:18) 25gr. [11(12:13:14)oz.] balls 4-ply medium-weight yarn.
For both garments: one pair each of No. 12 and No. 10 [US Nos. 1 and 3] needles.

Tension or Gauge: 15 sts and 19 rows to 2in. [5cm.] over st st (stockinette stitch) using No. 10 [US No. 3] needles.

Sizes
Sweater
To fit bust size 32(34:36:38)in. [81(86:91:97)cm.].
Length from shoulder, 19½(20:20½:21)in. [49·5(50·5:52:53)cm.].
Sleeve seam, 16½(16½:17:17)in. [42(42:43:43)cm.].

Cardigan
Length from shoulder, 25½(26:26½:27)in. [64·5(65·5:66·5:67·5)cm.].
Sleeve seam, 17(17:17½:17½)in. [43(43:44:44)cm.].
Note: Figures in parentheses ( ) refer to the larger sizes. Where there is only one figure this refers to all sizes.

Sweater back
Using No. 12 [US No. 1] needles, cast on 118(124:132:138) sts and work 24 rows in K1, P1 rib.
Change to No. 10 [US No. 3] needles and beg with a K row, st st (stockinette stitch) 8 rows.
Cont in st st (stockinette stitch) and inc 1 st at each end of the next row and every foll 12th row until there are 128(134:142:148) sts on the needle.
Cont in st st (stockinette stitch) on these sts until the work measures 12(12¼:12½:12¾)in. [30·5(31:31·5:32)cm.], ending with a P row.

Shape armholes
Cast off 9 sts at beg of next 2 rows. Dec 1 st at each end of the 6(8:10:12) foll rows. 98(100:104:106) sts remain. Work in pattern and st st (stockinette stitch) as follows:
1st row K1, *K8, P2, K1, P2, K8*, K until 22 sts remain, repeat from * to *, K1.
2nd row P1, *P7, K3, P1, K3, P7*, P until 22 sts remain from * to *, P1.
3rd row K1, *K6, P4, K1, P4, K6*, K until 22 sts remain from * to *, K1.
4th row P1, *P5, K5, P1, K5, P5*, P until 22 sts remain from * to *, P1.
5th row K1, *K4, P6, K1, P6, K4*, K until 22 sts remain from * to *, K1.
6th row P1, *P3, K7, P1, K7, P3*, P until 22 sts remain from * to *, P1.
7th row K1, *K2, P7, K3, P7, K2*, K until 22 sts remain from * to *, K1.
8th row P1, *P1, K7, P5, K7, P1*, P until 22 sts remain from * to *, P1.
9th row K1, *P7, K2, P1, K1, P1, K2, P7*, K until 22 sts remain, repeat from * to *, K1.
10th row P1, *K6, P2, K2, P1, K2, P2, K6*, P until 22 sts remain, repeat from * to *, P1.
11th row K1, *K7, P3, K1, P3, K7*, K until 22 sts remain from * to *, K1.
12th row P1, *P6, K4, P1, K4, P6*, P until 22 sts remain from * to *, P1.
13th row K1, *K5, P4, K3, P4, K5*, K until 22 sts remain from * to *, K1.
14th row P1, *P4, K4, P5, K4, P4*, P until 22 sts remain from * to *, P1.
15th to 26 rows Repeat from the 13th row back to the 2nd row inclusive. **
Repeat these 26 rows once more and the first 4(6:8:10) pattern rows again.

Shape shoulders
Cast off 6 sts at beg of next 6 rows then 5(6:7:8) sts at beg of 2 following rows. 52(52:54:54) sts.

Back neck band
Change to No. 12 [US No. 1] needles and work 8 rows in K1, P1 rib. Cast off in rib.

Front
Work as given for back until ** is reached. Repeat the first 6(8:10:12) rows again.

Shape neck
Next row Work 22 sts in pattern, K7(7:8:8) turn and leave remaining sts on a holder.
Keeping the continuity of the pattern, dec 1 st at neck edge of the next row and every following 4th row until 23(24:25:26) sts remain.
Cont in pattern without shaping until armhole matches back, ending at armhole end with a P row.

Shape shoulder
Cast off 6 sts at beg of next row and 2 following alternate rows. Work 1 row then cast off remaining 5(5:7:8) sts. With right side of work facing, slip first 40(42:44:46) sts on holder, rejoin yarn and work in pattern to end of row.
Complete to match first side.

Sleeves
Using No. 12 [US No. 1] needles cast on 50(54:58:62) sts. Work 24 rows in K1, P1 rib, inc 1 st at end of last row.
Change to No. 10 [US No. 3] needles and work in st st (stockinette stitch) for 4 rows, beg with a K row.
Inc 1 st at each end of next row and every foll 8th row 7 times then every 6th row a further 12 times. 89(93:97:101) sts.
Continue without shaping until sleeve measures 16½(16½:17:17)in. [42(42:43:43)cm.] or length required, ending with a P row.
Place a marker at each end of last row. Work 12 rows st st (stockinette stitch).

Shape top
Dec 1 st at each end of the next 6(6:8:8) rows.
Cast off 7 sts at beg of 8 following rows.
Cast off remaining 21(25:25:29) sts.

Front neckband
With right side of work facing and using No. 12 [US No. 1] needles, pick up and K 28 sts down left front neck, K across 40(42:44:46) sts at centre front, pick up and K 28 sts up right front neck 96(98:100:102) sts.
1st row Beg with P1, rib 25, K2 tog, P1 and mark the st, K2 tog, beg with P1, rib 16 (18:20:20), P2 tog, beg with K1, rib 18(18:18:20), K2 tog, P1 and mark this st, K2 tog, beg with P1, rib to end.
2nd row Rib 24, sl 1, K1, psso, K1, K2 tog, rib 33(35:37:39), sl 1, K1, psso, K1, K2 tog, rib to end.
Rib 6 more rows decreasing, as before at each side of the marked sts on each row.
Cast off in rib still decreasing as before.

Cardigan back
Using No. 12 [US No. 1] needles, cast on 128(136:144:150) sts.
Work 8 rows in K1, P1 rib, inc 1 st at end of last row. 129(137:145:151) sts.
Change to No. 10 [US No. 3] needles and work in st st (stockinette stitch) 2 rows. Now work the border pattern.
1st row K7(11:15:P1, K17), *P2, K1, P2, K17*, rep from * to * 4 times, P2, K1, P2, then K7(11:15:K17, P1).
2nd row P6(10:14:K2, P15), *K3, P1, K3, P15*, repeat from * to * 4 times, K3, P1, K3, then P6(10:14:K2, P15).
3rd row K5(9:13:P3, K13), *P4, K1, P4, K13*, repeat from * to * 4 times, P4, K1, P4, then K5(9:13:K13, P3).
4th row P4(8:K1, P11:K4, P11), *K5, P1, K5, P11*, repeat from * to * 4 times, K5, P1, K5, then P4(8:P11, K1:P11, K4).
5th row K3(7:P2, K9:P5, K9), *P6, K1, P6, K9*, repeat from * to * 4 times, P6, K1, P6, then K3(7:K9, P2:K9, P5).
6th row P2, K7, P1(P6, K7, P1:K3, P7, K7, P1:K6, P7, K7, P1), *K7, P7, K7, P1* repeat from * to * 4 times, K7, then P2(6:P7, K3:P7, K6).
7th row K1(5:P4, K5:P7, K5), *P7, K3, P7, K5*, repeat from * to * 4 times, P7, K3, P7, then K1(5:K5, P4:K5, P7).
8th row K7(K1, P3, K7:K5, P3, K7:P1, K7, P3, K7), *P5, K7, P3, K7*, repeat from * to * 4 times, P5, then K7(K7, P3, K1:K7, P3, K5:K7, P3, K7, P1).
9th row P6(P2, K1, P7:P6, K1, P7:K2, P7, K1, P7) *K2, P1, K1, P1, K2, P7, K1, P7*,

repeat from * to * 4 times, K2, P1, K1, P1, K2, then P6(P7:K1, P2:P7, K1, P6:P7, K1, P7, K2).
10th row K5, P2, K2(K2, P1, K6, P2, K2:K6, P1, K6, P2, K2:K1, P2, K6, P1, K6, P2, K2), *P1, K2, P2, K6, P1, K6, P2, K2*, repeat from * to * 4 times, P1, K2, P2, then K5(K6, P1, K2:K6, P1, K6:K6, P1, K6, P2, K1).
11th row K6, P3(K10, P3:K14, P3:P2, K15, P3), *K1, P3, K15, P3*, repeat from * to * 4 times, K1, P3, then K6(K10:K14:K15, P2).
12th row P5, K4(P9, K4:P13, K4:K3, P13, K4), *P1, K4, P13, K4*, repeat from * to * 4 times, P1, K4, then P5(P9:P13:P13, K3).
13th row K4, P4, K3(K8, P4, K3:P1, K11, P4, K3:P4, K11, P4, K3)* P4, K11, P4, K3*, rep from * to * 4 times, P4, then K4(K8:K11, P1:K11, P4).
14th row P3, K4, P5(P7, K4, P5:K2, P9, K4, P5:P1, K4, P9, K4, P5) *K4, P9, K4, P5*, repeat from * to * 4 times, K4, then P3(P7:P9, K2:P9, K4, P1).
15th to 26th rows Repeat from the 13th back to the 2nd row inclusive.
Repeat these 26 rows once and the 1st row again to complete border pattern.
Beg with a P row, work in st st (stockinette stitch) until work measures 18(18¼:18½:18¾)in. [45·5(46:46·5:47)cm.] ending with a P row.

Shape armholes
Cast off 14(16:18:20) sts at beg of next 2 rows. Work straight until armhole measures 7½(7¾:8:8¼)in. [19(19·5:20:20·5)cm.], ending with a P row.

Shape shoulders
Cast off 8(8:9:9) sts at beg of next 6 rows and then 7(8:7:7) sts at the beginning of 2 following rows. 39(41:41:43) sts remain.

Back neck border
Change to No. 12 [US No. 1] needles and work 8 rows in K1, P1 rib. Cast off in rib.

Pocket backs
(Two alike)
Using No. 10 [US No. 3] needles cast on 37 sts. Work 46 rows in st st (stockinette stitch). Leave sts on a spare needle until required.

Left front
Using No. 12 [US No. 1] needles, cast on 63(67:71:74) sts.
Work 8 rows in K1, P1 rib, dec 1 st at centre front edge of each row for mitred corner. 55(59:63:66) sts.
Change to No. 10 [US No. 3] needles. Work in st st (stockinette stitch) 2 rows. Work in pattern.
1st row K7(11:15:P1, K17), *P2, K1, P2, K17*, rep from * to * once, P2, K2.
2nd row P2, K3, *P15, K3, P1, K3*, repeat from * to * once. P6(10:14:P15, K2).
3rd row K5(9:13:P3, K13), *P4, K1, P4, K13*, repeat from * to * once, P4, K2.
4th row P2, K5, *P11, K5, P1, K5* repeat from * to * once, P4(P8:P11, K1:P11, K4).
5th row K3(7:P2, K9:P5, K9), *P6, K1, P6, K9* repeat from * to * once, P6, K2.
6th row P2, *K7, P7, K7, P1*, repeat from * to * once, K7, then P2(P6:P7, K3:P7, K6).
7th row K1(K5:P4, K5:P7, K5), *P7, K3, P7, K5*, repeat from * to * once, P7, K3.
8th row P4, *K7, P3, K7, P5*, repeat from * to * once, K7(K7, P3, K1:K7, P3, K5:K7, P3, K7, P1).
9th row P6(P2, K1, P7:P6, K1, P7:K2, P7, K1, P7), *K2, P1, K1, P1, K2, P7, K1, P7*, repeat from * to * once K2, P1, K2.
10th row P2, *K2, P2, K6, P1, K6, P2, K2, P1*, repeat from * to * once, K2, P2, then K5 (K6, P1, K2:K6, P1, K6:K6, P1, K6, P2, K1).
11th row K6, P3(K10, P3:K14, P3:P2, K15, P3) *K1, P3, K15, P3*, repeat from * to * once, K2.
12th row P2, *K4, P13, K4, P1*, repeat from * to * once, K4 then P5(P9:P13:P13, K3).
13th row K4, P4, K3(K8, P4, K3:P1, K11, P4, K3:P4, K11, P4, K3), *P4, K11, P4, K3*, repeat from * to * once.
14th row P4, *K4, P9, K4, P5*, rep from * to * once K4, then P3(P7:P9, K2:P9, K4, P1).
15th to 26th row Repeat from 13th row back to 2nd row inclusive. Rep these 26th rows once then the 1st row again.
Next row Work 12 sts in pattern. For pocket ribbing, beg with K1, rib 37. P to end.
Next row K6(10:14:17), rib 37. Work last 12 sts in pattern. Repeat last 2 rows once.
Next row Work 12 sts in pattern, cast off 37 sts in rib, P to end.
Pocket row K6(10:14:17), K across 37 sts of one pocket back, work last 12 sts in pattern.
Next row Work 12 sts in pattern, P to end.
Continue pattern until front measures same as back to armholes, ending with a P row.

Shape armhole and front edge
1st row Cast off 14(16:18:20), K until 14 sts remain, K2 tog for front shaping, work last 12 sts in pattern.
** Keeping the continuity of the pattern, dec by taking tog the 13th and 14th sts from front edge on every following 6th row until 31(32:34:34) sts remain.
Continue on these sts until armhole measures same as back ending with a P row.

Shape shoulder
Cast off 8(8:9:9) sts at beg of next row and 2 following alternate rows.
Work 1 row then cast off remaining 7(8:7:7) sts.

Right front
Work as for left front to armholes but reversing pocket ribbing rows, pocket rows and pattern.
1st pattern row will read K2, P2, *K17, P2, K1, P2*, repeat from * to * once, K7(11:15:K17, P1).
2nd row P6(10:14:K2, P15), *K3, P1, K3, P15*, repeat from * to * K3, P2. These 2 rows set the sts for the patt.

Shape front and armhole
1st row Work 12 sts in pattern, sl 1, K1, psso, K to end.
Cast off 14(16:18:20) sts.
P until 12 remain. Work these stitches in pattern stitch.
Work from ** to end as given on left front.

Front bands
(Both alike)
Using No. 12 [US No. 1] needles and with right side of work facing pick up and K172(176:180:184) sts from row ends of front.
Work 8 rows in K1, P1 rib, inc 1 st at lower edge on each row.
Cast off in rib.

Sleeves
Using No. 12 [US No. 1] needles cast on 62(62:70:70) sts.
Work 8 rows in K1, P1 rib, inc 1 st at end of last row.
Change to No. 10 [US No. 3] needles.
Work 2 rows in st st (stockinette stitch).
Work the 26 pattern rows as given for 1st (1st:2nd:2nd) sizes on back but working the stitches between * and * twice instead of 5 times.
Work the 1st row again.
Beg with a P row work st st (stockinette stitch) 3 rows. Inc 1 st at each end of the next row and every following 6th row until there are 91(95:99:103) sts. Continue on these sts until sleeve measures 17(17:17½:17½)in. [43(43:44)cm.], or to length required, ending with a P row. Place a marker at each end of last row.
Work st st (stockinette stitch) 16(18:20:22) rows.

Shape top
Cast off 9 sts at beg of next 8 rows.
Cast off remaining 19(23:27:31) sts.

To make up
Press pieces lightly under a damp cloth with a warm iron. Join shoulder seams, continuing seams across ribbing. Set in sleeves matching markers to sts cast off for armholes on both back and front. Join sleeve and side seams. Sew pocket backs in position on the wrong side on Cardigan and neatly join mitre corners at lower edge. Press all seams.

Jewelled with beads

18th-century baby's bonnet

This baby bonnet is a very good example of English white knitting and was probably knitted during the late 18th century. At this time knitting was a fashionable pastime in Britain and most hand knitting was worked with fine, white cotton on wire needles. Great skills were developed, as can be seen by the quality of this bonnet. Much of the delicate white knitting produced was used for making baby clothes which were, luckily, greatly treasured so that fine examples still exist today.

The bonnet is traditional in shape with the crown knitted in a lacy fan-shaped pattern with a double row of beads worked into the edge. The main part of the bonnet is also knitted in a very open lace pattern with single beads knitted into the fabric.

The bonnet is edged with a beautifully worked border of beadwork flowers, finished with a frill of net, edged with drawn-thread embroidery.

The beadwork flower border would have been rather difficult to work and considerable pre-planning would have been involved. Every bead must be threaded onto the yarn in sequence before knitting can be started. A chart is usually used and the pattern followed from the top left corner and so down to the bottom right. The design would have an odd number of rows and the last bead threaded onto the yarn from the chart would be the first to be knitted.

Knitting needles used for beaded work must be fine enough to form a loop of yarn smaller than the size of the bead, otherwise the bead falls through the loop to the back of the work. The needles used to knit the bonnet edge would have been extremely fine and probably made of wire. Cotton yarn was particularly suitable for this type of beadwork as the yarn had to be strong enough to maintain a firm tension.

Beaded knitting is fascinating to do and this pretty halter evening top uses beading for the edge band, the halter straps and for the belt. The beading pattern, which uses red, irridescent dark blue and turquoise blue beads, is worked on a pale blue ground. The design is abstracted from the bead edging of the baby's bonnet opposite.

The garment is knitted in a textured stitch which provides a contrast to the glitter of the beaded areas. The halter straps tie at the back of the neck. The top illustrated was knitted in Emu 4-ply Courtelle/Nylon yarn in dark and pale blue with red, dark blue and pale blue beads.

Perfect for informal evening wear, combining beautifully with either trousers or a long skirt, this beaded top has a novelty look which lends it an intriguing air.

Materials
6(7:8) 20gr. [5/6:7)oz.] balls of Courtelle/Nylon mixture 4-ply yarn in Navy (N) and 2[2] balls in Light Blue (L).
One pair each of Nos. 12 and 10 [US Nos. 1 and 3] needles.
1066(1139:1212) Red (A) No. 7 size beads, 810(851:891) Navy (B); 230(253:276) Pale Blue (C).
1 buckle with 1½in. [4cm.] bar.

Tension or Gauge: 16 sts to 2in. [5cm.] over the pattern and 10 sts over beaded pattern using No. 10 [US No. 3] needles.

Sizes
To fit bust sizes 32(34:36)in. [81(86:91cm.]. Side seam including band, 15½(16:16½)in. [39·5(41:42)cm.].
Note: Figures in parentheses ( ) refer to the larger sizes. Where there is only one figure given this refers to all sizes.

Back
Using No. 12 [US No. 1] needles and N, cast on 114(122:130) sts and work 4 rows in K1, P1 rib.
Change to No. 10 [US No. 3] needles.
Now work in pattern as follows:
1st row (right side) P.
2nd row P1, *P3 tog, K1, P1, K1 all into next st; repeat from * until 1 st remains, P1.
3rd row P.
4th row P1, *K1, P1, K1 all into next st, P3 tog; repeat from * until 1 st remains, P1.
These 4 rows form the pattern. Repeat them until work measures 8(8½:9)in. [20·5(21·5:23)cm.] end with a P row.

Shape side seam edge
Inc 1 st at each end of next row and every following 4th row until 130(138:146) sts.
Continue on these sts until work measures 14½(15:15½)in. [37(38:39·5)cm.] ending with a wrong-side row*. Cast off knitwise.

Front
Work as for back until * is reached.

Shape top
Cast off 12(14:16) sts at the beg of next 2 rows; 8(10:12) sts on 2 following rows; 6 sts on next 6 rows; then 5 sts on the 10 following rows. K tog the 4 remaining sts.

Right front strap
** Using No. 10 [US No. 3] needles and L cast on 131(137:143) sts and begin and end with a P row st st (stockinette stitch) 5 rows. Work in bead pattern as follows, working odd-numbered rows P and even-numbered rows K. Break off yarn. Thread 130(136:142) A beads on yarn and rejoin yarn.
1st row of charts 1, 2 and 3 *(Right side)* P1, * push A bead up to last st worked, P1; repeat from * to end**.
*** Break off yarn. Thread 2 B, 2 C and 1 B beads onto yarn.
2nd row of charts 2, 3 and 1 Begin at side seam edge and K45(48:51) to 15th st on chart 3, K5, push up 1 B bead, K2 (push up 1 C bead, K1), twice, K1, (push up 1 B bead, K1) twice, K2 – this is the 2nd st on chart 3, K72(75:78) ending at tie end.
Break off yarn. Thread 16 B, 3 C and 18 B beads onto yarn.
3rd row of charts 1, 3 and 2 P47(50:53), from chart 1, *P2, (P1, push up 1 B) 3 times, repeat from * 4 times more, from chart 3, P4, (push up 1 B, P1) 3 times, (push up 1 C, P1) 3 times, push up 1 B, P4 – this last st is the 15th st on chart 3 – from chart 2 ** (push up 1 B, P1) 3 times, P2; repeat from ** 4 times, P20(23:26).
Break off yarn. Thread up 19 B, 2 C, 16 B beads onto yarn.
4th row of charts 2, 3 and 1 K20(23:26), from chart 2 *K2, (push up 1 B, K1) 3 times, repeat from * 4 times, from chart 3 K3, push up 1 B, K1, (push up 1 C, K1) twice, (push up 1 B, K1) 4 times, K4, from chart 1 ** (K1, push up 1 B) 3 times, K2, repeat from ** 4 times, K47(50:53) sts.
Continue as follows working from charts 1, 3 then 2 for P rows and 2, 3 then 1 for K rows.
Break off yarn. Thread up 17 B, 1 A, 3 C, 19 B beads onto yarn.
5th row P47(50:53), repeat chart 1, 5 times, work from 2nd to 15th st on chart 3, then repeat chart 2, 5 times, P20(23:26).
Break off yarn. Thread up 14 B, 3 C, 3 A, 11 B beads onto yarn.
6th row K20(23:26), repeat from chart 2, 5 times, work from the 15th to 2nd st on chart 3, repeat chart 1, 5 times, K47/50:53).
7th to 11th rows Repeat from the 5th row back to 1st row inclusive.
Beginning and ending with a P row, st st (stockinette stitch) 5 rows. Cast off.

Left front strap
Work as for right strap from ** to **.
Now work as for right strap from *** to end, but begin 2nd row with tie end and K72(75:78) and end with K45(48:51) and following K rows with K47(50:53) and end K20(23:26) for side seam end. All P rows begin P20(23:26) and end P47(50:53).

Belt
Using No. 10 [US No. 3] needles and L, cast on 161(177:193) sts and beginning and ending with a P row, st st (stockinette stitch) 5 rows. Break off yarn.
Thread up 160(176:192) A beads, rejoin yarn and work the 1st row as on right strap. Break off yarn. Thread up *2 B, 2 C and 1 B beads; repeat from * 7(8:9) times. Rejoin yarn. Working odd-number rows P and even-numbered rows K, work from chart 3 only:
2nd row K9, then from 2nd row of chart 3, work from the 16th st to 1st st 8(9:10) times, K24. Break off yarn.
Thread up * 1 B, 3 C and 3 B beads; repeat from * 7(8:9) times. Rejoin yarn.
3rd row P24, then work from 1st to 16th st 8(9:10) times. P9. Break off yarn.
Thread up *4 B, 2 C and 1 B beads; repeat from * 7(8:9) times, rejoin yarn.
4th row K9, work from 16th st to 1st st 8(9:10) times, K24. Break off yarn. Thread up *2 B, 1 A, 3 C and 4 B beads; repeat from * 7(8:9) times, rejoin yarn.
5th row P24, work from the 1st to 16th st, 8(9:10) times, P9. Break off yarn. Thread up *4 B, 3 C, 3 A and 1 B beads; repeat from * 7(8:9) times, rejoin yarn.
6th row K9, work from 16th st to 1st st, 8(9:10) times, K24.
Now work from the 5th row back to 1st row inclusive.
Beginning with a P row st st (stockinette stitch) 5 rows. Cast off.

Back strap
Using No. 10 [US No. 3] needles and L, cast on 89(95:101) sts and beginning and ending with a P row, st st (stockinette stitch) 5 rows.
Break off yarn. Thread up 88(94:100) A beads, rejoin yarn and work as the 1st row in right strap.
Beginning and ending with a K row, st st (stockinette stitch) 9 rows.
Repeat from * to *.
Beginning and ending with a P row, st st (stockinette stitch) 5 rows, then cast off.

To make up
Press back and front lightly on the wrong side with a warm iron over a dry cloth. Join side seams. Pin out straps beaded side down on a soft pad and press as for back. Join row ends of back strap to side seam end of left and right front straps. Turn under the st st (stockinette stitch) rows so that the A beads form the edges, then join cast-on and cast-off edges of strap together. Neaten the ends of straps and sew 8 A beads to each end. With seams on straps to side seams on sweater sew straps in position so that centre of chart 3 pattern is in line with point on front, crossing right strap over left.

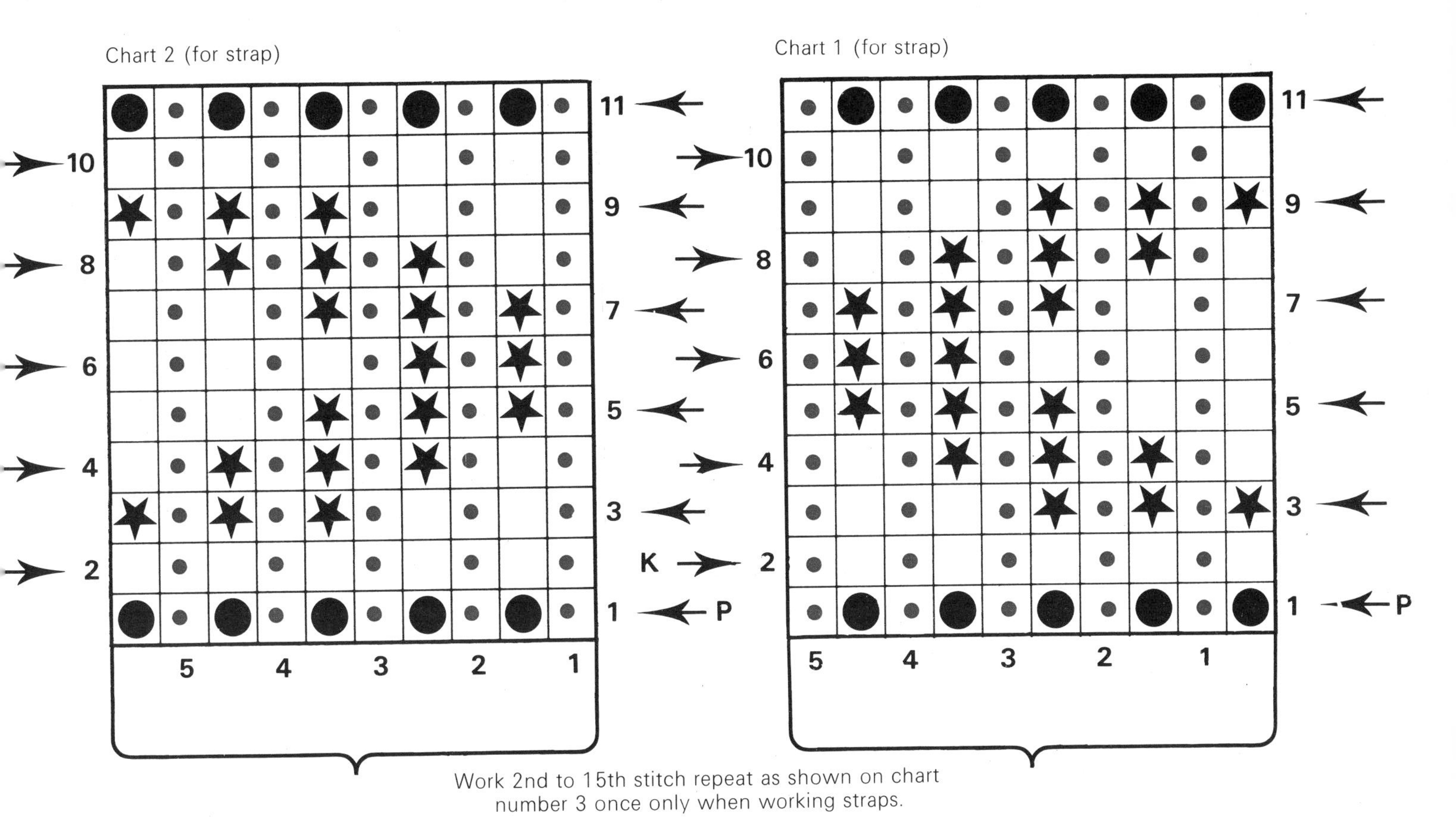

KEY TO CHART

- K or P stitch
- Colour A bead (red)
- Colour B bead (navy)
- Colour C bead (pale blue)

Chart 3 (for belt and straps)

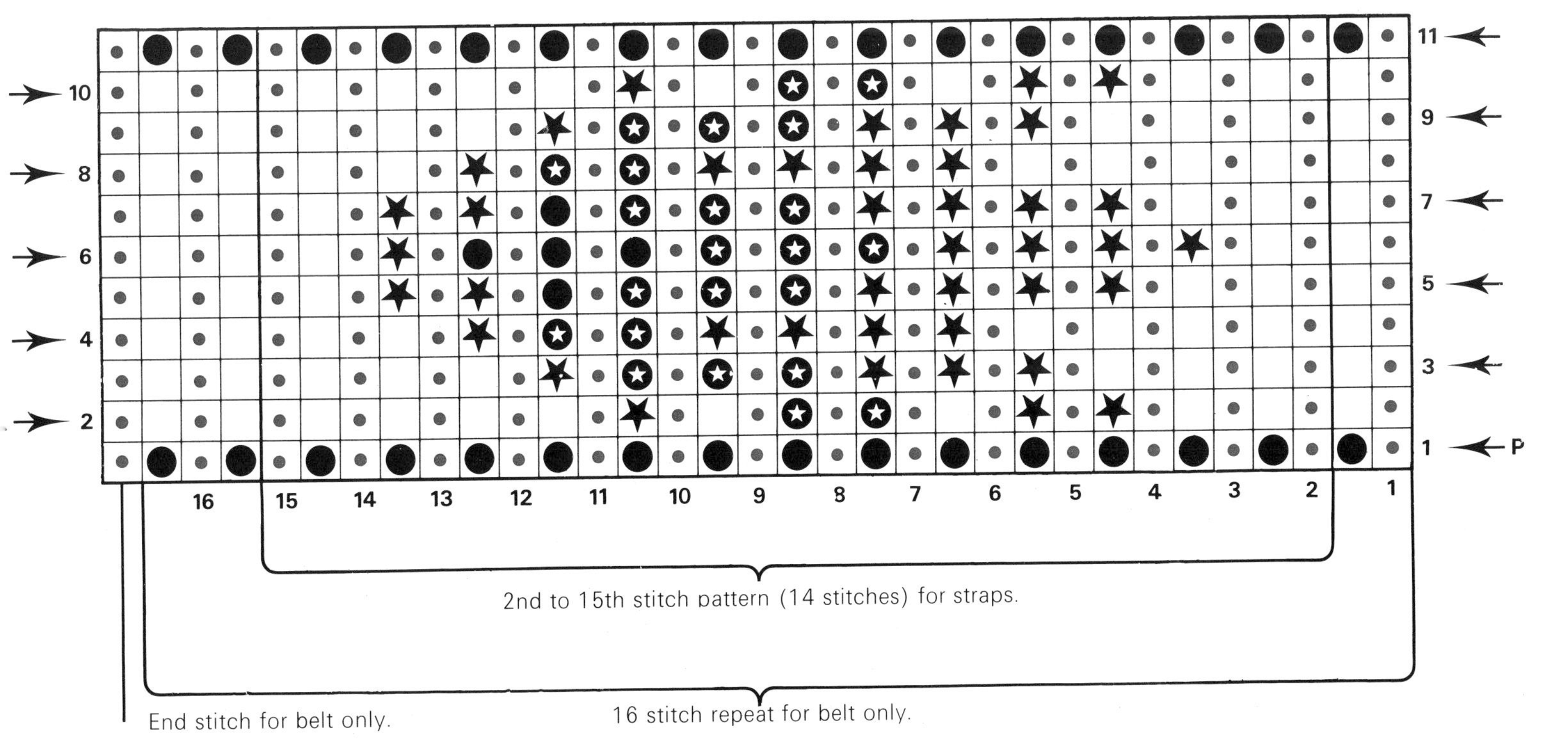

Making an heirloom

19th-century baby's dress

This beautiful baby dress was exhibited at the Great Exhibition of 1851 held in the Crystal Palace, London, and was awarded the Bronze Medal. The Exhibition, an idea of the Consort, Prince Albert, was organized to promote all areas of British art and industry and was a fanfare to the nation's confidence in its society, the Empire, British industry and taste.

The dress was knitted by a Miss Sarah Ann Cunliffe of Saffron Walden, in the county of Essex, and it is recorded that she worked seven hours a day for five months to complete the garment. Some 6,000 yards of fine sewing cotton were used in its construction.

A number of different patterns were used on this amazing dress although they do not appear to have been itemized or counted.

The dress is 22ins. (56cm.) long and the shape is conventional. The full skirt is gathered at the waist and the bodice has small buttons running across the front yoke. The hem, cuffs and neck edge are finished with delicately-worked lace knitting.

Lace knitting of the type used for this dress began in England with the introduction of fine cotton thread. As lace became more fashionable, so the skills of the hand-knitter grew. There was no existing lace-making tradition in Britain and knitted lace was a more easily-learned technique than traditional lace-making with its cushions and numbers of bobbins.

By 1850, when machine-made lace had become well-established, the home-knitter tended to restrict her output to edges, borders, mittens, mats and similar small items. By 1900, the skill of lace knitting had virtually disappeared. However, some patterns survived and their beauty can still be seen on the fine, wool shawls knitted on the Shetland Islands for the past 100 years.

Although machine knitted, this beautiful baby robe uses very similar lace patterns to that of the hand-knitted original. Three-ply baby wool has been used for this garment, rather than the fine sewing cotton of the 19th-century robe. The shape of this robe is similar to the original, too, except that the neckline and back fastening have been designed to be more practical.

The beauty of this robe is exceptional and such a dress might well become an heirloom.

The robe was knitted on a Knitmaster domestic knitting machine using Wendy 3-ply baby wool yarn in white.

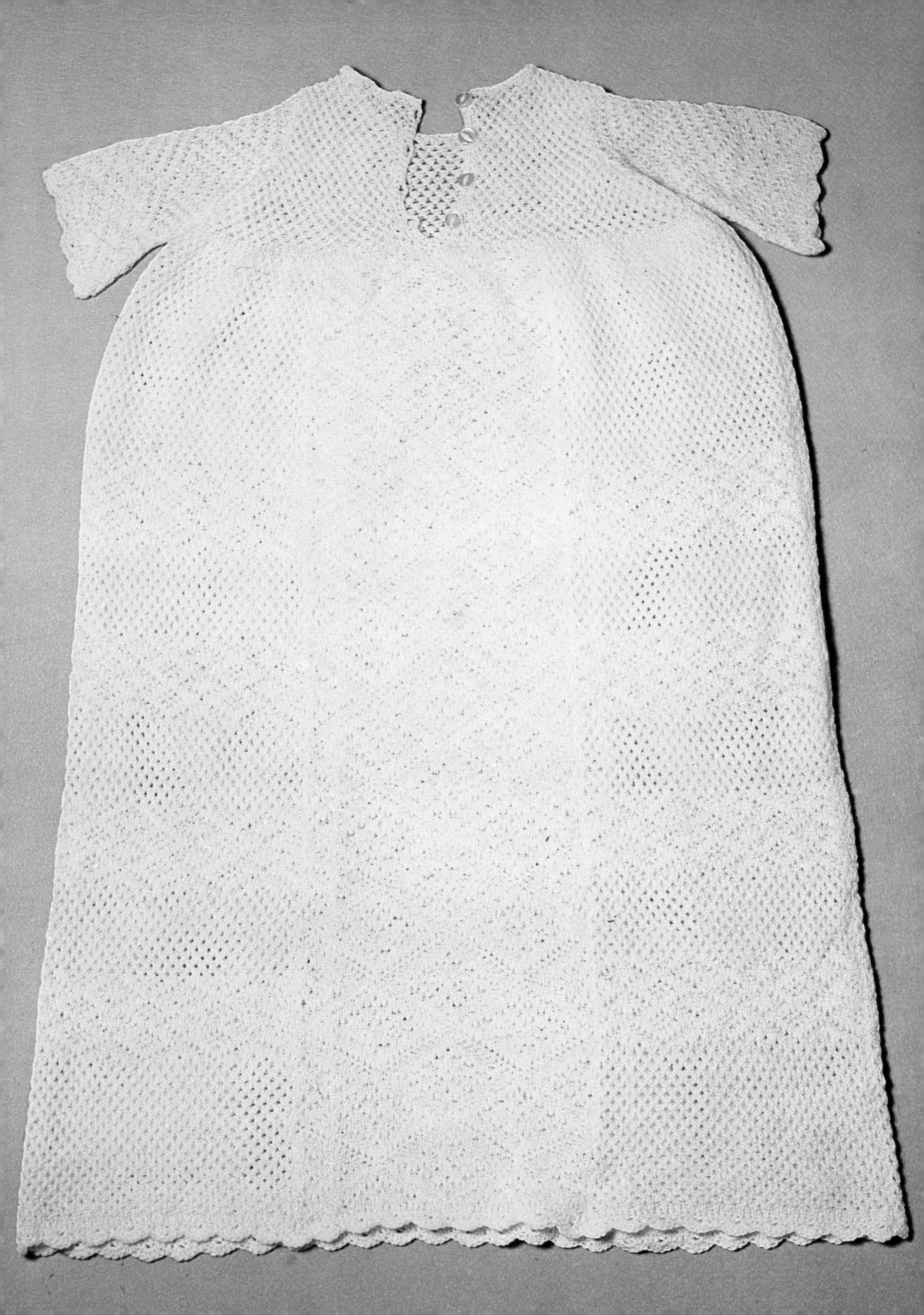

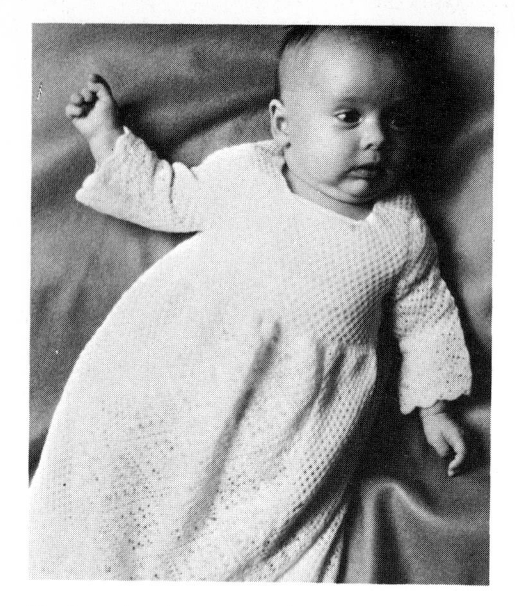

Designed to be treasured as an heirloom, this delicately worked baby robe compares favourably with the most beautiful robes of great-grandmother's day. This is a robe to be treasured and handed down.

Materials
6 25gr. [6 1oz.] balls of 3-ply baby yarn.
1 cone of No. 30 mercerised cotton thread.
No. 2·50 [US B/1] crochet hook.
3 small buttons.
For Knitmaster 321 and 323 automatic punch card knitting machines.

Size
To fit chest 18–20in. [45·5–50cm.].
Length from shoulder without edging, 29in. [73·5cm.]. Sleeve seam, 5in. [12·5cm.].

Tension or Gauge: Card No. 7 basic set, 31 sts and 42 rows to 4in. [10cm.].
Card No. 280 set 56, card No. 265 set 55, 31 sts and 44 rows to 4in. [10cm.].
Card No. 252 set 54, 30 sts and 44 rows to 4in. [10cm.]. Tension dial approximately 5.

Centre back and front panels
Insert card no. 265 A set 55 and lock to row 1. Cast on yarn by hand 52 sts. Set tension dial 5 and K 1 row. Thread cotton through feeder 1 and with cotton and yarn K 1 row. Thread cotton through feeder 2, release card and K 264 rows of lace pattern. K 8 rows with waste yarn and release from machine.

Side panels
(Knit 4)
Insert card No. 7 basic set and lock to row 1. Cast on yarn by hand 52 sts. Set tension dial 5 and K 1 row. With cotton and yarn, K 1 row. Release card and K 43 rows of lace. Remove card. *Insert card No. 280 A set 56 and lock to row 1. K 1 row. Release card and K 21 rows of lace pattern. Remove card. Insert card No. 7 basic set and lock to row 1. K 1 row. Release card and K 21 rows of lace pattern. Remove card.* Repeat from * to * twice more. Insert card No. 280 A and lock to row 1. K 1 row. Release card and K 21 rows. Remove card. Insert card No. 7 and lock to row 1. K 1 row. Release card and K 60 rows. K 8 rows with waste yarn and release from machine. Pin out and press skirt panels with a warm iron over a damp cloth.

Front bodice
Insert card No. 7 and lock to row 1. Carriage to left. Push 78 needles into B position. With wrong side of work facing you replace sts from centre front panel and side panels as follows: place 2 sts onto each needle. 78 sts. Set tension dial 5. With yarn and cotton K 1 row. Release card and work in lace pattern. K 14 rows.

Shape armholes
Cast off 4 sts at beg of next 2 rows, 2 sts at beg of next 8 rows. Dec 1 st at each end of next and following alternate rows. 50 sts. K 11 rows. 24 rows from beg of armhole.

Shape front neck
With a length of yarn cast off the centre 12 sts. K the sts at left by hand with waste yarn and take down to A position, work on the sts at right. Dec 1 st at beg of next 6 rows from neck edge. K 2 rows.

Shape shoulder
Cast off 7 sts at beg of next row from side edge. K 1 row. Cast off 6 sts.
Bring the needles at left from A position to B position, unravel waste yarn and work to match first side.

Right back bodice
Carriage at left. Insert card No. 7 and lock to row. 1. Push 39 needles into B position. Replace sts from one side panel and half of centre panel as follows. Place 2 sts onto each needle. 39 sts. Set tension dial to 5 and with yarn and cotton K 1 row. Release card and K 14 rows of lace pattern.

Shape armhole
Cast off 4 sts at beg of next row from side edge, 2 sts at beg of 4 alternate rows. Dec 1 st at beg of 2 alternate rows. 25 sts. K 25 rows.

Shape shoulder and back neck
Cast off 7 sts at beg of next 2 rows. Cast off 6 sts at beg of next row from side edge. Cast off 5 sts.

Left back bodice
Work to match right side reversing all shapings.

Sleeves
(Both alike)
Insert card No. 280A set 56 and lock to row 1. Cast on by hand with yarn 56 sts. Set tension dial 5 and K 1 row. With cotton and yarn K 1 row. Release card and work in lace pattern. Dec 1 st at each end of the next and every following 4th row to 46 sts. K 3 rows. Remove card. Insert card No. 252 A set 54 and K 32 rows.

Shape top
Cast off 4 sts at beg of next 2 rows, 2 sts at beg of next 8 rows. Dec 1 st at each end of the next and every alternate row to 6 sts. K 1 row. Cast off.

To make up
Pin out and press bodice and sleeves with a warm iron over a damp cloth. Join shoulders. Press. Stitch centre front panels to side panels of skirt. Set in sleeves. Join side and sleeve seams. With crochet hook work a row of double crochet [single crochet] all round neck edge. Work 2 rows of double crochet [s.c.] all round back opening, making 3 buttonhole loops on right side. Work a row of double crochet [s.c.] all round lower edge.

Shell edging: 1 sl st, *miss 2 sts; 5 tr [d.c.] in next st, miss 2 sts; 1 sl st.* Repeat from * to * to end. Work a row of d.c., [s.c.] and shell edging all round sleeve edges.

The baby dress exhibited at the Crystal Palace exhibition, London 1851.

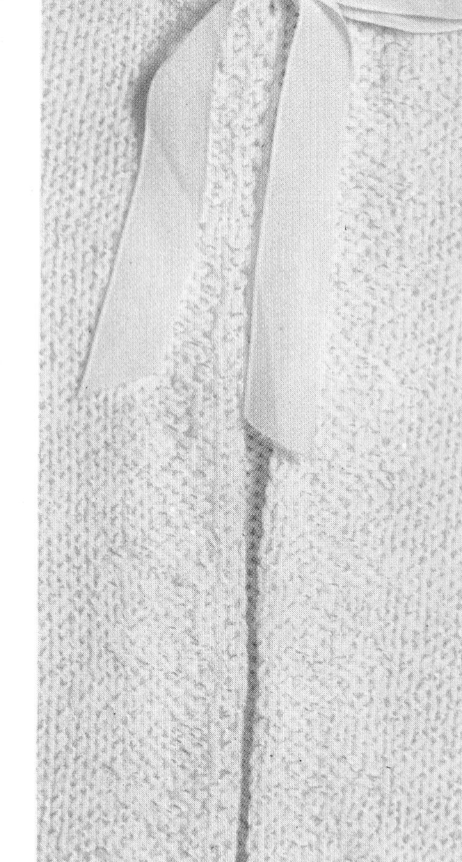

A touch of diamonds

17th-century child's jacket

This knitted jacket, made to fit a child, is very similar to the adult jacket illustrated on page 70. It is knitted in white cotton and the patterning is worked in purl stitch in crosses and diamonds.

Being a child's garment, the jacket has been frequently laundered and the fabric has subsequently felted, making the pattern rather difficult to see.

Like the adult garment, the pattern forms a double border around the bottom edge of the body and sleeves, down the front edges, round the armholes and down the length of the sleeves, both front and back. The jacket is knitted all-in-one, without seams, but seams have been simulated down the sides of the garment and down the sleeves.

Cotton jackets of this type seem to have been popular during the period when white knitting was fashionable. Several examples have survived, all having similar patterning and of the same general shape and construction.

When white Indian cotton was first imported into Britain, the most frequently used knitting patterns were those based on purl stitches. As finer cotton thread became available, lace knitting became more popular with home knitters.

The prettiness of this baby coat and hat is achieved not only with the glistening effect of the ripple yarn used but also with the placing of the patterning.

The original child's garment which inspired this modern baby outfit used purl and plain stitches to make a pattern of crosses and diamonds. The placing of the pattern areas has been successfully copied here. The pattern forms a double border round the coat edges and down the sleeves. The bonnet-style hat has the same patterning round the edge.

The edge-to-edge coat and the hat fasten with ribbon ties.

The coat and hat illustrated were knitted in Emu Ripple Courtelle in Ripple Yellow.

This beautiful baby coat and hat show the effects that can be achieved by using ripple yarn and also by a skilful placing of the pattern. This is quite a triumph of reconstruction since the original garment from which it draws its inspiration had "felted up", making the pattern difficult to see.

Materials
5(5:6) 20gr. [4(4:5)oz.] balls of nylon/rayon baby yarn with rippled effect.
One pair each of No. 9 and No. 11 [US Nos. 4 and 2] needles.
Stitch holder.
1½yds. [1·4m.] of ¾in. [2cm.] wide ribbon.

Tension or Gauge: 6 sts to 1in. [25mm.] in width over the st st (stockinette stitch) using No. 9 [US No. 4] needles.

Sizes
Coat
To fit chest sizes 17(18:19)in. [43(45:48)cm.].
Length from shoulder, 11¼(12:12¾)in. [28·5(30:32)cm.].
Sleeve seam, 5(5½:6¼)in. [12·5(13·5:16)cm.].

Hat
Hem to centre back 6in. [15cm.].
Round face edge 13in. [32·5cm.].
Note: Figures in parentheses ( ) refer to larger sizes. Where there is only one figure this refers to all sizes.

Coat back
Using No. 11 [US No. 2] needles, cast on 69(71:73) sts and beg with a K row, st st (stockinette stitch) 7 rows.
K 1 row to mark the hem line.
Change to No. 9 [US No. 4] needles.
Now work the border pattern.
1st row K4(5:6) *P2, K1, P2, K9*, repeat from * to * ending last repeat with K4(5:6).
2nd row P3(4:5), *K3, P1, K3, P7*, repeat from * to * ending last repeat with P3(4:5).
3rd row K2(3:4), *P4, K1, P4, K5, repeat from * to end.
4th row P1(2:3), *K4, P3, repeat from * to end.
5th row K0(1:2), *P4, K1, P1, K1, P1, K1, P4, K1; repeat from * to end.
6th row P4(5:6), *K2, P1, K2, P9; repeat from * to end.
7th row K3(4:5), *P2, K3, P2, K7; repeat from * to end.
8th row P2(3:4), *K3, P3, K3, P5, repeat from * to end.
9th to 15th rows Repeat from 7th row back to 1st row inclusive.
16th row K.
This completes the border pattern.
Working in st st (stockinette stitch), beg with a K row, dec 1 st at each end of next row and every following 6th(6th:8th) row until 53(57:61) sts remain.
Work 1(11:11) rows in st st (stockinette stitch).

Shape armholes
Cast off 5(6:7) sts at beg of next 2 rows.
Cont as follows:
1st row K2, P1, K1, P4, K until 8 sts remain, P4, K1, P1, K2.
2nd row P3, K4, P until 7 sts remain, K4, P3.
3rd row K2, P4, K until 6 sts remain, P4, K2.
4th row P2, K3, P until 5 sts remain, K3, P2.
5th row K2, P2, K until 4 sts remain, P2, K2.
6th to 9th row Repeat from 4th row back to 1st row inclusive.
10th row P2, K2, P until 4 sts remain, K2, P2.
11th row K3, P2, K until 5 sts remain, P2, K3.
12th row P3, K3, P until 6 sts remain, K3, P3.
13th and 14th rows Repeat 11th, then 10th row.
Repeat the last 14 rows once (once and 1st and 2nd rows again):(once and 1st to 4th rows again).

Shape shoulders
Cast off 5(6:6) sts at beg of next 2 rows, 6 sts at beg of 2 following rows.
Leave remaining 21(21:23) sts until required for neck band.

Left front
Using No. 11 [US No. 2] needles, cast on 29(30:31) sts and st st (stockinette stitch) 7 rows; then cast on 13 sts. 42(43:44) sts.
Next row K.
Change to No. 9 [US No. 4] needles.
Now work in pattern and set sts for front facing.
1st row K4(5:6), *P2, K1, P2, K9, repeat from * once, P2, K1, Sl 1 to mark edge of front, K6 for facing.
2nd row K2, P6, K3, *P7, K3, P1, K3, repeat from * to end.
3rd row K2(3:4), *P4, K1, P4, K5, repeat from * once, P4, K1, Sl 1, K6.
4th row K2, P7, *K4, P3, repeat from * 3 times, K4, P1(2:3).
These 4 rows set the sts for the pattern and front facing.
Keeping sl st and facing sts as set, continue in pattern until 15 pattern rows have been worked.
Now set sts for front pattern and continue front facing.
16th row K2, P6, K3, P3, K to end.
17th row K2 tog for side dec K until 12 sts remain, P4, K1 for pattern, sl 1, K6.
18th row K2, P7, K4, P to end.
Keeping sl st and facing sts as set, cont to work 7 sts in pattern inside sl st, pattern 4 (4:6) rows.
Cont as set and dec 1 st at side seam edge of next row and every following 6th(6th:8th) row until 34(36:38) sts remain.
Work straight until front measures same as back to armhole ending at side seam edge.

Shape armhole
1st row Cast off 5(6:7) sts. Work to end.
2nd row K2, P5, pattern 7, P to end.
Pattern 16(18:20) rows keeping the continuity of pattern at front edge; *at the same time* work 8 sts in pattern at armhole edge as given for back.

Shape neck
1st row Pattern until 13 sts remain, turn, leave these 13 sts on a stitch holder.
2nd row Dec 1, pattern to end.
Dec 1 st at neck edge of the 4(4:5) following alternate rows.
Cont as set until armhole measures same as back armhole ending at armhole end.

Shape shoulder
Cast off 5(6:6) sts at beg of next row.
Work 1 row then cast off 6 remaining sts.

Right front
Using No. 11 [US No. 2] needles, cast on 29(30:31) sts.
St st (stockinette stitch) 6 rows.
Break off yarn.
Cast on 13 sts onto free needle, turn, onto this needle K across sts on left-hand needle. 42(43:44) sts.
K 1 row to mark hem line.
Change to No. 9 (US No. 4] needles.
Now work in pattern and set sts for front facing.
1st row K6, sl 1, K1, P2, *K9, P2, K1, P2; repeat from * once K4(5:6).

2nd row P3(4:5), *K3, P1, K3, P7; repeat from * once, K3, P6, K2.
3rd row K6, sl 1, K1, P4, *K5, P4, K1, P4; repeat from * once, K2(3:4).
4th row P1(2:3), K4, *P3, K4; repeat from * 3 times, P7, K2.
These 4 rows set the pattern and sts for front facing.
Work in pattern as set, complete as for left front, reversing all shapings.

Sleeves
(Both alike)
Using No. 11 [US No. 2] needles, cast on 27(29:33) sts and work 7 rows in st st (stockinette stitch).
K 1 row to mark the hem line.
Change to No. 9 [US No. 4] needles.
Now work in st st (stockinette stitch) with centre pattern panel.
1st row K7(8:10), place a marker after last st, for pattern panel of 13 sts; K4, P2, K1, P2, K4, place a marker after last st, K to end.
2nd row P to first marker, for pattern panel P3, K3, P1, K3, P3, P to end.
3rd row K to marker, K2, P4, K1, P4, K2, K to end.
4th row P to marker, P1, K4, P3, K4, P1, P to end.
5th row Inc 1, K to marker, P4, K1, P1, K1, P1, K1, P4, P until 1 st remains, inc 1.
Continue in pattern as follows and *at the same time* inc 1 st at each end of every 8th(8th:10th) row following previous increase row.
6th row K to marker, P4, K2, P1, K2, P4, P to end.
7th row K to marker, K3, P2, K3, P2, K3, K to end.
8th row P to marker, P2, K3, P3, K3, P2, P to end.
9th to 14th row Repeat from 7th row back to 2nd row inclusive.
These 14 rows form the pattern.
Continue in pattern until the 5th inc row has been worked and there are 37(39:43) sts on the needle.
Continue on these sts until sleeve seam measures 5(5½:6½)in. [12·5(13·5:16)cm.] from hemline (or for length of sleeve required) ending with a wrong side row.

Shape top
Cont in pattern, cast off 5(6:7) sts at beg of next 2 rows.
Dec 1 st at each end of next row and every alternate row until 13 sts remain.
Cast off.

Neckband
Join shoulder seams.
Slip the first 6 sts on each front onto a double-pointed needle and fold to wrong side.
With right side of work facing you and using No. 11 [US No. 2] needles, K the sl st on right front, *then K next 6 sts tog with corresponding sts on back needle*, pick up and K 15 sts from neck edge, K across the sts of back, pick up and K15 sts from neck edge, repeat from * to *, K the sl st. 65(65:67) sts.
Work in rib as follows:
1st row K2, *P1, K1, repeat from * ending K2.
2nd row K1, *P1, K1, repeat from * to end.
Repeat these 2 rows 5 times.
Cast off loosely in rib.

To make up
Press pieces lightly on the wrong side with a cool iron over a dry cloth. Set in sleeves. Join sleeve and side seams. Turn in facings so that sl st forms the edge and catch in position.
Turn up at hem line all round lower edge of coat and sleeves and catch cast-on edge in position on wrong side. Neaten edges of facing. Press seams. Fold neckband in half and sew cast-off edge to neck edge. Cut ribbon into two pieces and thread one length through neck band.

Hat
Using No. 11 [US No. 2] needles, cast on 75 sts.
1st row K.
2nd row K3 for border, P until 3 remain, K3.
Repeat these 2 rows twice and then 1st row again.
K 1 row to form the hem line.
Change to No. 9 [US No. 4] needles.
Keeping the 3 border sts at each end as set and the centre 69 sts in pattern, work the 16 rows of border pattern as given on back for 1st size.
Beg with a K row, st st (stockinette stitch) 20 rows.

Shape crown
1st row *K9, K2 tog; repeat from * twice, K29, K2 tog, K9, K2 tog 70 sts.
2nd and each wrong side row P.
3rd row *K8, K2 tog; repeat from * 6 times.
5th row *K7, K2 tog; repeat from * 6 times.
Cont as set, working 1 st less before each dec until 14 sts remain.
Next row K2 tog across sts. Break off yarn, threading yarn into darning needle, thread through remaining sts, draw up and fasten off with a back stitch, then join row ends ending at last row of border.

To make up
Press as for jacket. Turn under at hem line and sew cast-on edge in position. Cut remaining piece of ribbon in two and sew to each side of bonnet.

Bright as a pin!

Pin cushions of the 18th century

This pin cushion is evidence of the increasing skill of the English home knitter in the 18th century. Knitted in silk thread on fine steel needles the cushion is finely and evenly knitted and has a working tension or gauge of 28 stitches and 30 rows to one inch (25mm.).

The cushion has a pattern of stylized geometric flowers and leaves and has the name "C. Osboldeston" worked into the design. The cushion is knitted in two circular pieces and then sewn together. The braid, to which the pin cushion is stitched, may have been handwoven on a tablet loom.

In the 18th century, hand knitting in England had become very much a fashionable pastime. Knitting skills had developed to such an extent that very ambitious patterns were being attempted, using finer and finer yarn. Beaded boxes, handbags, pin cushions, as well as delicate baby clothes, were being produced. The skills shown by home knitters were further developed with the importation of white cotton thread from India and a tradition of white, lace knitting grew up.

The refinement of design and colour and the delicacy of the knitting itself were peculiar to the 18th century. With the coming of the 19th century, restraint began to disappear and, with few exceptions, British knitting designs became more florid in colour.

This delightful bib-dress and cardigan develops one of the stylized flower motifs on the 18th century pin cushion. The whole, eight-petalled flower is used on the bib-front and as an all-over pattern on the cardigan.

The dress has ribbing at the waist for a pretty fit and the edge of the skirt is bordered with ribbing and a band of three-coloured geometric patterning. The cardigan is finished with a neat, ribbed welt and cuffs using the dark blue colour.

The dress and cardigan illustrated were knitted in Mademoiselle Pingouin yarn in Rust Red, Blue and Yellow.

It's warm and snug and at first glance seems a typical folk garment. In fact, the design for this delightful girl's bib dress and cardigan came from a Victorian pin-cushion.

Materials
Bib-front dress
2(3:3:4) 50gr. [4(6:6:7)oz.] balls of standard 4-ply yarn in blue, main colour (M), 1 ball in yellow, light colour (LT) and 1 ball in red, dark colour (DK).
Cardigan
2(2:2:3) 50gr. [4(4:4:6)oz.] balls in main colour and 2(2:3:3) 50gr. [4(4:6:6)oz.] balls in dark colour.
For both garments, one pair each of Nos. 12 and 10 [US Nos. 1 and 3] needles.
4 ⅜in. [1cm.] wide buttons, for Bib-front dress and 6 for Cardigan.

Tension or Gauge: 14 sts to 2in. [5cm.] over st st (stockinette stitch) using No. 10 [US No. 3] needles.

Sizes
To fit a girl of 7(8:9:10) years.
Bib-front dress
Total length, 24(25½:26:27)in.
[61(64·5:66:68·5)cm.].

Cardigan
Total length, 15(15½:16:16½)in.
[38(39·5:41:42)cm.].
Sleeve seam, 11(12:13:14)in.
[28(30·5:33:35·5)cm.].
Note: Figures in parentheses ( ) refer to the larger sizes. Where there is only one figure this refers to all sizes.

Dress skirt
Using No. 10 [US No. 3] needles and DK yarn, cast on 110(114:118:122) sts and work in rib as follows:
1st row K2, *P2, K2; repeat from * to end.
2nd row P2, *K2, P2; repeat from * to end.
Repeat these 2 rows twice and 1st row again.
K 1 row to mark the hem line.
Rib 8 rows, dec 1 st at each end of last row.
108(112:116:120) sts.
Now work in st st (stockinette stitch), beg with a K row.
St st (stockinette stitch) 2 rows LT and 2 rows M. Work border pattern.
1st row *K3 DK, K1 M; repeat from * to end.
2nd row *P1 M, P3 DK; repeat from * to end.
3rd row *K1 M, K1 DK; repeat from * to end.
4th row *P1 DK, P1 M; repeat from * to end.
5th row K1 DK, *K1 M, K3 DK; repeat from * ending with 2 DK.
6th row P2 DK, *P1 M, P3 DK; repeat from * ending with 1 DK.
Break off DK.
St st (stockinette stitch) 2 rows LT. Break off LT and cont with M only.
Cont in st st (stockinette stitch) until work measures 11½(12½:13:13½)in.
[29(31·5:33:34)cm.] from hem line ending with a K row.
Dec row P2(4:6:8), P2 tog, *P4, P2 tog; repeat from * 16 times, P to end.
90(94:98:102) sts.
Break off M and join in DK and K 1 row.
Change to No. 12 [US No. 1] needles and work 18 rows in rib as given at beg.
Divide sts for dress top.
Next row Cast off 17(18:19:20) sts, rib the next 26(27:28:29) sts, take 2 sts tog, rib 27(28:29:30) sts. Cast off the remaining 17(18:19:20) sts in rib and fasten off yarn.

Dress bib-front
Using No. 10 [US No. 3] needles and M, rejoin yarn to wrong side of remaining 55(57:59:61) sts. **
Beg with a P row, st st (stockinette stitch) 2(4:4:4) rows.
Next row P5(6:7:8) sts and place a marker after last stitch to mark end of motif; P45 and place a marker after last stitch to mark beg of motif; P5(6:7:8).

Motif for Bib-front
(*Note:* It is not necessary to weave in the yarns but care must be taken not to draw the yarn tightly across the back of the work or it will become puckered, and to avoid a gap when picking up colours from previous row, always twist the yarns before working the next stitch).
1st row With M, K5(6:7:8), for motif of 45 sts. 15M, 15DK, 15M, then 5(6:7:8)M.
2nd row With M, P5(6:7:8), for motif 14M, 17DK, 14M, then 5(6:7:8)M.
These two rows set the stitches for the motif.
Now work from the 3rd to 57th row of bib-front, following chart A.
With M, st st (stockinette stitch) 2(2:4:4) rows.
Divide sts for neck and shoulders.
Next row P10(11:11:12) sts, cast off 35(35:37:37) sts, P to end and work on the last set of sts.

Shoulder straps
Work in st st (stockinette stitch) for 2½(3:3:3½)in. [6·5(7·5:7·5:9)cm.], then cast off.
Rejoin M to neck edge of remaining sts and complete second strap to match.

Dress top, back
Work as for bib-front until ** is reached.
With M, cont in st st (stockinette stitch) until work measures same as front to neck, ending with a K row.
Divide sts for neck and complete as given for front.

Ribbed borders *(Four alike)*
With right side of work facing you, using No. 12 [US No. 1] needles and yarn M, pick up and K 85(89:91:95) sts from side edges of dress top.
Beginning and ending 1st row with K1, work 5 rows in single rib. Cast off in rib.

Back and front neck ribbing
(Both alike)
With right side of work facing you and using No. 12 [US No. 1] needles and yarn M, pick up and K 37(37:39:39) sts from those cast off at centre front.
Work 5 rows in single rib, dec 1 st at each end of every row. Cast off in rib.

Side neck ribbing *(Four alike)*
With right side of work facing you and using No. 12 [US No. 1] needles and yarn M, pick up and K 21(25:25:29) sts from edges of straps.
Work 5 rows in single rib, dec 1 st on each row at mitred corner only. Cast off in rib.

Buttonhole bands *(Two alike)*
With right side of front facing you and using No. 12 [US No. 1] needles and yarn M, pick and K19(21:21:23) sts across front shoulder straps.
Work 2 rows in single rib.
Buttonhole row Rib 4, cast off 2, rib until 6 sts remain, cast off 2, rib to end.
Next row Work in rib, casting on 2 sts over those cast off to complete buttonholes. Rib 1 row then cast off in rib.

Button bands *(Two alike)*
Work as for buttonhole bands across back shoulder straps, omitting buttonholes.

To make up
Do not press. Join side seams on dress skirt. Turn up at marked hem line all round skirt and catch cast-on edge in position. Join mitred corners of neck ribbing and edges of side ribbing to skirt. Sew two buttons to each back shoulder strap to correspond with buttonholes.

Cardigan back
Using No. 12 [US No. 1] needles and M, cast on 102(106:110:114) sts and work 17 rows in rib as given for dress.
Inc row Rib 3(3:3:7), *inc 1, rib 23(49:49:49); repeat from * 3 (1:1:1) times, inc 1, rib to end. 107(109:113:117) sts.
Change to No. 10 [US No. 3] needles and join in DK and st st (stockinette stitch) 2 rows.
Work two-colour pattern as follows:
1st row K1(2:4:6) DK; work from motif, chart B across the next 105 sts, then with DK K1(2:4:6).
2nd row P1(2:4:6) DK, work from the motif chart B across the next 105 sts, then with DK P1(2:4:6).
These 2 rows set the sts for the two-colour pattern. Work from the 3rd to 42nd row on chart B.

Cont in pattern until work measures 8(8½:8½:9)in. [20·5(21·5:21·5:23)cm.] ending with a P row.

Shape armholes
Cast off 17 sts at beg of next 2 rows.
On 73(75:79:83) sts, cont in pattern until armhole measures 6½(6½:7:7)in. [17(17:18:18)cm,] ending with a P row.

Shape shoulders
Cast off 12 sts at beg of next 2 rows; 12(12:13:14) sts at beg of 2 following rows.
Cast off remaining 25(27:29:31) sts.

Left front
Using No. 12 [US No. 1] needles and yarn M cast on 50(50:54:54) sts and work 17 rows in rib.
Inc row Rib 2(2:10:4), *inc 1, rib 22; repeat from * once (2:0:2) times, inc 1, rib to end. 53(54:56:58) sts.
Change to No. 10 [US No. 3] needles.
Join in DK yarn and st st (stockinette stitch) 2 rows**.
Work the two-colour pattern as follows:
1st row K1(1:3:5) DK, pattern across the next 51 sts from chart B, K1(2:2:2) DK.
2nd row P1(2:2:2) DK, pattern across 51 sts from chart B, P1(1:3:5) DK.
These 2 rows set the sts for the two-colour pattern.
***Work from the 3rd to 42nd row of two-colour chart B.
Continue as set until work measures same as back to armhole, ending at armhole end.

Shape armhole
Cast off 17 sts at beg of next row. On 36(37:39:41) sts cont in pattern until armhole measures 4in. [10cm.] ending at neck edge.

Shape neck
Cast off 5 sts at beg of next row, then dec 1 st at neck edge on the 7(8:9:10) following rows.
On 24(24:25:26) sts cont in pattern until armhole measures same as back to shoulder ending at armhole end.

Shape shoulder
Cast off 12 sts at beg of next row; 12(12:13:14) sts on following alternate row and fasten off.

Right front
Work as for left front until ** is reached.
Work the two-colour pattern as follows:
1st row K1(2:2:2) DK, pattern across the next 51 sts from chart B, K1(1:3:5) DK.
2nd row P1(1:3:5) DK, pattern across next 51 sts, P1(2:2:2) DK.
These 2 rows set the stitches for the right front.
Work from *** to end as given on left front.

Sleeves
(Both alike)
Using No. 12 [US No. 1] needles and yarn M, cast on 46(46:50:50) sts and work in K2, P2 rib for 17 rows.
Inc row Rib 2(2:4:4), *inc 1, rib 6(6:20:20); repeat from * 5(5:1:1) times, inc 1, rib to end. 53 sts remain on all sizes.
Change to No. 10 [US No. 3] needles, join in DK yarn and st st (stockinette stitch) 2 rows.
Work the two-colour pattern from chart B as follows:
1st row K1 DK, work from chart across the next 51 sts, K1 DK.
2nd row P1 DK, work in pattern across 51 sts, P1 DK.
These 2 rows set the sts for the sleeves.
Working from chart B and beg with 3rd row, pattern 2 rows.
Cont in pattern inc 1 st at each end of next row and every following 4th row until there are 85(85:91:91) sts on the needle, working the inc sts into the pattern as they occur.
Cont in pattern on these sts until sleeve seam measures 11(12:13:14)in. [28(30·5:33:35·5)cm.], (or for sleeve seam length required), ending with a P row.
Place a marker at each end of the last row, then pattern 16(16:18:18) rows. Cast off.

Neck band
Join shoulder seams.
With right side of work facing you, using No. 12 [US No. 1] needles and yarn M, pick up and K89(91:101:103) sts. Beginning and ending 1st row with K1, work 7 rows in K1, P1 rib. Cast off in rib.

Buttonhole band
With right side of work facing you, using No. 12 [US No. 1] needles and yarn M, pick up and K95(101:101:107) sts along right front edge.
Work 3 rows in single rib.
1st buttonhole row Rib 4(5:5:6), cast off 2, *rib next 14(15:15:16) sts, cast off 2; repeat from * 4 times, rib to end.
2nd buttonhole row Work in rib casting on 2 sts over those cast off to complete buttonholes.
Rib 2 rows then cast off in rib.
Button band
Work as for buttonhole band but omit the buttonholes.

To make up
Do not press. Set in sleeves, sewing the edges above the markers to the stitches cast off for armholes on both back and front, and cast-off edge to edges of armholes. Join sleeve and side seams. Sew on buttons.

MOTIF CHART A

KEY TO CHART
■ RED
• BLUE
★ YELLOW

1 REPEAT

1 REPEAT

MOTIF CHART B
KEY TO CHART
■ RED
• BLUE

Sweater from Egypt

Fragment of Arab knitting

This fragment is one of the few surviving examples of Arab coloured knitting. The earliest examples of the craft, found at Bahnasa, in Egypt, were thought to have been knitted by Copts, an Egyptian Christian sect. These early scraps of knitting were very simple in pattern although the garments – the sandal socks with a separate big toe piece for instance – were quite advanced in construction.

It is thought that the Arabs very quickly learned the skill of knitting from the Copts and it was during their period of domination (from 400 AD to 1100 AD), that the introduction and development of patterning with colour came about.

This was one of the most important developments in the history of hand knitting because the type of patterns produced by the Arabs became the basis of almost the whole of folk knitting in Europe and the near East. This was probably because the patterns were geometric and were therefore the easiest to form with the knitted stitch.

The patterns were invariably in bands of different widths, broad alternating with narrow, each band containing designs made up of different shapes. The colours were almost always on a dark ground.

This is true of almost all the folk knitting of the Near and Middle East and of eastern and southern Europe, whereas in the folk knitting of Scandinavia and the northern islands the ground colour is light in tone.

This particular fragment can give only a very vague impression of Arab coloured knitting were very simple in pattern just discernable and the use of strong colour on a dark ground can be seen.

The piece was knitted on fine needles and the complicated nature of the design would have required considerable skill. Unfortunately, we can only guess at the purpose for which this piece of knitting was intended.

Brilliantly inspired by the patterning of the mysterious Egyptian fragment of knitting which is shown above, this beautiful sweater has an all-over geometric motif worked in white on a blue background. A colourful border pattern is worked on the elasticated wrists on the sleeves and at the bloused, draw-string waist. The border patterns and motifs are an exact reproduction of the ancient Egyptian patterning and indicate quite clearly how the coloured knitting of the 10th century influenced the folk knitting of the world.

The sweater illustrated is knitted in Hayfields Beaulon 4-ply yarns in Royal Blue, White, Red and Emerald.

A girl who knows her blouson sweater has stood the test of time. . . . The border patterns and motifs exactly reproduce early Egyptian patterning.

Materials
9(10:11) 25gr. [8(9:10)oz.] balls of Nylon-mixture 4-ply yarn in Royal blue (RB); 4(5:6) 4[5:6] in Cream (C); 1 in Meadow Green (MG); 1(1:2) 1[1:2] in Lipstick Red (LR).
One pair each of Nos. 10 and 12 [US Nos. 3 and 1] needles.
Length of elastic for wrists.
Tension or Gauge: 16 sts to 2in. [5cm.] in width using No. 10 [US No. 3] needles.

Sizes
To fit bust sizes 32(34:36)in. [81(86:91)cm.].
Length from shoulder, $20\frac{1}{2}$($20\frac{1}{2}$:$20\frac{1}{2}$)in. [52(52:52)cm.].
Sleeve seam, $18\frac{1}{2}$($18\frac{1}{2}$:$18\frac{1}{2}$)in. [47(47:47)cm.].
Note: Figures in ( ) parentheses refer to larger sizes. Where there is only one figure this refers to all sizes.

Front
Using No. 12 [US No. 1] needles and Cream (C), cast on 115(122:129) sts and work 7 rows in st st (stockinette stitch) ending with a K row.
K 1 row on wrong side of work to mark hem line.
Beginning with a K row, st st (stockinette stitch) 3 rows.

Casing row P51(55:58) sts, cast off 2, P next 8(7:8) sts, cast off 2, P to end.
K 1 row casting on 2 sts over those cast off.
St st (stockinette stitch) 3 rows.
Change to No. 10 [US No. 3] needles.
Inc row K4(5:6), inc 1, *K4, inc 1; repeat from * until 5(6:7) sts remain, K to end. 137(145:153) sts.
P 1 row.
Join in Lipstick Red yarn (LR).
Work 2 rows LR, 1 row C, 4 rows LR, 1 row C, 2 rows LR.
Continue in st st (stockinette stitch) and work from chart A for the 34in. [86cm.] size, and from chart B for 32in. [81cm.] and 36in. [91cm.] sizes.
Work from 1st to 59th row, then work from the 38th to 59th row – the last 22 rows form the main pattern. Place a marker at each end of the last row to mark beginning of armholes.
Continue to repeat from the 38th to 59th row until work measures $15\frac{1}{2}$in. [40cm.] from hem line ending with a right side row. Now divide the sts for neck and shoulders.
Next row Pattern 58(61:65) sts and leave on a spare needle for right front shoulder, pattern 21(23:23) sts and leave on stitch-holder for neck band, pattern to end and work in the last set of 58(61:65) sts.

Left front shoulder
Shape neck
Dec 1 st at neck edge on the next 9 rows, then 5 following alternate rows. 44(47:51) sts.
Continue in pattern until work measures 20in. [51cm.] from hem-line ending at armhole end.

Shape shoulder
Cast off 8(7:7) sts at beg of next row; 7(8:9) on 4 following alternate rows.
Work 1 row then cast off remaining 8 sts.
Rejoin yarn to neck edge of 58(61:65) sts and pattern to end of row.

Right front shoulder
Complete as left front shoulder.

Back
Work as for Front until ** is reached, omitting the "holes".
Now work from chart A for 34in. [86cm.] size and chart C for 32in. [81cm.] and 36in. [91cm.] sizes.
Work from 1st to 59th row, then repeat from 38th to 59th row – last 22 rows form main pattern – placing a marker at each end of last row to mark beginning of armholes.
Continue to work from 38th to 59th row until work measures same as front to shoulder, ending with a wrong side row.

Shape shoulder
Cast off 8(7:7) sts at beg of next 2 rows; 7(8:9) sts on following 4 rows.

Shape back neck
1st row Cast off 7(8:9) sts, pattern next 17(18:19) sts and work on these 18(19:20) sts; turn, leaving the remaining sts on a spare needle.
2nd row P2 tog, pattern to end.
3rd row Cast off 7(8:9) sts, pattern until 2 remain, K2 tog.
4th row As 2nd row.
Cast off remaining 8 sts.
With right side of work facing you, slip the next 43(45:45) sts onto a stitch-holder and leave until required for neck band; rejoin yarn to remaining sts and pattern to end of row.
1st row Cast off 7(8:9) sts, pattern until 2 remain, P2 tog.
2nd row K2 tog, pattern to end.
3rd row As 1st.
Work 1 row then cast off remaining 8 sts.

Sleeves
Using No. 12 [US No. 1] needles and C, cast on 57 sts and st st (stockinette stitch) 7 rows.
K 1 row on wrong side to mark hem line.
St st (stockinette stitch) 8 rows.
Inc row K1, inc 1 st in each of the remaining 56 sts. 113 sts.
St st (stockinette stitch) 2 rows in LR, 1 row C, 4 rows LR, 1 row C, 2 rows LR.
Change to No. 10 [US No. 3] needles.
Work from the 1st to 17th row as on chart A.
With Royal blue (RB), st st (stockinette stitch) 2 rows.
Repeat from 38th to 59th rows 5 times and first 4 of these rows again, or until sleeve seam measures $18\frac{1}{2}$in. [47cm.] from hem line.
Cast off.

Tie
Using No. 12 [US No. 1] needles and [RB] cast on 5 sts.
1st row K2, P1, K2.
2nd row K1, *P1, K1; repeat from * once.
Repeat these 2 rows until tie measures 58in. [147cm.] or for length required, then cast off.

Neck band
Join right shoulder seam.
Using No. 12 [US No. 1] needles and C, pick up and K 45 sts from left front neck edge, K across the sts at centre front, dec 4 sts evenly, pick up and K 45 sts from row ends of right front neck edge, 6 sts from right back neck edge, K across the sts of back, dec 4 sts evenly, pick up and K 5 sts from left back neck edge. 157(161:161) sts.
Beginning with a P row, st st (stockinette stitch) 9 rows.
P next row to mark hem line, then beginning with a P row, st st (stockinette stitch) 9 rows.
Cast off.

To make up
Press all parts lightly with a warm iron over a dry cloth. Join left shoulder seam, continuing seam across neck band. Fold neck band in half and catch cast-off edge to inside neck edge. Sew cast-off edge of sleeves to back and front between the markers.
Join sleeve and side seams. Turn under all round on marked hem line and catch cast-on edge in position.
Cut elastic to required length for wrists and join ends. Turn up sleeves on marked hem line, place elastic inside and catch cast-on edge in position.
Press seams.
Thread tie through hem.

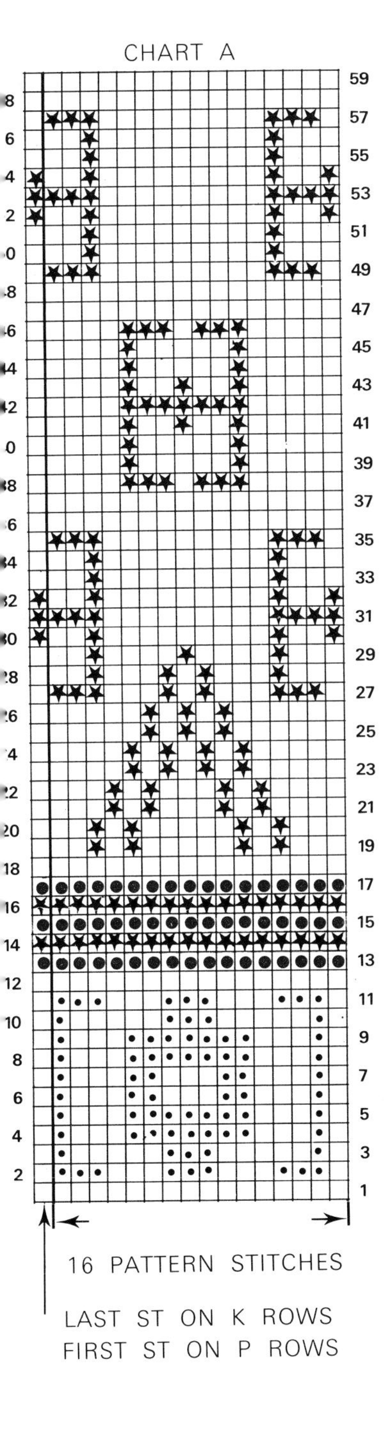

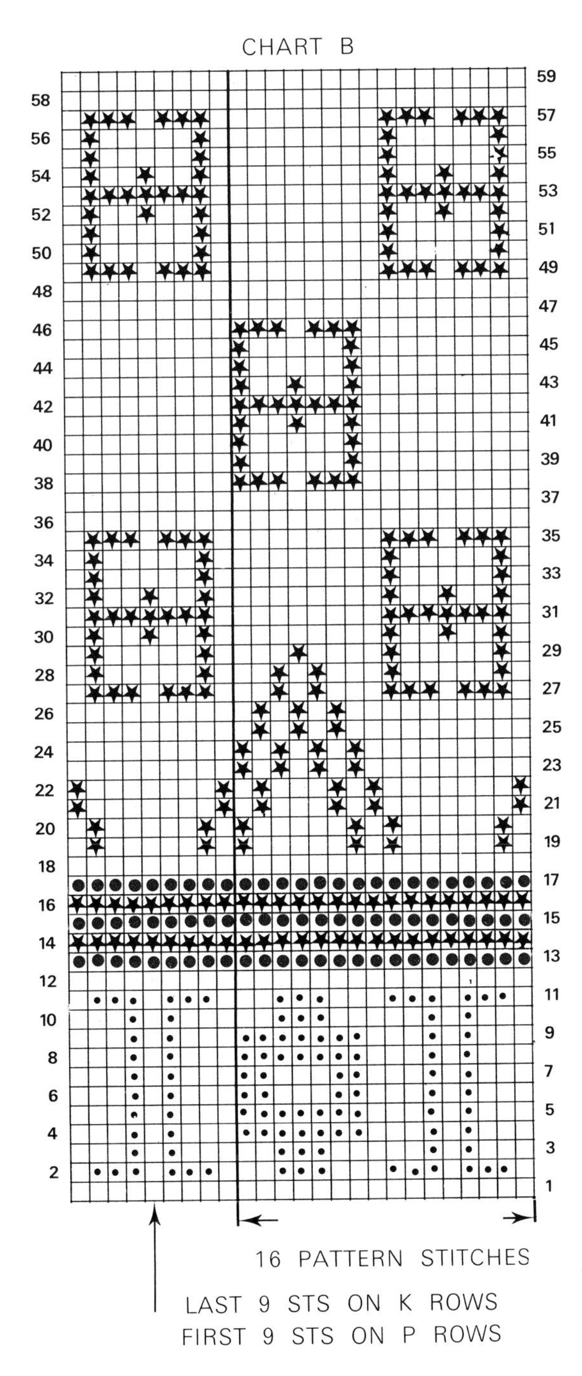

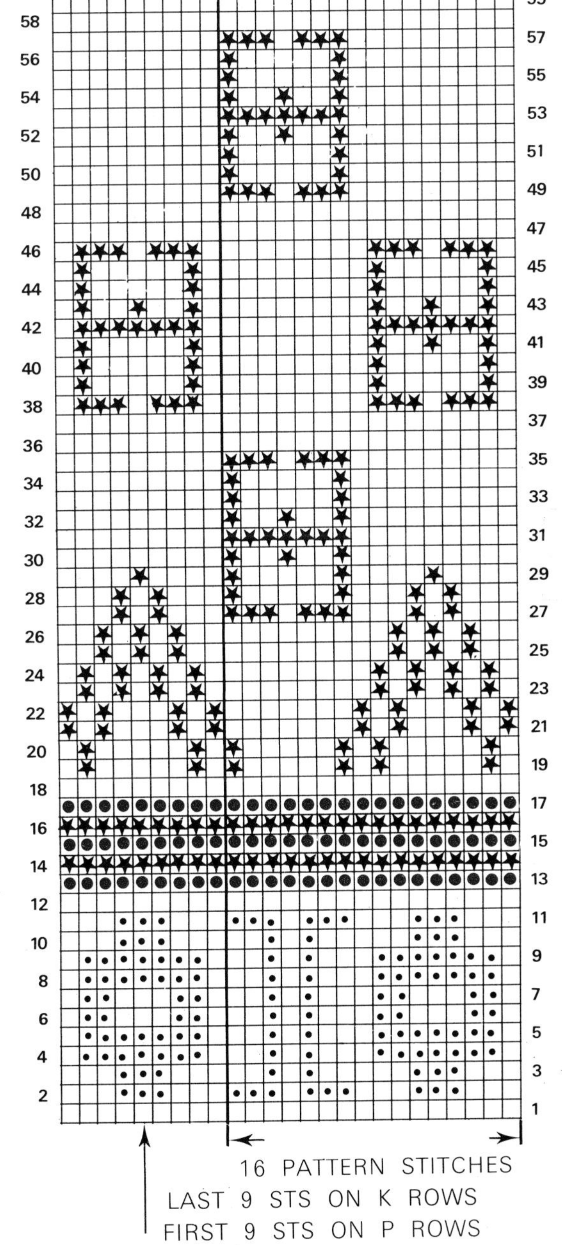

KEY TO CHARTS

• GREEN
✶ CREAM
● RED

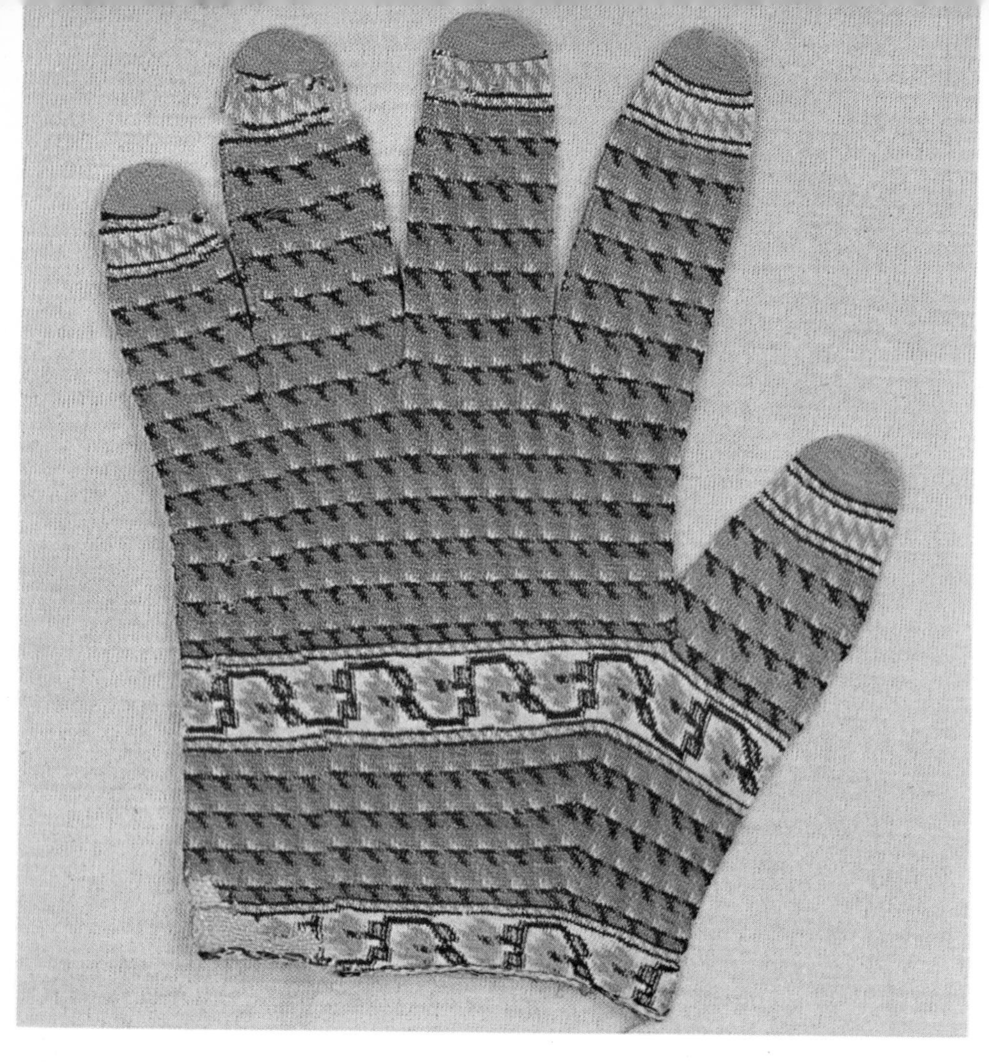

Allure from Kashmir

Glove from 18th-century Kashmir

This man's glove was among a group of garments found in Kashmir in northern India and is supposed to have been knitted in the early part of the 18th century. The patterning therefore might well be the result of European colonial influences on a folk tradition. The community in which this glove was found was not isolated, as is the case with other folk areas in the world, but was close to the old trade routes through northern India.

The glove is made of wool, probably taken from goats or sheep, which were herded on the north-west slopes, and the yarn would have been hand-spun within the community. Probably the same type of yarn was used to weave the cloth and carpets for which this part of India became famous and the bright, rich colours have much in common with the woven fabrics of the area.

The patterning on the glove is curious. It has two bands of a type of geometric floral pattern on a light ground, one at the wrist, the other mid-way across the palm. This is outlined and stands out quite clearly from the background pattern of richer, darker colours. Narrower, lighter bands also recur around the tips of each finger, which are finished off in a plain colour.

The standard of knitting is quite high, both in the execution of the pattern and in the shaping of the glove. The thumb has been knitted on and was shaped in the process. Each of the fingers was knitted in the round and shaped while being knitted. The surface of the fabric has a slightly strange texture which suggests that it was probably knitted on fine, hook needles in the Eastern manner, which slightly distort the loop. The use of the hook needle, however, allows knitting to be done at great speed and with considerable regularity, producing an evenness of fabric.

The combination of bands of pattern on an area of speckled design is similar in some ways to the approach used in the folk knitting of Scandinavia and northern Europe. It appears that, given the same basic route followed by Arab coloured knitting, this form of patterning is the result of a natural evolution which developed quite independently thousands of miles apart.

A girl of today with all the allure of Kashmir in this brightly patterned winter rig of warm scarf, gloves and cap.

An exact reproduction of the Kashmir glove patterning, this cap, scarf and gloves set shows clearly the influence of the Egyptian geometric patterning on folk knitting. Modern yarns cannot hope to reproduce exactly the subtle colours of the original vegetable dyes but the yarn colours chosen for the garments illustrated are nevertheless subtle and the effect is glowing and rich.

The cap is a simple pull-on and is shaped in the making. The scarf has an all-over pattern on one side, with deep, patterned borders. The reverse side is in a plain colour but bordered to match the front.

The set illustrated was knitted in Madame Pingouin 3-ply yarns.

Materials
5 50gr. [9 1oz.] balls of lightweight Double Knitting [Knitting worsted] yarn Ecru (colour 1), 2 [4 1oz.] balls each of Black (colour 2), Green (colour 3), Ochre (colour 4), Red (colour 5) and Blue (colour 6).
1 [2 1oz.] ball [s] in Turquoise (colour 7) used only for gloves.
One pair each of Nos. 9, 10 and 11 [US Nos. 4, 3 and 2] needles.

Tension or Gauge: 12 sts and 16 rows to 2in. [5cm.] using No. 9 [US No. 4] needles.

Sizes
Scarf 50in. [127cm.] long and approximately 7in. [18cm.] wide.
Hat Will fit an average size adult head.
Gloves Size 7.

Scarf
Using No. 9 [US No. 4] needles and colour 2, cast on 44 sts.
Working in st st (stockinette stitch) across all the sts, work the first 43 rows as shown on chart A*, changing yarn colours as indicated. Now work from the 44th to 55th rows; repeat these 12 rows until scarf measures 46in. [117cm.] ending with a 52nd row.
**Work from the 43rd row back to the 1st row inclusive, but using colour 6 instead of colour 5 and colour 4 instead of colour 3.
Cast off.

Lining for scarf
Work as for main part until * is reached.
Using colour 1 only, work in st st (stockinette stitch) until lining measures 46in. [117cm.] ending with a P row.
Work from ** to end as for scarf.

To make up
Do not press. With right side of scarf facing right side of lining, join long edges. Turn to right side then neaten cast-on and cast-off edges.

Hat
Using No. 10 [US No. 3] needles and colour 6, cast on 108 sts and work 9 rows in st st (stockinette stitch).
K 1 row on wrong side to mark hemline.
St st (stockinette stitch) 9 rows.
Change to No. 9 [US No. 4] needles and using colour 6 instead of colour 3, work from the 12th to 23rd rows as on chart A, then from the 44th to 55th rows.
P 1 row in colour 2, K 1 row in colour 1, P 1 row in colour 2. Working with colour 5 only, st st (stockinette stitch) 8 rows.

Shape top
Dec row K7, (K 1 st less here on each repeat of this row), * sl 1, K1, psso, K1, K2 tog, K13, (K 2 sts less here on each repeat of this row), repeat from * 4 times, sl 1, K1, psso, K1, K2 tog, K to end.
St st (stockinette stitch) 3 rows.
Repeat these 4 rows twice.
Now decrease as before on next row and every following K row until 24 sts remain, P 1 row.
Next row K2 tog all along the row.
Break off yarn leaving a long end, thread it into a tapestry needle and draw yarn through remaining stitches. Secure with a back stitch.
Join edges to form back seam. Turn up all round at marked hem line and sew cast-on edge in position.

Gloves
Left hand
Using No. 11 [US No. 2] and colour 1, cast on 48 sts and work 18 rows in K1, P1 rib.
Change to No. 9 [US No. 4] needles and K 1 row.
Divide the sts for back and palm.
Next row P24 and work on these sts for back of hand. Leave the remaining 24 sts on a stitch holder.

Back of Glove
Working in st st (stockinette stitch), work from the 1st to 13th row on chart B, then 2nd to 13th rows again.
Break off yarn and leave these 24 sts on a stitch holder.
With wrong side of work facing you, sl the first 4 sts onto a stitch holder for thumb, then rejoin colour 1 and P the remaining 20 sts for palm.
Now work from * to * as on back of hand.
Break off yarn and leave these stitches on a spare needle.
With wrong side of work facing you rejoin colour 2 to the 24 sts on a stitch holder, P these sts, cast on 4 for base of thumb, then P across the 20 sts of palm. 48 sts.
Now work from the 15th to 17th row but repeating *first* 24 sts only of chart B.

Fingers
Next row With colour 1, P31, turn, cast on 2 with colour 2, then K16 for 1st finger.
***1st finger** Work the first 8 rows on chart B. Work 1 row colour 2, 1 row colour 1, and 1 row colour 2.
**Work from the 35th to 43rd rows on chart A but using colour 4 instead of colour 5.

Shape top
Using colour 4, P 1 row and K 1 row.
Next row P2 tog all along row.
Break off yarn leaving a long end, thread it into a tapestry needle and draw it through remaining sts tightly. Secure with a back stitch.
2nd finger Using colour 1, pick up and P 2 sts from base of previous finger.
P across first 6 sts at front of glove. Join in colour 2, cast on 2 sts. K these 2 sts then K 14 sts. 16 sts for 2nd finger. Now work from * as 1st finger but use colour 7 instead of colour 4.
3rd finger Work as for 2nd finger but use colour 3 instead of colour 7.
4th finger Pick up and P 2 sts from base of 3rd finger. With colour 1 P 5 sts.
Next row With colour 2 K across 12 remaining sts.
Work the first 4 rows only on chart B, then complete as 1st finger but use colour 5 instead of colour 4.
Thumb Rejoin colour 1 to wrong side of 4 sts on stitch holder and P these sts. Work the 1st and 2nd rows on chart B.
Continue in pattern and inc 1 st at each end of next row and every following 4th row until there are 16 sts.
Pattern 1 row.
Next row Cast on 2 sts, pattern to end; turn, cast on 2 sts.
Continue in pattern for 8 rows on these 20 sts.
P 1 row colour 2, K 1 row colour 1, P 1 row colour 2. Now work from ** as on first finger but use colour 6 instead of colour 4.

Right hand
Work as for left hand in reverse, i.e. when dividing stitches for back and palm, place first 24 sts on a stitch holder and work on the last 24 sts.

To make up
Do not press. Set in thumb, sewing shaped edge to opening on hand, then join remaining seam. Join seams on all fingers to complete glove.

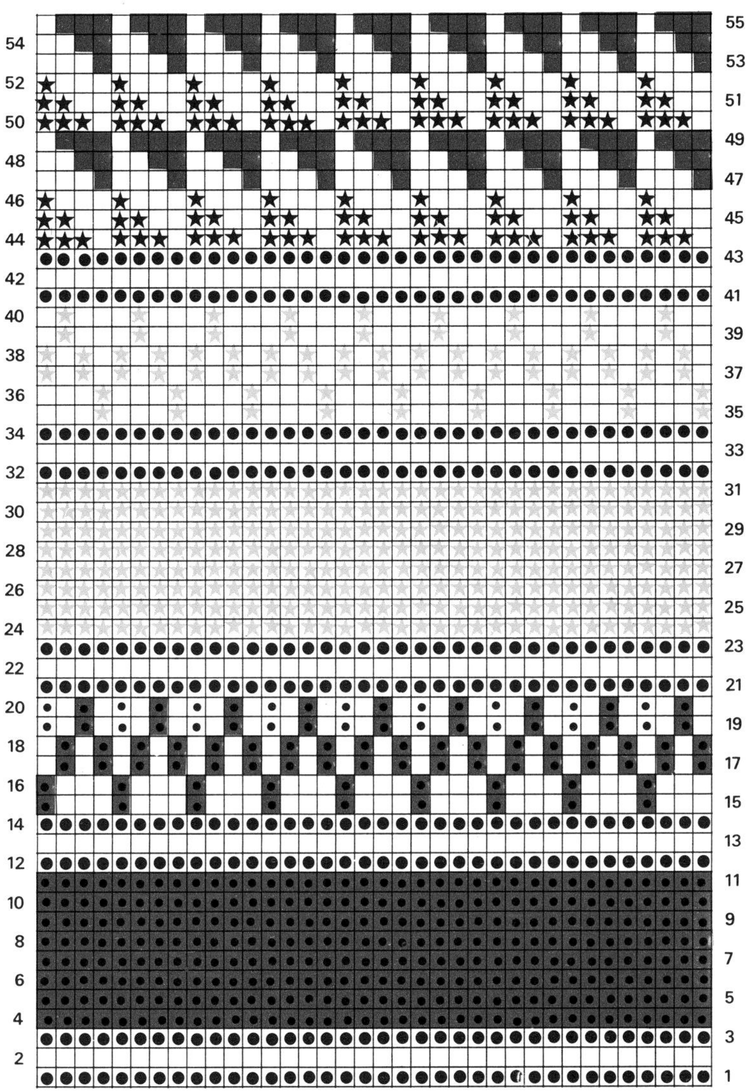

SCARF CHART A

Key for first 43 rows

- ■ OCHRE
- ● BLACK
- ☆ BLUE
- □ ECRU

Key for last 43 rows

- ■ GREEN
- ● BLACK
- ☆ RED
- □ ECRU

Main scarf pattern key – rows 44 to 55

- ■ GREEN
- □ ECRU
- ★ OCHRE

GLOVE CHART B

- □ ECRU
- ● BLACK
- ★ OCHRE
- ○ RED
- ● BLUE
- ▒ GREEN
- ☆ TURQUOISE

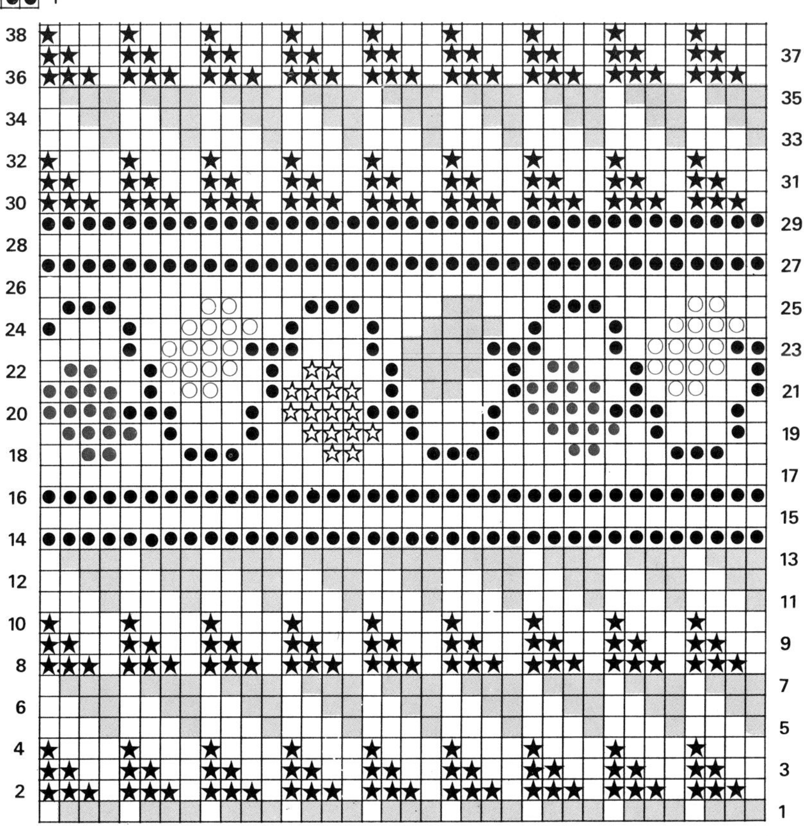

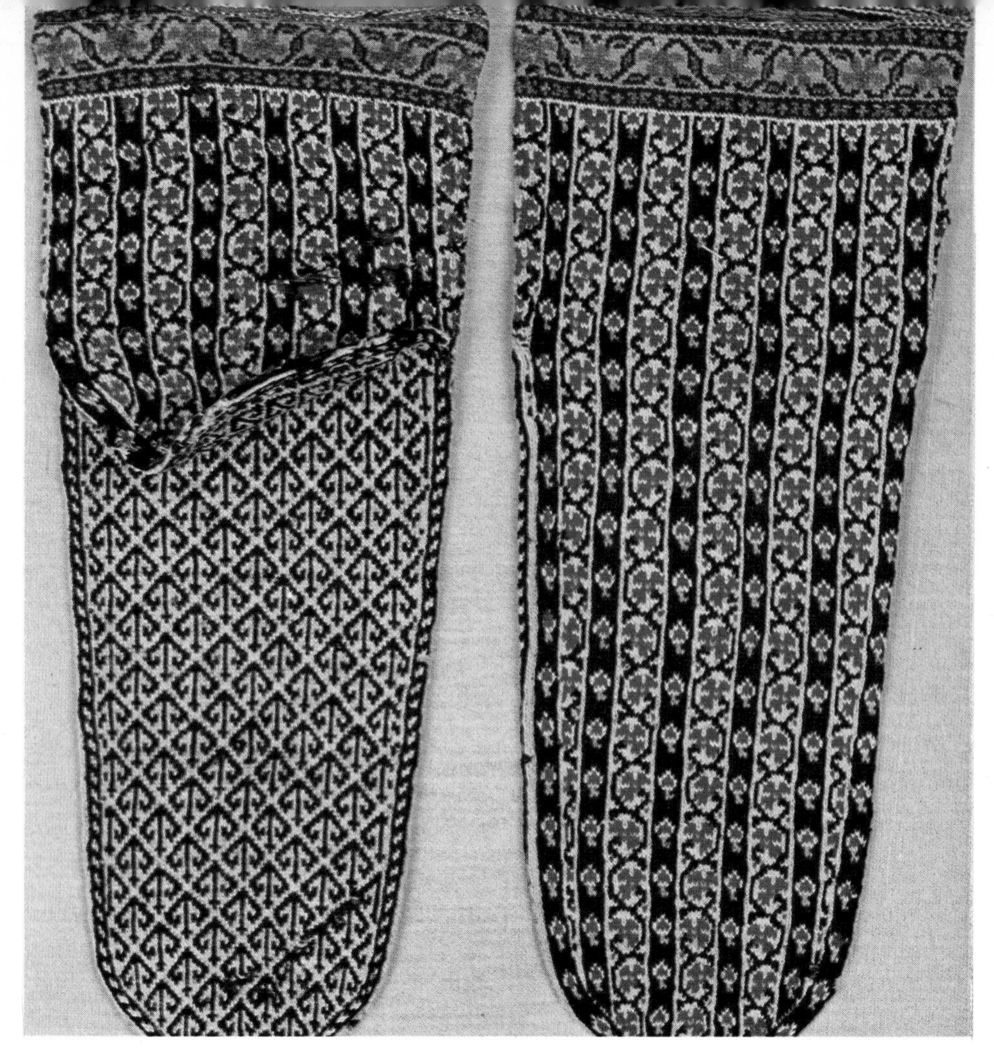

Cutting a handicap

Over-sock from 18th-century Kashmir

This sock is another superb example of the folk knitting produced in 18th-century Kashmir, in India. Like the man's glove on page 94, it is finely knitted with small-scale patterning. The yarn used is wool and is smoother and less wiry than the goat yarn used for the Kashmir glove.

The patterns on the two garments have certain similarities in the use of a formalized flower shape interspersed with a wandering dark-coloured line and the use of a band of pattern at the top of the sock. The patterns are also mixed, being both light on dark and dark on light. However, the interpretation of the pattern is more definite and clearer on the sock.

Apart from these similarities, the sock is quite different. The floral bands alternate with the dark stripes forming a very dominant vertical pattern which is rare in folk knitting where almost all bands of pattern run horizontally. The knitting is finely worked and even in texture and the sock has been adequately shaped during knitting with parts hand-sewn together afterwards. The heel is not sophisticated in shaping and not as cleverly constructed as the Arab sandal sock, made more than 1000 years earlier.

This type of decorative sock was probably worn on festive occasions and as an over-sock. The many float stitches on the back of the fabric indicate that it would have been difficult to put the sock directly on to the foot without damaging the fabric.

These knee-high socks are knitted in a nylonized yarn, chosen for its wearing qualities. The colours used – black, beige, green and white – are not similar in scheme to the original Kashmir socks but the patterning interprets the 18th-century design effectively.

The patterning on these socks runs vertically, as on the Kashmir example, in wide bands of beige patterned in green and black, alternating with a black stripe patterned in green. A band of green, black and white patterning is worked round the top of the socks and a ribbed edge ensures a neat and comfortable fit. The underside of the socks is knitted in black.

The socks illustrated were knitted in Wendy 4-ply nylonized yarns.

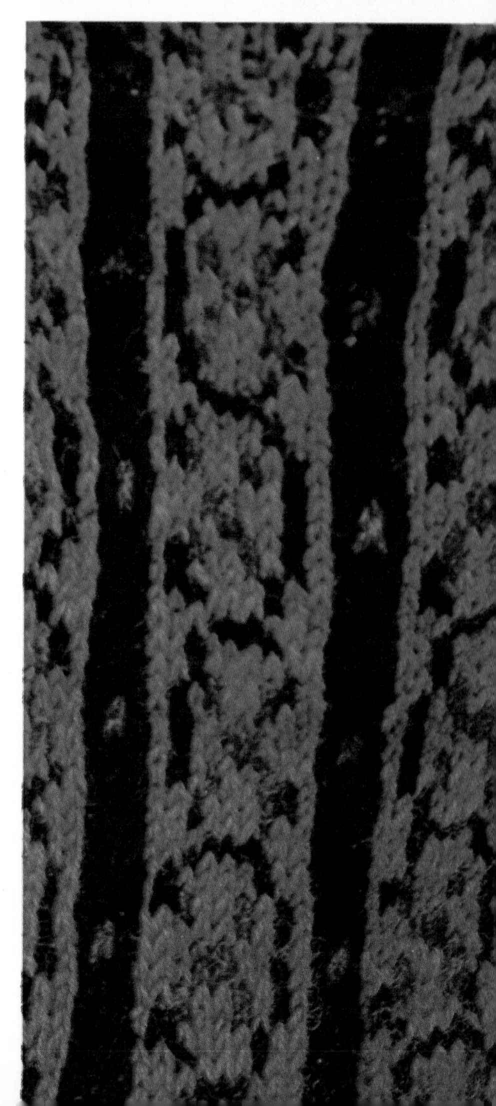

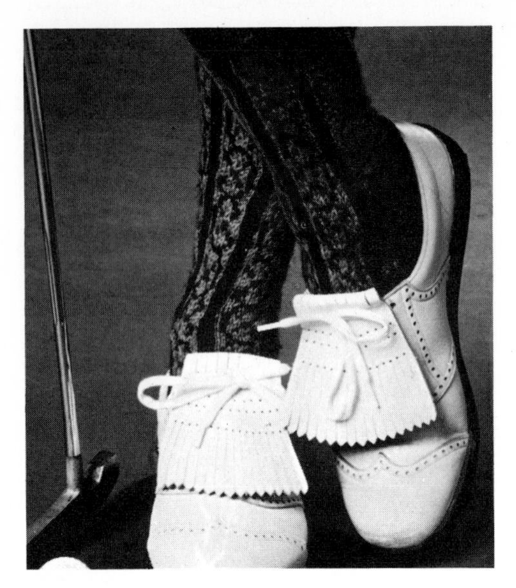

How to cut a dashing figure on the golf course – turn up in a pair of socks knitted from an 18th-century Kashmir design. It's enough to reduce any chap's handicap. Of course, it helps if the shoes have a touch of style, too. . . .

Materials
For any one size:
4 25gr. [4 1oz.] balls of Nylon mixture 4-ply yarn in Camel, 3 balls in Black (B), 2 balls in Green and 1 ball in White.
Set of 4 double-pointed No. 11 and No. 10 [US Nos. 2 and 3] needles.
Optional: 2–3yd. [2–3m.] shirring elastic.

Tension or Gauge: 16 sts to 2in. [5cm.] over the pattern using No. 10 [US No. 3] needles.

Measurements
Length to base of heel, 18in. [46cm].
Length of foot from back of heel to toe, $11(11\frac{1}{2}:12)$in. [28(29:30)cm.].
Note: Figures in parentheses ( ) refer to the larger sizes. Where only one figure is given this refers to all sizes.

To work a sock
(Two alike)
Using set of 4 No. 11 [US No. 2] needles and Black (B) cast on 84 sts, 28 sts on each of 3 needles.
Place a marker at beginning of 1st needle to mark the beginning of round.
Work 22 rounds of K1, P1 rib.
Change to set of No. 10 [US No. 3] needles. Work in st st (stockinette stitch) and work pattern from chart. (It is not necessary to weave in the yarns, but care must be taken not to draw the yarn tightly across the back of the work or it will become puckered.) There are 7 complete patterns all round. Work the 37 rounds as given on chart, then continue to repeat from the 16th to 37th round until work measures $7\frac{1}{2}$in. [19cm.].
Continue in pattern adjusting the sts over the decreasings.

Shape leg
1st round Sl 1, K1, psso, pattern until 2 sts remain, K2 tog.
Pattern 5 rounds.
Repeat last 6 rounds 4 times and 1st round again. 72 sts, 6 complete patterns.
Continue on these sts until work measures 15in. [38cm.], or for length of leg required, but finish on an even-numbered round.

Divide for heel
Next row Pattern 18, then sl the last 17 sts of 3rd needle on to end of this needle and work on these 35 sts for heel flap.
Divide the remaining 37 sts on 2 needles and leave for instep.

Heel flap
Use Black and 2 No. 10 [US No. 3] needles.
1st row Sl 1, P to last st, K1.
2nd row Sl 1, K to end.
Repeat these 2 rows 10 times and then 1st row again.

Turn heel
1st row K22, sl 1, K1, psso, turn.
2nd row P10, P2 tog, turn.
3rd row K10, sl 1, K1, psso, turn.
4th row P10, P2 tog, turn.
Repeat 3rd and 4th rows 10 times. 11 sts.
Break off yarn.
Pick up and K 17 sts from row ends of heel flap, K across the 11 sts, pick up and K 17 sts from row ends at other side of heel flap. 45 sts.
Work 1 row in K1, P1 rib.

Shape foot
1st row K1, sl 1, K1, psso, rib to last 3 sts, K2 tog, K1.
2nd row All rib.
Repeat these 2 rows 3 times. 37 sts.
Cont in rib on these sts until foot measures $6\frac{1}{2}(7:7\frac{1}{2})$in. [17(18:19)cm.] from 1st row of ribbing ending with a wrong side row. Rib first 19 sts onto a double-pointed needle, then sl the remaining sts onto another needle.
Break off yarn and leave sts until required.

Instep
Sl all sts onto a No. 10 [US No. 3] needle.
Rejoin yarns to right side of the 37 sts and work in rows. Cont in pattern until instep measures same as foot.
Break off yarns and sl these sts onto a double-pointed No. 10 [US No. 3] needle. Rejoin B yarn to the beg of the needle holding the 18 sts and, working in rounds of st st (stockinette stitch), shape toe as follows:
1st round 1st needle, K to last 3 sts, K2 tog, K1,
2nd needle, K1, Sl 1, K1, psso, K to last 3 sts, K2 tog, K1,
3rd needle, K1, Sl 1, K1, psso, K to end.
2nd round All K.
Repeat the last 2 rounds 10 times and the 1st round again then K sts on 1st and 2nd needles. Sl the sts off 3rd needle onto end of 1st. 13 sts on each of 2 needles. Graft or cast off tog the sts from 2 needles. Using a flat seam, join row ends of foot.

Optional finish:
On wrong side of ribbed top, thread shirring elastic through each K st on alternate rows.

KEY TO CHART

● BLACK
★ GREEN
☆ CAMEL

This enlargement from the knitted sock shows the exact area covered by the pattern on the left. This vertical pattern is unusual in folk knitting, where the pattern usually runs horizontally.

	●	☆	☆	●	☆	☆	☆	●	☆	☆	●	●	37
36	●	☆	●	☆	☆	☆	☆	●	☆	☆	●	●	
	●	☆	☆	★	☆	☆	★	☆	●	☆	●	●	35
34	●	☆	☆	★	☆	☆	★	☆	●	☆	●	●	
	●	☆	☆	☆	★	★	☆	☆	●	☆	●	★	33
32	●	☆	☆	☆	★	★	☆	☆	●	☆	●	★	
	●	☆	☆	★	☆	☆	★	☆	●	☆	●	●	31
30	●	☆	●	★	☆	☆	★	☆	●	☆	●	●	
	●	☆	●	☆	☆	☆	☆	●	☆	☆	●	●	29
28	●	☆	☆	●	☆	☆	☆	●	☆	☆	●	●	
	●	☆	☆	☆	●	●	●	☆	☆	☆	●	●	27
26	●	☆	☆	●	☆	☆	☆	●	☆	☆	●	●	
	●	☆	☆	●	☆	☆	☆	☆	●	☆	●	●	25
24	●	☆	●	☆	★	☆	☆	★	●	☆	●	●	
	●	☆	●	☆	★	☆	☆	★	☆	☆	●	●	23
22	●	☆	●	☆	☆	★	★	☆	☆	☆	●	★	
	●	☆	●	☆	☆	★	★	☆	☆	☆	●	★	21
20	●	☆	●	☆	★	☆	☆	★	☆	☆	●	●	
	●	☆	●	☆	★	☆	☆	★	●	☆	●	●	19
18	●	☆	☆	●	☆	☆	☆	☆	●	☆	●	●	
	●	☆	☆	●	☆	☆	☆	●	☆	☆	●	●	17
16	●	☆	☆	☆	●	●	●	☆	☆	☆	●	●	
	★	★	★	★	★	★	★	★	★	★	★	★	15
14	★	★	★	★	★	☆	★	★	★	★	★	☆	
	★	★	★	★	★	☆	★	★	★	★	★	☆	13
12	★	★	★	★	★	★	★	★	★	★	★	★	
											●	●	11
10	●	●	●					●	●	●			
			●	●			●	●					9
8			●	●			●	●	★				
		★	★	●	●		●	●	★	★	★		7
6	★	★		●	●		●				★		
				●	●		●					★	5
4	★			●			●				★		
	★	★		●		●				★	★		3
2		★	★		●			★	★				
			★				★						1

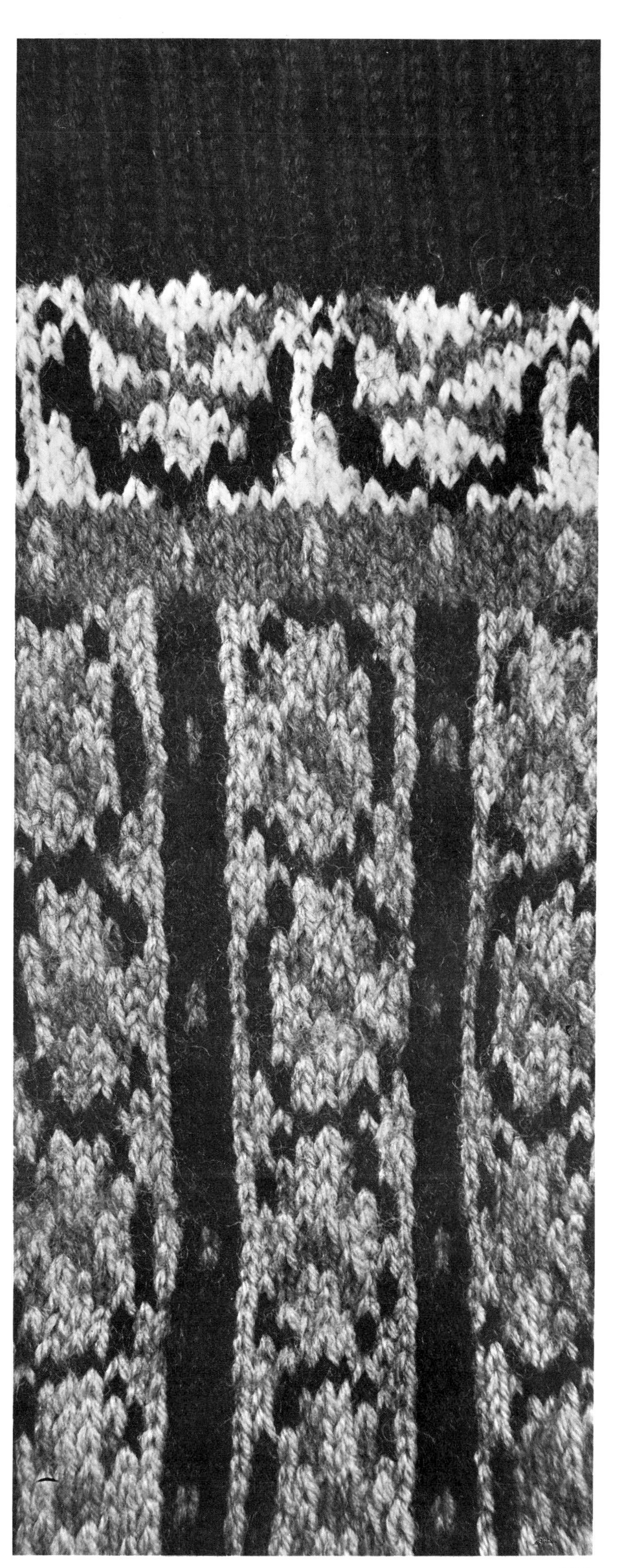

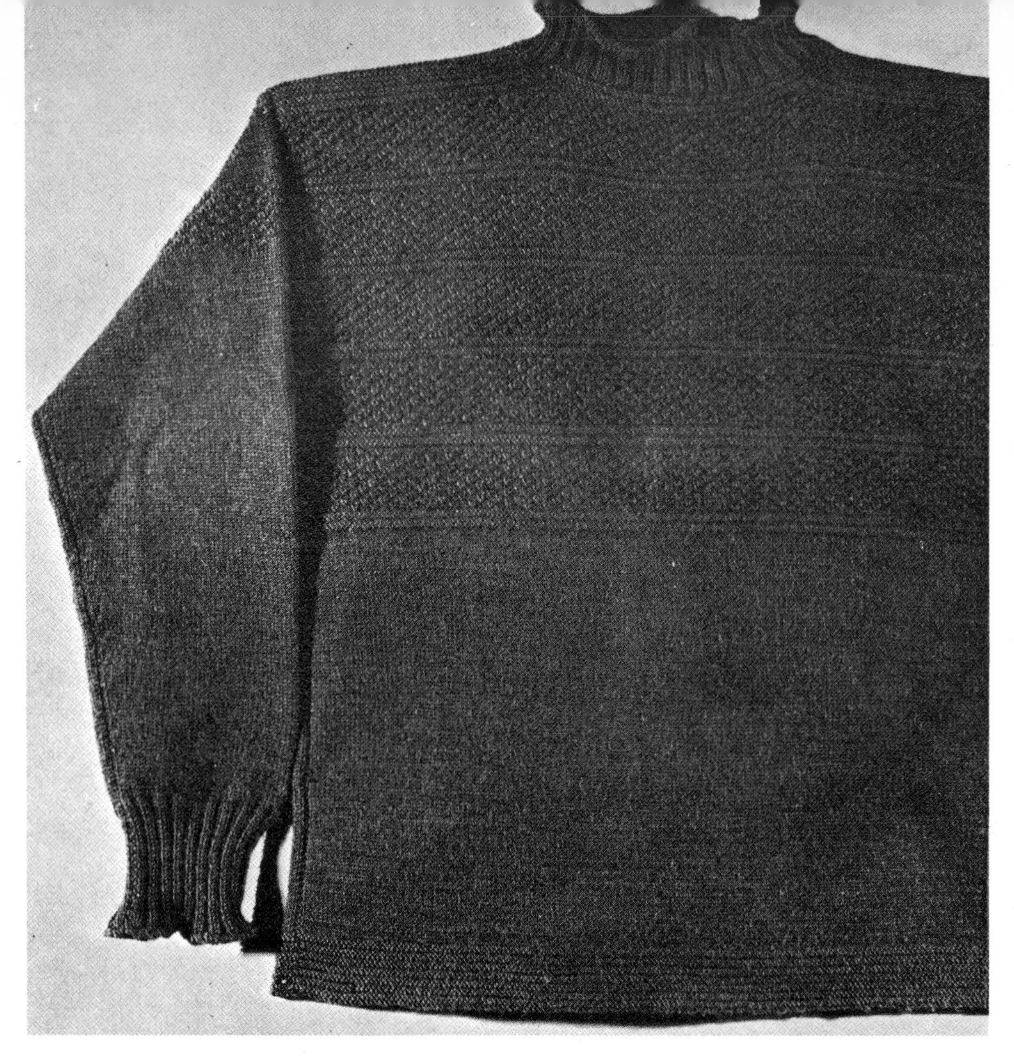

That unisex look

19th-century Guernsey sweater

The Guernsey sweater illustrated is a copy of one worn by a Mr Verril of Staithes, North Riding in the British county of Yorkshire during the 19th century. The sweater is a typical Guernsey or "Gansey", as it was colloquially known. The garment is square in shape and knitted "in the round" without seams. The yarn is a special wool known in the county of Yorkshire as "wassit" – a crisp, hard-wearing five-ply worsted yarn.

Like most Guernsey sweaters, this one is knitted in a dark blue yarn. It has a purl stitch section at the bottom, which is traditional. This was often knitted in double wool, as were the edges of the cuffs, to give extra strength to these areas. From the bottom edge, the sweater was knitted straight up to the under-arm level where gussets were worked. The bands of tuck and purl pattern were started just below the armhole and continued up the chest to the shoulder level where the little stripes of purl were concentrated into a shoulder strap pattern. This double band of purl stitch also appears at the top of the sleeve. The remainder of the sleeve is made of textured knitting. The sleeves of a Guernsey are knitted from the body by picking up all the stitches of the under-arm gusset and the body armhole, and then knitted in the round down to the cuff.

The texture and patterning of Guernseys, while beautiful, are also very practical because the techniques bring extra yarn into the chest area of the garment, thus providing additional warmth for the wearer.

This type of sweater used to be knitted by a fisherman's wife or sweetheart and the distinctive patterns were special to families or to the fishing villages. Most of the stitches and patterns used were named after objects in the fisherfolk's lives – cable or rope stitch, ladder-stitch anchors, diamonds (the shape of fishing nets) and many others which are still known in the villages and towns around British coasts.

One of those splendid all-purpose jackets a man can wear almost anywhere. Perfect for informal country days and even a very serviceable "smoking" jacket or, come to think of it, useful as a beach robe when the sun goes in. There's a definite touch of unisex about it – so beware. It could easily stray into someone else's wardrobe.

Guernsey knitting traditionally uses plain and purl patterning in different parts of the garment and this smart, three-quarter-length jacket successfully follows Guernsey traditions. The yoke areas are worked in a combination of blocks of purl stitches divided by bands of plain knitting. Double bands of purl and plain stitches are worked across the yokes. The cuffed sleeves have a band of similar patterning near the top of the arm and the jacket is edged with bands of plain and purl knitting. The tie belt picks up the yoke patterning again.

Traditional Guernsey sweaters were knitted in the round and without seams. This jacket is knitted in separate pieces and sewn together afterwards.

The jacket illustrated was knitted in Marney Blarney Bainin yarn in Ecru.

Materials
26(27:28:29) 50gr. [46(50:50:52)oz.] balls of special Aran quality yarn.
One pair each of Nos. 7, 8 and 9 [US Nos. 6, 5 and 4] needles.
One No. 9 [US No. 4] circular needle for front borders.
No. 8 [4·00mm.] crochet hook for loops.
5 toggle fasteners.

Tension or Gauge: 9 sts and 12 rows to 2in. [5cm.] over the st st (stockinette stitch) using No. 7 [US No. 6] needles.

Sizes
To fit chest sizes 38(40:42:44)in. [97(102:107:112)cm.].
Length from shoulder, 36(36½:37:37½)in. [91(93:94:95cm.].
Sleeve seam with cuff turned back, 19(19½:19½:20)in. [48(49:49:50)cm.].
Note: Figures in parentheses ( ) refer to the larger sizes. Where there is only one figure this refers to all sizes.

Back
Right half back
*Using No. 9 [US No. 4] needles, cast on 46(48:51:53) sts and work in ridge pattern as follows:
1st row (right side) P.
2nd row K.
3rd row K.
4th row P.
Repeat these 4 rows 4 times and 1st and 2nd rows again.*
Change to No. 7 [US No. 6] needles and work in st st (stockinette stitch) with centre back border.
1st row K.
2nd row P.
3rd row K until 5 sts remain, P5.
4th row K5, P to end.
Continue as set until work measures 16in. [40cm.] ending with a 2nd patt row.
Next row K until 5 sts remain, cast off these 5 sts. Leave remaining sts on stitch holder.

Left half back
Work as for right half from * to *.
Change to No. 7 [US No. 6] needles and work in st st (stockinette stitch) with centre back border.
1st row K.
2nd row P.
3rd row P5, K to end.
4th row P until 5 remain, K5.
Continue as set until work measures same as right half but ending with a 3rd pattern row.
Now join left and right half backs.
Next row P41(43:46:48), K4, then K tog the last st of left half with 1st st of right half, P remaining sts of right half.
86(90:96:100) sts.
Working in st st (stockinette stitch) beginning with a K row, work 10 rows. Inc 1 st at each end of next row and 2 following 16th rows.
On 92(96:102:106) sts continue in st st (stockinette stitch) until work measures 27½in. [70cm.] ending with a P row and inc (inc:dec:dec) 1 st at end of last row.
93(97:101:105) sts.
Now work yoke pattern as follows:
1st row P.
2nd and 3rd rows K.
4th row P1, *K3, P1; repeat from * to end.
5th row K1, *P3, K1; repeat from * to end.
6th row As 4th row.
7th row K.
8th row K2, *P1, K3; repeat from * ending K2.
9th row P2, *K1, P3; repeat from * ending P2.
10th row As 8th row.
11th row K.
12th to 19th rows Repeat 4th to 11th rows once.
20th row K.
21st and 22nd rows P.
These 22 rows form the yoke pattern.
Continue in pattern until yoke measures 8½(9:9½:10)in. [22(23:24:25)cm.] ending with a right side row.
Divide sts for neck and shoulders.
Next row Pattern 41(42:43:44), cast off next 11(13:15:17) sts, pattern to end and work on the last set of 41(42:43:44) sts.

Right back shoulder
1st row Cast off 8(9:10:11) sts for shoulder, pattern to end.
2nd row Cast off 3 sts for neck, pattern to end.
3rd row Cast off 8 sts, pattern to end.
Repeat last 2 rows twice, then fasten off.
Rejoin wool to right side of 41(42:43:44) and pattern to end of row.

Left back shoulder
Complete as right shoulder.

Pocket backs
(Two alike)
Using No. 7 [US No. 6] needles, cast on 34 sts and work in K2, P2 rib, beginning and ending right side rows with P2 and wrong side rows with K2, rib 33 rows.
Next row K4, *K2 tog, K4; repeat from * to end.
Leave remaining 29 sts on holder until required.

Right front
Using No. 9 [US No. 4] needles, cast on 45(47:50:52) sts and work the 22 rows of ridge pattern as on Back.
Change to No. 7 [US No. 6] needles and beginning with a K row, work in st st (stockinette stitch) until work measures 7½in [19cm.] ending with a K row.*
Now work for pocket fronts as follows:
Next row P8(9:10:11), inc 1, *P2, K2, P2, inc 1 K1 repeat from * 3 times, P to end.
50(52:55:57) sts.
1st row K8(9:11:12), P2, *K2, P2; repeat from * 7 times, K to end.
2nd row P8(9:10:11), K2, *P2, K2; repeat from * 7 times, P to end.
Repeat these 2 rows 16 times.
Next row K8(9:11:12), cast off next 34 sts firmly in rib, K to end.
Pocket row P8(9:10:11), P across the 29 sts of one pocket back, P to end.
** On 45(47:50:52) sts, st st (stockinette stitch) 28 rows.
Beginning on left front, inc 1 st at end of next row and 2 following 16th rows.
48(50:53:55) sts.
Continue in st st (stockinette stitch) until work

measures same as back to yoke, ending with a P row, inc 1 at beginning of last row on 38in. and 40in. [97 and 102cm.] sizes only. 49(51:53:55) sts.**
Now work the yoke pattern.
1st, 2nd and 3rd rows as on back yoke.
4th row *P1, K3; repeat from * ending with K4(2:4:2).
5th row P4(2:4:2), K1, *P3, K1; repeat from * to end.
6th row As 4th row.
7th row K.
8th row K2, *P1, K3; repeat from * ending K2(4:2:4).
9th row P2(4:2:4), *K1, P3; repeat from * ending P2.
10th row As 8th row.
11th row K.
12th to 19th rows Repeat 4th to 11th rows.
20th row K.
21st and 22nd rows P.
Pattern 22(24:26:28) rows ending at front edge.

Shape neck and shoulder
Cast off 8(9:10:11) sts at beginning (neck edge) of the next row, 2 sts on the 3 following alternate rows and 1 st on next 3 alternate rows.
Cast off 8 sts at beg (armhole end) of next row and 2 following alternate rows.
Work 1 more row then cast off remaining sts.

Left front
Work as for right front until * is reached.
Now work for pocket fronts as follows:
Next row P8(9:11:12), inc 1, *P2, K2, P2, inc 1 K; repeat from * 3 times, P to end. 50(52:55:57) sts.
1st row K8(9:10:11), P2, *K2, P2; repeat from * 7 times, K to end.
2nd row P8(9:11:12) K2, *P2, K2; repeat from * 7 times, P to end.
Work 32 rows as set.
Next row K8(9:10:11) sts, cast off firmly the next 34 sts in rib, K to end.
Pocket row P8(9:11:12), now P across the 29 sts of other pocket back, P to end.
Work from ** to ** as on right front.
Now work the yoke pattern.
1st, 2nd and 3rd rows As given on back.
4th row K4(2:4:2), P1, *K3, P1; repeat from * to end.
5th row *K1, P3; repeat from * ending with P4(2:4:2).
6th row As 4th row.
7th row K.
8th row K2(4:2:4), *P1, K3; repeat from * ending K2.
9th row P2, *K1, P3; repeat from * ending with P2(4:2:4).
10th row As 8th row.
11th row K.
12th to 19th rows Repeat 4th to 11th rows.
20th row K.
21st and 22nd rows P.
Pattern 23(25:27:29) rows.

Shape neck and shoulder as given for right front.

Sleeves
(Two alike)
Using No. 8 [US No. 5] needles, cast on 58(62:66:70) sts and work 22 rows in K2, P2 rib.
Change to No. 9 [US No. 4] needles and rib a further 22 rows.
Next row Rib 10(14:18:22), *P2 tog, rib 14; repeat from * to end. 55(59:63:67) sts.
Change to No. 7 [US No. 6] needles and, beginning with a K row, st st (stockinette stitch) 8 rows.
Inc 1 st at each end of next row and every following 6th row until there are 75(79:83:87) sts.
Continue on these sts until sleeve measures 18(18½:18½:19)in. [46(47:47:48)cm.], ending with a P row, inc 1 at each end of last row. 77(81:85:89) sts.
Repeat the 22 rows of yoke pattern as given on back, then st st (stockinette stitch) 2 rows.

To shape top
Cast off 6 sts at beginning of next 4(2:2:6) rows, 8 sts on each of the 4(6:6:4) following rows.
Cast off the remaining 21(21:25:21) sts.
With right side facing you and using No. 7 [US No. 6] needles, pick up and K 77(81:85:89) sts across cast off edges of sleeve.
K 1 row and P 2 rows.
Cast off purlwise.

Right front border
Using circular needle, pick up and K 12 sts from front edges of ridge pattern, 115 sts from front edges of st st (stockinette stitch) and 29(31:33:35) sts from yoke. 156(158:160:162) sts.

1st row K.
2nd and 3rd rows P.
4th row K.
Repeat these 4 rows once and 1st and 2nd rows again. Cast off purlwise.

Left front border
Work as for right front but begin at neck of yoke pattern.

Collar
Using No. 8 [US No. 5] needles, cast on 118(122:126:130) sts and work as follows:
1st row K4, *P2, K2; repeat from * ending K4.
2nd row K2, *P2, K2; repeat from * to end.
Repeat these 2 rows 7 times.
Change to No. 9 [US No. 4] needles and work a further 6 rows.
Cast off 12 sts at beg of next 4 rows; 14(15:16:17) at beg of 2 following rows.
Cast off remaining 42(44:46:48) sts.

Belt
Using No. 8 [US No. 5] needles, cast on 11 sts and work in pattern as follows:
1st row K1, P3, K1, P3, K1, P1, K1.
2nd row K2, P1, K3, P1, K4.
3rd row As 1st row.
4th row K1, P9, K1.
5th row K1, P1, K1, P3, K1, P3, K1.
6th row K4, P1, K3, P1, K2.
7th row As 5th row.
8th row As 4th row
Repeat these 8 rows until belt measures 54 in. [138cm.], or to length required.
Cast off.

To make up
Press st st (stockinette stitch) and pockets lightly on the wrong side with a hot iron over a damp cloth. Join shoulder seams. Set in sleeves, sewing the cast off edge to edges of yoke on both back and fronts. Join sleeve seams, placing seam allowance on outside for 3in. [8cm.] at wrist. Sew pocket backs to wrong side. Catch the cast-off edge of right half back behind left half back border. Leaving front borders free, sew cast-off edges of collar neatly to neck edge. Press seams, front borders then outer edge of collar so that it lies flat. Press belt well, stretching as you press. Sew toggles vertically to first row of border, the first toggle 5 stitches below neck edge and the remaining 4 at equal intervals, ending 11in. [28cm.] from cast-on edge.

Loops
(Make 5)
Using crochet hook, make a chain 3in. [7cm.] long. Sew loops to left front opposite toggles.

A lad from Aran

Sweater from the Isles of Aran

The Isles of Aran lie off the west coast of Ireland at the outer edge of Galway Bay. There are three main islands, Inishmore, Inishman and Inisheer. The islanders lead an isolated life and, of necessity, are very self-sufficient. Aran women weave their own tweed fabric and are famous for their knitting.

It is generally supposed that knitting was first brought to the islands by missionaries of the Christian church and that these men had learned their skills from the Egyptian Copts. Several of the patterns appear to have a religious significance, as, for instance, the Tree of Life and the Trinity stitch.

The most prominent pattern in Aran knitting is the interlaced or plaited pattern. This is said to have been originated from the design of the Celtic cross, used on early Irish illuminations and which can still be seen, carved in stone, in many parts of Ireland.

Aran garments are usually very simple in shape but differ from the Guernsey garment in that they are patterned all over the front, back and sleeves. The actual knitting construction is not so tight and dense as the Guernsey, thus giving the impression of a heavier yarn being used.

Aran sweaters are not necessarily knitted in the round (without seams), but are knitted in pieces and then sewn together afterwards. Aran patterning also works from a centre panel with the repeat worked on both sides towards the side of the garment. Aran sweaters thus almost always have a vertical patterning.

The sweater illustrated has a very distinctive pattern made up of double moss stitch diamonds outlined, heavy herring-bone stitch, fine single cable stitch and a heavier cable stitch.

Knitted in an authentic Aran yarn, this warm, hooded sweater is a suitable garment for a boy or a girl.

The design uses Aran patterns in a typical way, plain knitting contrasting with purl and giving textural interest to the garment. Two thick cables run from the shoulder line to the waist with a central panel of outlined diamond shapes. The neckline closes with a toggle fastening and the hood is worked in purl stitches to link with the shoulder and chest areas.

The garment illustrated was knitted in Lister Aran yarn in Irish Cream.

Sure and it's the perfect sweater for a boy – or a pretty young colleen, for that matter. And it has that distinctive and ancient patterning which instantly proclaims its origin – Yes, Aran, of course.

Materials
7(8:9) 50gr. [13(15:16)oz.] balls of special Aran quality yarn.
One pair each of Nos. 6 and 8 [US Nos. 7 and 5] needles.
Cable needle.
2 toggle fastenings.
6in. [15cm.] of braid or cord.

Tension or Gauge: 9 sts and 11 rows to 2in. [5cm.] over the st st (stockinette stitch) using No. 6 [US No. 7] needles.

Special abbreviations for this design:
C3b Slip next st on cable needle and place at back of work, K2 then P1 from cable needle.
C3f Slip next 2 sts on cable needle and bring to front of work, P1 then K2 from cable needle.
C8 Slip next 4 sts on cable needle and bring to front of work, K4 then K4 from cable needle.

Sizes
To fit chest sizes 26(28:30)in. [66(71:76)cm.].
Length from shoulder, 17½(18½:19½)in. [45(47:50)cm.].
Sleeve seam, 11½(12½:13½)in. [29(31·5:34)cm.].
Note: Figures in parentheses () refer to the larger sizes. Where there is only one figure this refers to all sizes.

Back
Using No. 8 [US No. 5] needles, cast on 64(68:72) sts and work 10 rows in K1, P1 rib*.
Change to No. 6 [US No. 7] needles and, beginning with a K row, work in st st (stockinette stitch) until work measures 11½(12:12½)in. [29(31:32)cm.], ending with a P row.
Now work in reversed st st (stockinette stitch) beginning with a P row.

Shape armholes
Cast off 4(5:6) sts at beg of next 2 rows.
Dec 1 st at each end of next row and every following P row until 50(52:54) sts remain.
Continue in reversed st st (stockinette stitch) until armhole measures 6(6½:7)in. [15(16·5:18)cm.], ending with a K row.

Shape shoulders
Cast off 8 sts at beg of next 2 rows, 8(8:9) sts on 2 following rows.
Cast off remaining 18(20:20) sts.

Front
Work as for back until * is reached. Change to No. 6 [US No. 7] needles.
Now work in cable and diamond pattern as follows:
1st row K9(10:11), * for cable panel P2, K8, P2*, K6(7:8); for diamond pattern P2, C3b, C3f, P2, then K6(7:8), repeat from * to *, K to end.
2nd row P9(10:11), *for cable panel K2, P8, K2*, P6(7:8); for diamond panel, K2, P2, K2, P2, K2, then P6(7:8), repeat from * to *, P to end.
3rd row K9(10:11), *P2, K8, P2*, K5(6:7), P2, C3b, P2, C3f, P2, K5(6:7); repeat from * to *, K to end.
4th row P9(10:11), *K2, P8, K2*, P5(6:7), K2, P2, K4, P2, K2, P5(6:7), repeat from * to *, P to end.
5th row K9(10:11), *P2, C8, P2*, K4(5:6), P2, C3b, P4, C3f, P2, K4(5:6), repeat from * to *, K to end.
6th row P9(10:11), *K2, P8, K2*, P4(5:6), K2, P2, K6, P2, K2, P4(5:6), repeat from * to *, P to end.
7th row K9(10:11), *P2, K8, P2*, K3(4:5), P2, C3b, P6, C3f, P2, K3(4:5), repeat from * to *, K to end.
8th row P9(10:11), *K2, P8, K2*, P3(4:5), K2, P2, K8, P2, K2, P3(4:5), repeat from * to *, P to end.
9th row K9(10:11), *P2, K8, P2*, K2(3:4), P2, C3b, P8, C3f, P2, K2(3:4), repeat from * to *, K to end.
10th row P9(10:11), *K2, P8, K2*, P2(3:4), K2, P2, K10, P2, K2, P2(3:4), repeat from * to *, P to end.
11th row K9(10:11), *P2, K8, P2*, K3(4:5), P1, C3f, P8, C3b, P1, K3(4:5), repeat from * to *, K to end.
12th row P9(10:11), *K2, P8, K2*, P3(4:5), K2, P2, K8, P2, K2, P3(4:5), repeat from * to *, P to end.
13th row K9(10:11), *P2, K8, P2*, K4(5:6), P1, C3f, P6, C3b, P1, K4(5:6), repeat from * to *, K to end.
14th row As 6th row.
15th row K9(10:11), *P2, C8, P2*, K5(6:7), P1, C3f, P4, C3b, P1, K5(6:7), repeat from * to *, K to end.
16th row As 4th row.
17th row K9(10:11), *P2, K8, P2*, K6(7:8), P1, C3f, P2, C3b, P1, K6(7:8), repeat from * to *, K to end.
18th row As 2nd row.
19th row K9(10:11), *P2, K8, P2*, K7(8:9), P1, C3f, C3b, P1, K7(8:9), repeat from * to *, K to end.
20th row P9(10:11), *K2, P8, K2*, P7(8:9), K2, P4, K2, P7(8:9), repeat from * to *, P to end.
These 20 rows form the pattern.
Continue in pattern until work is 1 row less than back to armholes, ending with a right-side row.
Divide stitches for neck and shoulders.
Next row Pattern 32(34:36) and leave on holder until required, pattern to end and work on the last set of sts.

Left front shoulder
Shape armhole
1st row Cast off 4(5:6), P next 4 sts, pattern 12, P to end.
Continue in reversed st st (stockinette stitch), with cable panel as set, and dec 1 st at armhole end on each alternate row until 25(26:27) sts remain.
Continue on these sts until armhole measures 4(4½:5)in. [10(11·5:13)cm.], ending at neck edge.

Shape neck
Cast off 5(6:6) sts at beg of next row.
Now dec by working tog the 2nd and 3rd sts from neck edge of the next row and every following alternate row until 16(16:17) sts remain.
Continue in pattern on these sts until armhole measures the same as back, ending at armhole end.

Shape shoulder
Cast off 8 sts at beg of next row, and 8(8:9) sts on following alternate row. Fasten off.
Rejoin yarn to neck edge of 32(34:36) sts and pattern to end of row.
Complete to match first side.

Sleeves
(Two alike)
Using No. 8 [US No. 5] needles, cast on 32(34:38) sts and work 14 rows in K1, P1 rib.

Change to No. 6 [US No. 7] needles and, beginning with a K row, st st (stockinette stitch) 4 rows.
Continue in st st (stockinette stitch) and inc 1 st at each end of next row and every following 6th row until there are 48(50:54) sts on the needle.
Continue on these sts until sleeve seam measures 11½(12½:13½)in. [29(31·5:34)cm.] – (or to sleeve seam length required) ending with a P row.

Shape top
Working in reversed st st (stockinette stitch) beginning with a P row, cast off 4(5:6) sts at beginning of next 2 rows.
Dec each end of next row (3rd:3rd) row, then every P row until 14 sts remain, then cast off.

Hood
Using No. 6 [US No. 7] needles, cast on 64(68:72) sts and, beginning with a P row, work in reversed st st (stockinette stitch) until work measures 9in. [23cm.] ending with a K row.

Shape hood
1st row P29(31:33), P2 tog, P2, sl 1, P1, psso, P to end.
2nd row K.
3rd row P28(30:32), P2 tog, P2, sl 1, P1, psso, P to end.
Continue in this way, dec 2 sts on each P row until 50(54:58) sts remain, then cast off.

To make up
Press all parts, except the ribbing, on the wrong side with a warm iron over a damp cloth. Join shoulder seams. Set in sleeves. Join sleeve and side seams.
Fold cast-off edge of hood in half and join with a flat seam. Sew cast-on edge of hood to neck edge, easing in any fullness. Press seam.
Sew a toggle to each front approximately 11 rows down from neck edge.
Make cord or braid into loops and sew in the position shown in the illustration.

A detail from the Aran sweater

A cap for Andy

Pullover from the Shetland Islands

The Shetland Islands, which lie off the north coast of Scotland, have all the characteristics of other folk knitting centres. The Islands form an isolated community, subject to the vagaries of the North Sea, which is notorious for storms and bitterly cold winds. The land is poor and the islanders struggle to make a meagre living.

As a result of the poor grazing, the sheep of the Shetlands have developed a special quality of fleece from which the now-famous wool is spun. This yarn was very seldom dyed, which is why the traditional Shetland patterning, unlike that of the Fair Isles, is always in natural tones – cream, black, brown, beige and grey – the soft colours forming a pattern on a ground of cream or ecru.

The traditional patterns of Shetland have much in common with the folk traditions of Scandinavia, eastern Europe and the Middle East and all of these seem to have a direct link with the scraps of knitting found in various parts of the ancient Arab empire. In Shetland, these patterns have been tempered by designs taken from nature. In this pullover, for instance, patterns seem to have been evolved from the shapes of flowers or snowflakes.

The broad bands of patterns are separated by narrow bands of geometric designs. Within the bands, the pattern colours and the ground colour alternate every few rows. Thus black and brown alternate to make the pattern on pale grey or ecru ground.

The traditional shape of the Shetland sweater is very much the same as that of the Guernsey garment, square in shape and knitted in the round, without seams. Evenness of tension or gauge is absolutely essential in this type of patterned knitting for, should the "float" threads at the back of the work be of different lengths, the front of the fabric becomes buckled and distorted.

Two of the patterns in the original Shetland pullover have been chosen in the design of this peaked cap. The yarn colours have been specially selected and matched to reproduce as closely as possible the natural fleece colours which would have been used for the pullover.

The cap follows a traditional Shetland shape and is made up of six panels, finished off with a leather-covered button on top. The peak is stiffened.

The cap illustrated was knitted in Sirdar Double Knitting yarn in Ivory, Turf Brown, Black, Silver Cloud and Camel.

A thoroughly traditional Shetland-shaped cap gives that touch of originality in a modern setting. But it looks just as good – indeed, distinctly piquant – on a girl, so here's another one for the joint wardrobe.

Materials
1 25gr. [1oz.] ball of Double Knitting [knitting worsted] yarn in each of the following colours: Ivory, Camel, Silver, Black and Turf Brown.
1 pair of No. 7 [US No. 6] needles.
Elastic for head band 1in. [25mm.] wide.
1 button 1in. [25mm.] wide.
Piece of stiff card for peak.

Tension or Gauge: 11 sts to 2in. [5cm.] in width over the pattern.

Size
Cap will fit an average size adult head and is made up of three A panels and three B panels (see charts).

Panel A
Using No. 7 [US No. 6] needles and Camel, cast on 30 sts and beg with a K row, work in st st (stockinette stitch). Work the 41 rows as given in the chart, dec each end of rows where indicated.
Leave remaining 4 sts on a stitch-holder.
Work 2 panels more from A chart.
Work 3 panels as B chart.
Press each panel lightly with a hot iron over a damp cloth. Alternating A and B panels, join panels together leaving last seam free.
Press seams.

Headband
Using No. 7 [US No. 6] needles and Camel, pick up and K 25 sts from cast-on edge of 2 panels and 24 sts on each of the remaining 4 panels. 146 sts.
Beg with a P row, work from the 2nd to 9th row as on chart A.
Cast off with Camel.

Peak
(Two pieces alike)
Using No. 7 [US No. 6] needles and Camel, cast on 41 sts.
Inc row Inc in 1st st, K until 1 st remains, inc 1. 43 sts.
Beg with a P row, work from the 1st to 9th row on chart C for peak, inc 1 st at each end of every row. 61 sts.
10th row With Camel, inc in 1st st, K1, *K2 tog, K4, rep from * until 5 sts remain, K2 tog, K2, inc 1 in last st. 53 sts.
11th row With Ivory, inc 1, P until 1 st remains, inc 1.
12th row Inc 1, K3, *K2 tog, K3, rep from * until 1 st remains, inc 1. 47 sts.
Cast off. Press as for panels.

To make up
Slip the 4 sts at top of each panel onto a length of yarn, draw up and fasten off with a back stitch, then join remaining seam. With right sides tog, join cast-on and shaped edges of peak together, leaving cast-off edge open, turn to right side and press.
Using peak for a pattern, cut card to shape.
Slip inside peak. Sew peak to headband.
Cut elastic to required size. Join into a ring.
Sew one edge to cast-off edge of headband.
Sew button to centre top of cap.
Place cap flat, peak uppermost, and lightly press round outer edge so that the 10th row of each panel forms the double edge.

PANEL A CHART

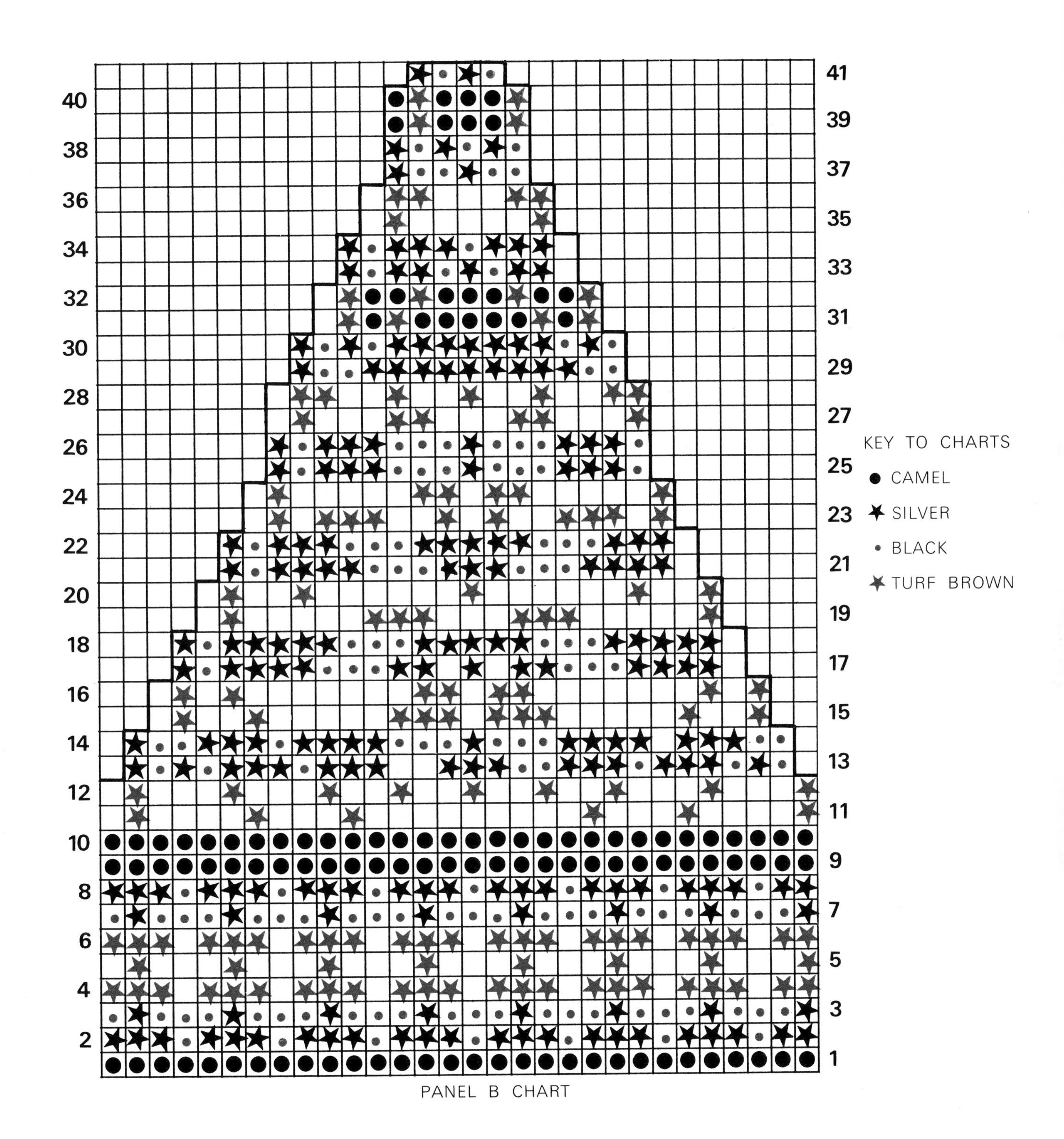

PANEL B CHART

C CHART

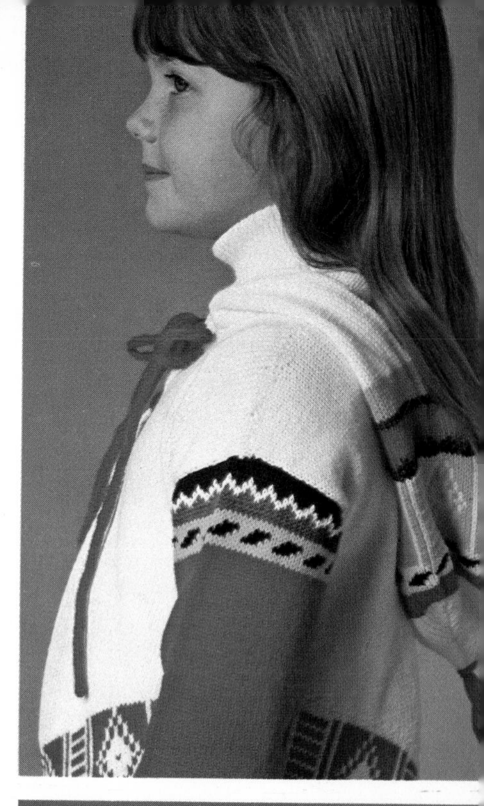

Little Miss Poncho

Socks from Albania

This highly decorative pair of socks was knitted in Albania and was probably part of a festive costume. The socks are knitted in extremely coarse woollen thread in strong colours. The knitting itself is quite different from most examples of folk knitting in that it is crudely and unevenly worked and there are several knitting faults. The shaping of the socks is extremely simple.

The same pair of socks has been used as the basis for the boys' garments on page 118, and we tell you more about the ancient pattern on that page.

The charm of all folk knitting is apparent in this colourful winter set for a girl. The hooded pop-over, designed to look like a peasant poncho, is banded with a deep border of brilliantly colourful geometric patterning. Red predominates in the colouring but, as in the original Albanian sock, the patterning is both horizontal and vertical, both light on a dark ground and dark on a light ground. Kneesocks and mittens with the same patterning match the pop-over top. The set of pop-over, mittens and socks illustrated were knitted on a Knitmaster 321 domestic knitting machine in standard 4-ply yarn.

Materials
Standard 4-ply yarn in the following quantities and colours.
Popover top 6(7 :9:10) 25gr. [6(7:8:9)oz.] balls in Red (colour 1); 6(7:9:10), [6(7:8:9)oz.] balls in White (colour 2); 1(1:2:2), [1(1:2:2)oz.] in Royal Blue (colour 3); 1(1:2:2), [1(1:2:2)oz.] in Yellow (colour 4); 1, [1 1oz.] in Green (colour 5).
Mittens 1 25gr. [1 1oz.] balls in colour 1; 1(1:2:2), [1(1:1:2)oz.] in colour 2; 1, [1 1oz.] in colour 5.
Socks 4(5:6:7) 25gr. [4(5:6:7)oz.] balls in colour 1; 1(1:1:2), [1(1:1:2)oz.] in colour 2; 1(1:1:2), [1(1:1:2)oz.] in colour 3; 1(1:1:2), [1(1:1:2)oz.] in colour 4; 1(1:1:2), [1(1:1:2)oz.] in colour 5.
2 stitch holders.
For Knitmaster 321 and 323 automatic punch card knitting machines.

Tension or Gauge: 30 sts and 42 rows to 4in. [10cm.] measured over the stocking stitch (stockinette stitch), tension dial approx 6··.

See Page 121 for colour chart.

30 sts and 40 rows to 4in. [10cm.] measured over pattern, tension dial approximately 7··.
Note: Figures in parentheses ( ) refer to larger sizes. Where there is only one figure this refers to all sizes.

Sizes
To fit chest sizes 22(24:26:28)in. [56(61:66:71)cm.].

Popover pattern
Knit 8 rows colour 4 and 1 row colour 2. Release card. Work in pattern. With colour 2 in feeder 1 and colour 1 in feeder 2, K 2 rows. With colour 5 in feeder 1 and colour 1 in feeder 2, K 2 rows. K 3 rows colour 5 and 2 rows colour 3. With colour 3 in feeder 1 and colour 4 in feeder 2, K 3 rows. K 2 rows colour 3. With colour 1 in feeder 1 and colour 2 in feeder 2, K 46 rows.

Popover left back
Insert card into machine and lock on row 1. Using colour 4, cast on 71(79:87:95) sts by hand. Row counter 000. Tension dial at 8·. Working in pattern K 2 rows. *Dec 1 st at left edge and inc 1 st at right edge of next row, K 1 row. Dec 1 st at left edge of next and following alternate row, K 1 row.* Repeat from * to * 7 more times. Dec 1 st at left edge and inc 1 st at right edge of next row. **K 1 row. Dec 1 st at left edge of next and following 3rd row. Inc 1 st at right edge of next row.** Repeat from ** to ** 2 more times. 52(60:68:76) sts. Row counter 069. Remove card. Tension dial at 6··. Change to stocking stitch (stockinette stitch) and continue in colour 2 throughout. K 2 rows without shaping (1 row only for right back and left front). Carriage at left.
Always taking yarn round first inside needle in D position, push 50(58:66:74) needles at opposite end to Carriage into D position, K 2 rows. With all latches open, push 2 inside needles at opposite end to Carriage from D position down into C position on next and every following alternate row 21(16:14:9) times in all, K 1 row. With all latches open, push 3 inside needles at opposite end to Carriage from D position down into C position on next and every following alternate row 2(8:12:18) times in all, K 1 row.
With all latches open, push remaining 2 needles at opposite ends to Carriage from D position down into C position, K 2 rows. *** Dec 1 st (2 sts in) at right edge of next and every following 5th (4th:4th:4th) row 3(7:11:15) times in all. 49(53:57:61) sts. K 0(2:2:2) rows without shaping. Carriage at right. Mark right edge with yarn. K 53 (55:57:59) rows without shaping. Carriage at left.

Shape shoulder
Always taking yarn round first inside needle in D position, push 6(7:8:8) needles at opposite end to Carriage into D position, K 2 rows. Push 6(7:7:8) needles at opposite end to Carriage into D position on next and following alternate row. K 1 row. Push 6(6:7:8) needles at opposite end to Carriage into D position, K 2 rows. Push 6(6:7:7) needles at opposite end to Carriage into D position, K 2 rows. With all latches open, push 30(33:36:39) needles at opposite end to Carriage from D position into C position. Cast off 19(20:21:22) sts beg of next row. Using waste yarn, K 8 rows. Release from machine.

Right back
Follow instructions for left back but reverse the shapings by noting alteration in number of rows worked and reading left for right and vice versa.

Right front
Follow instructions for left back to ***.
2nd and 3rd sizes only Dec 1 st (2 sts in) at right edge of next row, K 3 rows.
4th size only Dec 1 st (2 sts in) at right edge of next and following 4th row, K 3 rows.
All sizes Carriage at left.

Front opening
Cast off 5 sts at beg of next row. Dec 1 st (2 sts in) at right edge of next and every following 5th(4th:4th:4th) row 3(6:10:13) times in all. 44(48:52:56) sts. K 0(2:2:2) rows without shaping. Carriage at right. Mark right edge with waste yarn. K 45(45:53:53) rows without shaping. Carriage at left.

Shape neck
Cast off 7(7:6:6) sts at beg of next row, K 1 row. Cast off 2 sts at beg of next and following alternate row, K 1 row. Dec 1 st beg of next and every following alternate row 2(3:5:6) times in all, K 1 row. Carriage at left.

Shape shoulder
Dec 1 st at left edge. Always taking yarn round first inside needle in D position, push 6(7:8:8) needles at opposite end to Carriage into D position, K 2 rows. Push 6(7:7:8) needles at opposite end to Carriage into D position on next and following alternate row, K 1 row. Push 6(6:7:8) needles at opposite end to Carriage into D position, K 2 rows With all latches open, push 24(27:29:32) needles at opposite end to Carriage from D position down into C position, K 1 row. Using waste yarn, K 8 rows. Release from machine.

Left front
Follow instructions for right front but reverse the shapings by noting alteration in number of rows worked and reading left for right and vice versa.

Sleeves
(both alike)
Graft shoulders. Insert card into the machine and lock on row 1. Push 77(81:85:89) needles to B position. With purl side facing you, pick up 77(81:85:89) sts evenly between marked points and place onto needles. Tension dial at 6··. Using colour 3, K 4 rows. Tension dial at 7··. Release card. Work in pattern. With colour 3 in feeder 1 and colour 2 in feeder 2, K 2 rows. With colour 5 in feeder 1 and colour 2 in feeder 2, K 2 rows. K 3 rows colour 5 and 2 rows colour 4. With colour 4 in feeder 1 and colour 3 in feeder 2, K 3 rows. K 2 rows colour 4. Remove card. Tension dial at 6··. Change to stockinette stitch and continue in colour 1 throughout. K 2(6:8:10) rows without shaping. Dec 1 st (2 sts in) both ends of next and every following 8th(9th:10th:11th) row 11 times in all. 55(59:63:67) sts. K 14(16:20:24) rows without shaping. Tension dial at 7··, K 1 row. Tension dial at 5··, K 12 rows. Cast off.

Front bands
(2 alike)
Push 40(49:59:68) needles to B position. With right side of work facing you, pick up 40(49:59:68) sts evenly along front opening and place onto needles. Inc 1 st at lower edge. 41(50:60:69) sts. Tension dial at 5··. Using colour 2, K 3 rows. Transfer the 4th(6th:6th:5th) and every following 5th st onto its adjacent needle, leaving empty needles in B position. K 3 rows. Tension dial at 6··, K 1 row. Tension dial at 5··, K 3 rows. Transfer sts as before. K 4 rows. Using waste yarn, K 8 rows. Release from machine.

Right side of hood
Using colour 2, cast on by hand 18 sts. Tension dial at 6··, K 2 rows (knit 1 row extra for left side of hood). Cast on 2 sts beg of next and every following alternate row 8 times in all, K 1 row. Inc 1 st beg of next and every following alternate row 4(5:6:7) times in all, K 1 row. Cast on 16(17:18:19) sts beg of next row. 54(56:58:60) sts. K 4 rows without shaping. Inc 1 st at right edge of next and following 10th(11th:12th:13th) row, K1(2:3:4) rows. Carriage at left. Always taking yarn round first inside needle in D position, push 4 needles at opposite end to Carriage into D position next and every following alternate row 10 times in all, K 1 row. With all latches open, push 40 needles at opposite end to Carriage from D position down into C position, K 1 row. Using colour 4, K 7 rows. Inc 1 st at right edge of next row. 57(59:61:63) sts. Using colour 5, K 2 rows. Using colour 1, K 3 rows. Carriage at left. Using nylon cord, K49(51:53:55) sts at right by hand, taking needles down into A position.

Shape front facing
K 2 rows. Dec 1 st at right edge of next 7 rows, K 1 row. Fasten off remaining st. Unravel nylon cord, bringing needles to correct position. Using waste yarn, K 8 rows. Release from machine.

Left side of hood
Follow instructions for right side of hood but reverse the shapings by noting alteration in number of rows worked and reading left for right and vice versa.

Top of hood
Insert card into the machine and lock on row 1.
Using colour 1, cast on by hand 62 sts. Tension dial at 6··, K 1 row. Dec 1 st both ends of next 8 rows, K 1 row. 46 sts. Carriage at right. Push 49(51:53:55) adjacent needles at left and right into B position. With purl side of right side of hood facing you, replace sts from last

row knitted in colour 1 onto needles at right. With purl side of left side of hood facing you, replace sts from last row knitted in colour 1 onto needles at left. 144(148:152:156) sts. K 6 rows without shaping. Tension dial at 7··. Release card. Work in pattern. With colour 1 in feeder 1 and colour 5 in feeder 2, K 2 rows. With colour 3 in feeder 1 and colour 5 in feeder 2, K 1 row. Lock card on row 15. With colour 3 in feeder 1 and colour 5 in feeder 2, K 1 row. Release card. With colour 4 in feeder 1 and colour 2 in feeder 2, K 22 rows. Lock card on row 8. With colour 4 in feeder 1 and colour 2 in feeder 2, K 1 row. Release card. K 2 rows colour 2. With colour 2 in feeder 1 and colour 3 in feeder 2, K 3 rows. K 2 rows colour 2. Remove card. Tension dial at 6··. and all top seams of hood. Press. Mitre corners of facings, turn facings to inside and catch down. Sew hood into position. Press. Thread cord through eyelet holes in front bands. Cut 12in. [30cm.] lengths of yarn in all colours to make tassels. Attach one tassel to top of hood. Attach tassels round lower edge of popover top. Give garment a final pressing.

Right mitten
Insert card into the machine and lock on row 9.
Push 38(44:47:50) needles to B position. Arrange needles for 2 × 1 ribbed welt. Tension dial at 4··. Cast on using waste yarn, K 8 rows (knit 1 row extra for left mitten only). Carriage at right. Using colour 2, K 20 rows. Tension dial at 5··, K 1 row. Tension dial at 4··, K 20 rows. Turn up a hem. Carriage at left. Inc 2(0:1:2) sts. 40(44:48:52) sts. Tension dial at 7··. Release card. Work in pattern. K 1 row colour 5. *With colour 5 in feeder 1 and colour 1 in feeder 2, K 3 rows. Lock card on row 10. K 1 row colour 5. Release card.* Working in pattern as given from * to *, inc 1 st both ends of next and every following 3rd(5th:5th:7th) row 3 times in all. 46(50:54:58) sts. Lock card on row 15. K 1 row colour 5. Carriage at right.
Using the same method as for making button-holes, work thumb opening over 8(9:10:11) sts at left. Release card. With colour 1 in feeder 1 and colour 2 in feeder 2, knit 22 rows. Change to stockinette stitch. Using colour 1, K 1 row. Carriage at left.

Shape top
Using nylon cord, K108(111:114:117) sts at right by hand taking needles down into A position.

1st section
K 1 row. Dec 1 st both ends of next row, K 2 rows. Using colour 2, dec 1 st both ends of next and following 4th row, K 1 row. Dec 1 st both ends of next and every following alternate row 12(13:13:14) times in all, K 1 row. Cast off 2 sts beg of next 2 rows. Fasten off remaining 2(1:2:1) sts.

2nd section
Unravel nylon cord over next 36(37:38:39) needles bringing needles to correct position. Follow instructions for 1st section.

3rd and 4th sections
Follow instructions for 2nd section.

Cord
Using colour 1, make a 3 stitch cord to the required length.

To make up
Pin out each piece to size and steam carefully with a hot iron over a wet cloth. Join centre back, centre front, side and sleeve seams. Press. Turn up 12 rows at lower edge of sleeves and catch down on the inside. Fold front bands in half onto outside. Pin into position and backstitch through the open loops of the last row knitted in colour 2. Unravel waste yarn. Sew lower edges into position. Join back seam Lock card on row 9. With colour 1 in feeder 1 and colour 2 in feeder 2, K 1 row. Release card. K 1 row colour 5. Working in pattern as given from * to * throughout, K1(1:5:5) rows without shaping. Carriage at left. Note row number showing on pattern panel. Using nylon cord, K23(25:27:29) sts at right by hand taking needles down into A position. K left part as follows: always taking yarn round first inside needle in D position, push 2 needles at opposite end to Carriage into D position on next 8(8:10:10) rows. Push remaining 7(9:7:9) needles to D position. With Carriage at left, set card at number previously noted and lock. Take Carriage to right. Unravel nylon cord, bringing needles to correct position. Release card. Knit right part as for left part.
Set front lever/russol lever at 11. Using waste yarn, K 8 rows in stockinette stitch. Release from machine.

Thumb
Place 8(9:10:11) st loops from both edges of thumb opening onto 2 stitch holders. With purl side of work facing you, place both sets of sts back onto machine leaving 1 empty needle between. Pick up loop from the st below and place onto empty needle. 17(19:21:23) sts. Tension dial at 7··. ** Lock card on row 10. K 1 row colour 2. Release card. Work in pattern. With colour 2 in feeder 1 and colour 1 in feeder 2, K 3 rows. ** The last 4 rows from ** to ** form 1 pattern which should be repeated throughout. K12(14:14:16) rows. Break off yarn, leaving end long enough to sew thumb seam. Thread end through all stitches and draw up.

Left mitten
Follow instructions for right mitten but reverse the shapings by noting alteration in number of rows worked and reading left for right and vice versa.

To make up
Join thumb and side seams. Graft sts together. Unravel waste yarn. Press lightly with a hot iron over a wet cloth.

Socks
(both alike)
Insert card upside down into the machine so that row 4 shows upside down at left side.
Push 71(77:83:89) needles to B position. Arrange needles for 2 × 1 ribbed welt. Tension dial at 4··. Cast on using waste yarn, K 7 rows. Carriage at left. Using colour 3, K 20 rows. Tension dial at 5··, K 1 row. Tension dial at 4··, K 20 rows. Turn up a hem, Dec 1 st at right edge. 70(76:82:88) sts. Carriage at right. Row counter 000. Tension dial at 6··. Using colour 2, K 1 row. Dec 1 st both ends of next row, K 2 rows. K 4 rows colour 4. Tension dial at 7··. Release card. Work in pattern. K 2 rows colour 5. With colour 5 in feeder 1 and colour 3 in feeder 2, dec 1 st both ends of next row, K 2 rows. K 1 row colour 5. Lock card so that row 27(27:50:50) shows upside down at left side. K 2 rows colour 5. Release card. With colour 1 in feeder 1 and colour 2 in feeder 2, dec 1 st at both ends of 6th(6th:11th:11th) and following 10th(10th:20th:20th) rows, K7(7:15:15) rows. K 2 rows colour 3. With colour 3 in feeder 1 and colour 4 in feeder 2, dec 1 st both ends of next row, K 2 rows. K 2 rows colour 3 and 3 rows colour 5. With colour 5 in feeder 1 and colour 1 in feeder 2, K 2 rows. With colour 2 in feeder 1 and colour 1 in feeder 2, dec 1 st both ends of next row, K 1 row. Remove card. Tension dial at 6··. Change to stockinette stitch and continue in colour 1 throughout. Knit 21(21:20:20) rows without shaping (adjust length at this stage, if desired). Carriage at left. Dec 1 st (2 sts in) both ends of next and every following 16th row 4(5:6:7) times in all. 50(54:58:62) sts. K 5 rows without shaping. Carriage at left.

Instep
Break off yarn. Slip 12(13:14:15) sts at left (right on 2nd sock) and 13(14:15:16) sts at right (left on 2nd sock) onto 2 stitch holders. 25(27:29:31) sts. Join in yarn.
K26(36:46:56) rows without shaping (Adjust length of instep, if desired.)

Shape toe
Always taking yarn round first inside needle in D position, push 1 needle at opposite end to Carriage into D position on next 10 rows and 2 needles at opposite end to Carriage into D position on next 4 rows. With all latches open, push 2 inside needles at opposite end to Carriage from D position down into C position on next 4 rows and 1 inside needle at opposite end to Carriage from D position down into C position on next 10 rows.

Sole
K26(36:46:56) rows without shaping. (Adjust length of sole as on instep if desired.)

Shape heel
Follow instructions for toe from * to *. Using waste yarn, K 8 rows. Release from machine.

To make up
Pin out each piece to size and steam carefully with a hot iron over a wet cloth. Join back seam. Press. Graft stitches from top of heel to stitches at lower edge of leg. Join side of foot seams. Press. Give final pressing.

Ready for anything

Socks from Albania

This is the same pair of Albanian socks shown on page 114. Here we show their versatility by using them for the basis of boys' garments.

The patterns on the socks are different from most folk traditions and strangely mixed, being both vertical and horizontal, dark on light and light on dark. All are geometric in design and therefore simple to form in a knitted stitch. There are also areas of all-over pattern, such as the diagonal birdseye broken by a fine stripe.

The vertical and horizontal patterning is, as we have said, typical of this rather unusual style of European folk knitting. It shows a more sophisticated design talent than is usually to be found in straight-forward folk knitting and allows for subtle permutations to be made both in the actual design and in the use of colours.

The Albanian festive socks were almost a natural source of inspiration for this delightful winter set for a boy. The brilliant colouring of the peasant patterning adapts easily to modern fashion and, although the set was knitted on a Knitmaster 321 domestic knitting machine, the patterning could be worked by hand, working row by row from the charts. The sweater is zip-fronted and the matching cap has ear-flaps which tie under the chin. The predominant colouring of this version of the Albanian knitted sock is blue.

Any young man in this colourful winter set can be said to be ready for anything from a snowball fight to a trip to reindeer-land. Again, the influence here is Albanian.

Materials
Standard 4-ply yarn in the following quantities and colours:
Jacket 5(6:7:8) 25gr. [5(6:7:8)oz.] balls in Royal Blue (colour 1); 4(5:6:7), [4(5:6:7)oz.] in White (colour 2); 1(1:1:2), [1(1:1:2)oz.] in Green (colour 3); 1(1:1:2), [1(1:1:2)oz.] in Yellow (colour 4); 1(1:1:2), [1(1:1:2)oz.] in Red (colour 5).
Mittens 1 25gr. [1 1oz.] ball in colour 1; 1(1:1:2), [1(1:1:2)oz.] in colour 2; 1, [1 1oz.] in colour 4.
Hat 1 25gr. [1 1oz.] ball in colour 1; 1, [1 1oz.] in colour 2; 1, [1 1oz.] in colour 3; 1, [1 1oz.] in colour 5.
14(14:16:16)in. [36(36:41:41)cm.] open-ended or separated zip fastener.
4·50mm. [US G/6] crochet hook.
2 stitch holders.
Tension or Gauge: 30 sts and 42 rows to 4in. [10cm.] measured over stocking stitch (stockinette stitch), tension dial approximately 6·· 30 sts and 40 rows to 4in. [10cm.] measured over pattern, tension dial approximately 7··.

Sizes
To fit chest sizes 22(24:26:28)in. [56(61:66:71)cm.].
Note: Figures in parentheses ( ) refer to the larger sizes. Where there is only one figure this refers to all sizes.

Jacket
Back
Insert card into the machine and lock on row 1. Push 95(101:110:119) needles to B position. *Arrange needles for 2 × 1 ribbed welt. Tension dial at 4. Cast on using waste yarn, K 7 rows (K 1 row extra for left front only). Carriage at left. Using colour 1, K15(15:20:20) rows. Tension dial at 5, K 1 row. Tension dial at 4, K15(15:20:20) rows. Turn up a hem. Carriage at right. * Inc 0(2:1:0) sts. 95(103:111:119) sts. ** Row counter 000. Tension dial at 6, K 1 row. K 6 rows colour 3 and 1 row colour 5. Tension dial at 7, release card. Work in pattern. With colour 5 in feeder 1 and colour 1 in feeder 2, K 2 rows. With colour 4 in feeder 1 and colour 1 in feeder 2, K 2 rows. K 3 rows colour 4 and 2 rows colour 3. With colour 3 in feeder 1 and colour 5 in feeder 2, knit 3 rows. K 2 rows colour 3. With colour 1 in feeder 1 and colour 2 in feeder 2, K 45 rows.
Lock card on row 8. With colour 1 in feeder 1 and colour 2 in feeder 2, K 1 row. Release card. K 2 rows colour 4. With colour 4 in feeder 1 and colour 1 in feeder 2, K 3 rows. K 1 row colour 4. Lock card. K 1 row colour 4 and 1 row colour 3. Lock card on row 1. K 1 row colour 3. Release card. With colour 3 in feeder 1 and colour 5 in feeder 2, K 2 rows. With colour 1 in feeder 1 and colour 5 in feeder 2, K 1 row. Lock card on row 1. With colour 1 in feeder 1 and colour 5 in feeder 2, K 1 row. Release card. With colour 1 in feeder 1 and colour 2 in feeder 2, Knit 2 rows. Remove card. Tension dial at 6··, change to stockinette stitch and continue in colour 2 throughout. K9(9:25:25) rows without shaping. Row counter 092(092:108:108). Carriage at right.** Mark both edges with waste yarn. K 53(55:57:59) rows without shaping. Carriage at left.

Shape shoulders
Always taking yarn round first inside needle in D position, push 7(8:8:9) needles at opposite end of carriage into D position on next 6(2:8:4) rows. Push 6(7:7:8) needles at opposite end to carriage into D position on next 4(8:2:6) rows. Cast off remaining 29(31:33:35) sts in centre. With all latches open, push 33(36:39:42) needles at right from D position down into C position. Using colour 2, K 1 row. Using waste yarn, K 8 rows. Release from machine. With all latches open, push 33(36:39:42) needles at left from D position down into C position. Using colour 2, K 1 row. Using waste yarn, K 8 rows. Release from machine.

Right front
Insert card into the machine and lock on row 1. Push 47(50:56:59) needles to B position. Follow instructions for back from * to * inc 1(2:0:1) sts. 48(52:56:60) sts. Follow instructions for back from ** to **. Mark right edge with waste yarn.
K 41(41:39:39) rows without shaping. Carriage at left.

Shape neck
Cast off 8 sts beg of next row, K 1 row. Cast off 2 sts beg of next and following alternate row, K 1 row. Dec 1 st beginning of next and every following alternate row 3(4:5:6) times in all. 33(36:39:42) sts. K3(3:5:5) rows without shaping. Carriage at left.

Shape shoulder
Always taking yarn round first inside needle in D position, push 7(8:8:9) needles at opposite end to Carriage into D position on next row, K 1 row. Push 7(7:8:9) needles at opposite end to Carriage into D position on next row, K 1 row. Push 7(7:8:8) needles at opposite end to Carriage into D position on next row, K 1 row. Push 6(7:8:8) needles at opposite end to Carriage into D position on next row, K 1 row. With all latches open, push 27(29:32:34) needles at opposite end to Carriage from D position down into C position, K 1 row. Using waste yarn, Knit 8 rows. Release from machine.

Left front
Follow instructions for right front but reverse the shapings by noting alteration in number of rows worked and reading left for right and vice versa.

Sleeves *(Both alike)*
Graft shoulders to join seams. Insert card into the machine and lock on row 1. Push 77(81:85:89) needles to B position. With purl side facing you, pick up 77(81:85:89) sts evenly between marked points and place onto needles. Tension dial at 6··, Using colour 4, K 4 rows. Tension dial at 7··, release card. Work in pattern. With colour 4 in feeder 1 and colour 2 in feeder 2, K 2 rows. With colour 5 in feeder 1 and colour 2 in feeder 2, K 2 rows. K 3 rows colour 5 and 2 rows colour 3. With colour 3 in feeder 1 and colour 4 in feeder 2, K 3 rows. K 2 rows colour 3. Remove card. Tension dial at 6··. Change to stockinette stitch and continue in colour 1 throughout. K 2(6:8:10) rows without shaping. Dec 1 st (2 sts in) both ends of next and every following 8th(9th:10th:11th) row 11 times in all. 55(59:63:67) sts. K 14(16:20:24) rows without shaping. Tension dial at 7·· K 1 row. Tension dial at 5··, K 12 rows. Cast off.

Pocket
Insert card into the machine and lock on row 1. Push 23 needles to B position. Arrange needles for 2 × 1 ribbed welt. Tension dial at 4··. Cast on using waste yarn, K 7 rows. Carriage at left. Using colour 2, K 8 rows. Tension dial at 5··, K 1 row. Tension dial at 4··, K 8 rows. Turn up hem. Carriage at right. Tension dial at 7··, K 2 rows colour 3. Release card. Work in pattern. With colour 3 in feeder 1 and colour 5 in feeder 2, K 2 rows. With colour 2 in feeder 1 and colour 5 in feeder 2, K 1 row. Lock card on row 1. With colour 2 in feeder 1 and colour 5 in feeder 2, K 1 row. Release card. With colour 2 in feeder 1 and colour 1 in feeder 2, K 2 rows. Remove card. Tension dial at 6··, change to stockinette stitch and continue in colour 2 throughout. K 16 rows without shaping. Using waste yarn, K 8 rows. Release from machine.

Neckband
Push 86(92:98:104) needles to B position. With right side of work facing you, pick up 86(92:98:104) sts evenly around neck edge and place onto needles. Tension dial at 4··, Using colour 2, K 1 row. Transfer sts for 2 × 1 ribbed welt. Push empty needles down into A position. K 12 rows. Tension dial at 5··, K 1 row. Tension dial at 4··, K 14 rows. Using waste yarn, K 8 rows. Release from machine.

To make up
Pin out each piece to size and steam carefully with a hot iron over a wet cloth. Join side and

sleeve seams, press. Turn up 12 rows at lower edge of sleeves and catch down on the inside. Fold neckband in half onto outside, pin into position and backstitch through the open loops of the last row knitted in colour 2. Unravel waste yarn. Neaten open ends. Graft lower edge of pocket into position. Catch down side edges. Work 1 row of double crochet [US single crochet] along both front edges. Sew in zip fastener. Give final pressing.

Mittens

Right mitten

Insert card into the machine and lock on row 9. Push 38(44:47:50) needles to B position. Arrange needles for 2 × 1 ribbed welt. Tension dial at 4··, cast on using waste yarn, K 8 rows. (Knit 1 row extra for left mitten only.) Carriage at right. Using colour 2, K 20 rows. Tension dial at 5··, K 1 row. Tension dial at 4··, K 20 rows. Turn up a hem. Carriage at left. Inc 2(0:1:2) sts. 40(44:48:52) sts. Tension dial at 7··. Release card. Work in pattern. K 1 row colour 4. *With colour 4 in feeder 1 and colour 1 in feeder 2, K 3 rows. Lock card on row 10. K 1 row colour 4. Release card.* Working in pattern as given from * to *, inc 1 st both ends of next and every following 3rd(5th:5th:7th) row 3 times in all. 46(50:54:58) sts. Lock card on row 15. K 1 row colour 4. Carriage at right. Using the same method as for making buttonholes, work thumb opening over 8(9:10:11) sts at left. Release card. With colour 1 in feeder 1 and colour 2 in feeder 2, K 22 rows. Lock card on row 9. With colour 1 in feeder 1 and colour 2 in feeder 2, K 1 row. Release card. K 1 row colour 4. Working in pattern as given from * to * throughout. K1(1:5:5) rows without shaping. Carriage at left. Note row number showing on pattern panel. Using nylon cord, K23(25:27:29) sts at right by hand taking needles down into A position.

Knit left part as follows: always taking yarn round first inside needle in D position, push 2 needles at opposite end to Carriage into D position on next 8(8:10:10) rows. Push remaining 7(9:7:9) needles to D position. With Carriage at left, set card at number previously noted and lock. Take Carriage to right. Unravel nylon cord, bringing needles to correct position. Release card. K right part as for left part.

Set front lever/russol lever at 11. Using waste yarn, K 8 rows in stockinette stitch. Release from machine.

Thumb

Place 8(9:10:10) st loops from both ends of thumb opening onto 2 stitch holders. With purl side of work facing you, place both sets of sts back onto machine, leaving 1 empty needle between. Pick up look from the st below and place onto empty needle. 17(19:21:21) sts. Tension dial at 7··. **Lock card on row 10. K 1 row colour 2. Release card. Work in pattern. With colour 2 in feeder 1 and colour 1 in feeder 2, K 3 rows.** The last 4 rows from ** to ** form 1 pattern which should be repeated throughout. K11(14:14:16) rows.

Break off yarn leaving end long enough to sew the thumb seam. Thread end through all stitches and draw up.

Left mitten

Follow instructions for right mitten but reverse the shapings by noting alteration in number of rows worked and reading left for right and vice versa.

To make up

Join thumbs and side seams. Graft stitches together. Unravel waste yarn. Press lightly with a hot iron over a wet cloth.

Hat

Main part

Insert card into the machine and lock on row 1.

Cast on using waste yarn, 144(148:152:160) sts. Tension dial at 5··, K 7 rows. Carriage at left. Using colour, K 6 rows. Tension dial at 7··, K 1 row. Tension dial at 6··, K 6 rows. Turn up a hem. Carriage at right. Tension dial at 7··. Release card. Work in pattern. With colour 4 in feeder 1 and colour 5 in feeder 2, K 2 rows. With colour 1 in feeder 1 and colour 5 in feeder 2, K 1 row. Lock card on row 15. With colour 1 in feeder 1 and colour 5 in feeder 2, K 1 row. Release card. With colour 3 in feeder 1 and colour 2 in feeder 2, K 22 rows. Lock card on row 8. With colour 3 in feeder 1 and colour 2 in feeder 2, K 1 row. Release card. K 2 rows colour 2. With colour 2 in feeder 1 and colour 5 in feeder 2, K 3 rows. K 2 rows colour 2. Remove card. Tension dial at 6··. Change to stockinette stitch. Using colour 1, K 1 row. Carriage at left.

Shape top

Using nylon cord, K108(111:114:117) sts at right by hand taking needles down into A position.

1st section K 1 row. Dec 1 st both ends of next row, K 3 rows. Using colour 2, dec 1 st both ends of next and following 4th row, K 1 row. Dec 1 st both ends of next and every following alternate row 12(13:13:14) times in all, K 1 row. Cast off 2 sts beg of next 2 rows. Fasten off remaining 2(1:2:1) sts.

2nd section Unravel nylon cord over next 36(37:38:39) needles bringing needles to correct position. Follow instructions for 1st section.

3rd and 4th sections Follow instructions for 2nd section.

Ear pieces

(Two alike)

Insert card into the machine and lock on row 15.

Using colour 1, cast on by hand 29 sts. Tension dial at 6··, K 3 rows. K 3 rows colour 4 and 6 rows colour 3. Tension dial at 7··. Release card. Work in pattern. With colour 1 in feeder 1 and colour 2 in feeder 2, K 13 rows. Dec 1 st both ends of next and every following 4th row 4 times in all, K 1 row. Dec 1 st both ends of next and every following alternate row 3 times in all, K 1 row. Cast off 2 sts beg of next 2 rows. Cast off remaining 11 sts.

To make up

Pin out each piece to size and steam carefully with a hot iron over a wet cloth. Join back seam and all top seams. Press. Sew ear pieces into position on cap. Work 2 rows of double crochet [US single crochet] around ear pieces. Make 2 cords and tassels and attach to ear pieces. Give final pressing.

CHART FOR PUNCH CARD FOR GIRLS AND BOYS WINTER OUTFITS

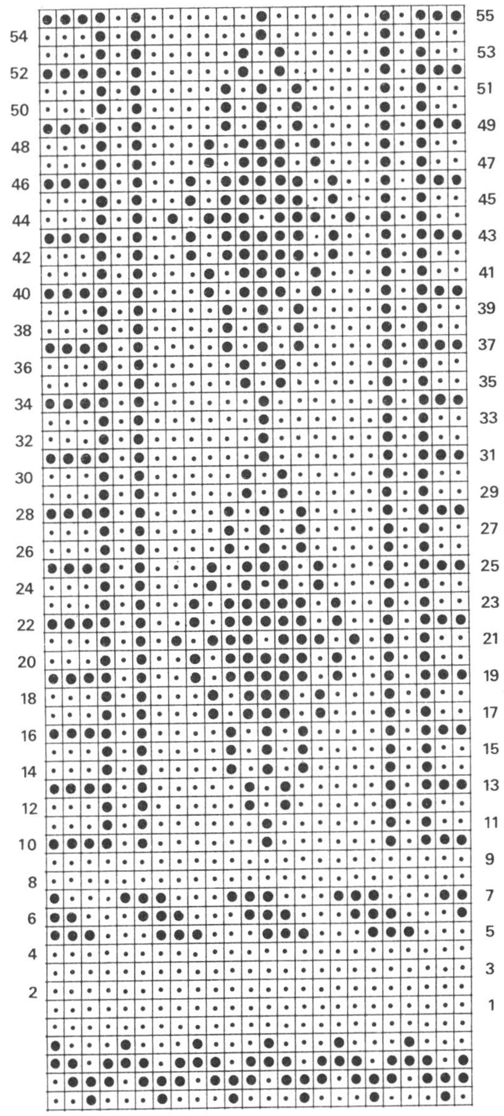

A peasant theme

Bag from Greek folk costume

Whenever knitting was introduced into a culture where embroidery was already well established, coloured pattern knitting tended to be used on the same areas of garments as embroidery would have been. Bags of similar shape to the one illustrated formed part of the male folk costumes of Greece and Albania and were usually woven and embroidered.

The complete folk costume consisted of a half-length tunic embroidered along the hem, up the side seams and around the neck and armholes. Over this was worn a jacket which also had embroidery round the neck, round the hem and along the sleeves. A belt was worn around the hips under the jacket and from this hung an embroidered bag. The embroidery often picked up the motifs of the tunic and jacket.

The bag illustrated might have been made from an old, worn-out garment but, as the fabric is in reasonably good condition, it was almost certainly knitted as a bag and it can be assumed that the patterns were repeated on a garment.

The pattern is made up of a border of triangles, black on ecru, followed by a diabolo-shaped pattern on red, outlined in ecru on a black ground. This pattern edges the main part of the bag on which there is a series of diamond shapes in red and ecru on a black ground.

The bag is seamed at the side and there is a drawstring closure at the top. The yarn used is a crisp, hard wool which gives clarity to the stitches, intensity to the colours and is also very hard wearing.

The three-colour patterned border of this heavy, zip-fronted sweater uses the decoration in exactly the same way as the original garment may have used it. The border design has been taken from the Greek bag shown above and the tunic and jacket which would have been worn with the bag would have had the patterning repeated on the hem.

The sweater has raglan sleeves for extra comfort and ease of movement and the ribbed collar matches the cuffs. The deep, ribbed welt picks up the red of the black, white and red patterning.

The garment illustrated was knitted in Hayfields "Gaylon" Thickerknit yarn.

In this zip-fronted sweater the modern version uses the decoration in very much the same way as in the original garment. Here the border design is taken from the Greek bag on the previous page.

Materials
15(16) 50gr. [27(29)oz.] balls of thick-knit yarn in Black, 2(3) [4(6)oz.] balls in Red and 1(2) [2(4)oz.] balls in White.
One pair each of No. 7 and No. 5 [US No. 6 and 8] needles.
22in. [56cm.] open-ended (separating) zip fastener.
2 pieces of lining fabric 7in. × 6in. [18cm. × 15cm.] for pockets.

Tension or Gauge: 8 sts and 11 rows to 2in. [5cm.] using No. 5 [US No. 8] needles.

Sizes
Suitable for chest size 38–40in. (41–43in.) [97–102cm. (104–109cm.)].
Length, 25½(26)in. [65(66)cm.].
Sleeve seam, 18(18½)in. [46(47)cm.].
Note: Figures in parentheses ( ) refer to the larger sizes. Where there is only one figure this refers to both sizes.

Special abbreviation for this design:
Up1 Pick up the loop lying between needles and knit or purl into back of it.

Fronts and Back
(in one piece)
Using No. 7 [US No. 6] needles and red yarn, cast on 152(164) sts and work in rib as follows:
1st row K3, *P2, K2, repeat from * ending last repeat with K3.
2nd row P3, *K2, P2; repeat from * ending P3.
Work 17 rows more in rib.
Inc row P4(10), up1, *P9, up1; repeat from * until 4(10) remain, P4(10).
169(181) sts.
Join in white yarn and K 1 row and P 1 row.
Join in black yarn and change to No. 5 needles [US No. 8].
Working in st st (stockinette stitch), beg with a K row and work the 20 rows of pattern as shown on chart.
Break off red and white yarns and continue with black yarn only.
K 1 row.
Now work for 1st pocket opening:

Next row P25(26), turn, leaving the remaining sts on a spare needle and work on the 25(26) sts.
1st row K2 tog, K to end.
2nd row P until 2 remain, P2 tog.
Repeat these 2 rows 8 more times, then leave remaining 7(8) sts on a stitch holder.
Break off yarn.
With wrong side of work facing you, rejoin yarn to sts on spare needle and P119(129) sts, turn and leave remaining 25(26) sts on a spare needle.
On the 119(129) sts continue in st st (stockinette stitch) and inc 1 st at each end of every row until there are 155(165) sts on the needle. Break off yarn and leave these sts on a stitch holder.
Rejoin yarn to wrong side of the 25(26) sts and P to end of row.
Now work for 2nd pocket opening.
1st row K until 2 remain, K2 tog.
2nd row P2 tog, P to end.
Repeat these 2 rows 8 times more, then K 1 row.
With the needle holding the 7(8) sts, K across the 155(165) sts on the stitch holder and 7(8) sts on stitch holder at end of row.
On 169(181) sts, beginning with a P row, st st (stockinette stitch) 21 rows, or until work measures 15¾in. [40cm.].
Now divide the sts for fronts and back.
Next row K42(45) for right front, cast off 1, K the next 82(88) sts for back, cast off 1, K to end and work on the last 42(45) sts.

Left front
Shape armhole
1st row P until 4 remain, P2 tog, P2.
2nd row K2, sl 1, K1, psso, K to end.
3rd to 6th rows Repeat 1st and 2nd rows twice.
7th row As 1st row.
8th row K.
9th row P.
10th row As 2nd row.
11th row P.
12th row K.
Repeat 7th to 12th rows 3 times and 7th to 11th row again.

Shape neck
1st row K to last 5(6) sts, cast off these sts.
Rejoin yarn to neck edge.
2nd row P2 tog, P until 4 remain, P2 tog through backs of loops P2.
3rd row K until 2 sts remain, K2 tog.
4th row P2 tog, P to end.
Cast off remaining 17(19) sts.

Back
Rejoin yarn to wrong side of the 83(89) sts.

Shape armholes
1st row P2, P2 tog, P until 4 remain, P2 tog through backs of loops, P2.
2nd row K2, sl 1, K1, psso, K until 4 remain, K2 tog, K2.
3rd to 7th row Repeat these 2 rows twice more and 1st row again.
8th and 9th row K 1 row and P 1 row.
10th row As 2nd.
11th row P.
12th row K.
Repeat 7th to 12th rows 4 times and the 7th to 9th rows again.
Continue as follows:
Repeat 2nd row then 1st row.
Repeat last 2 rows 6(7) times more and 1st of these rows again.
Cast off remaining 19(21) sts.
Rejoin yarn to wrong side of remaining 42(45) sts.

Right front
Shape armhole
1st row P2, P2 tog, P to end.
2nd row K until 4 remain, K2 tog, K2.
3rd to 6th row Repeat 1st and 2nd rows twice.
7th row As 1st.
8th and 9th row K 1 row, P 1 row.
10th row As 2nd.
11th row P.
12th row K.
Repeat 7th to 12th rows 3 times and 7th to 11th rows again.

Shape neck
Cast off 5(6) sts, K to end.
Complete to match left front, reversing the shapings.

Left sleeve
With No. 7 [US No. 6] needles and black yarn, cast on 40(42) sts.
1st row P1(2), K2, *P2, K2; repeat from * to last 1(2) sts, P1(2).
2nd row K1(2), P2, *K2, P2, repeat from * to last 1(2) sts, K1(2).
Rib 15 more rows.
Inc row P1(2), inc 1, *P4, inc 1; repeat from * until 3(4) sts remain, P to end. 48(50) sts.
Change to No. 5 [US No. 8] needles.
Beginning with a K row, st st (stockinette stitch) 8 rows.
Continue in st st (stockinette stitch) and inc 1 at each end of the next row and every following 10th row until there are 62(64) sts.
Continue on these sts until sleeve measures 18(18½)in. [46(47)cm.] (or to length required), ending with a P row.

Shape top
1st row K2, sl 1, K1, psso, K until 4 remain, K2 tog, K2.
2nd row P.
Repeat these 2 rows 19(20) times and 1st row again. 20 sts.
St st (stockinette stitch) 2 rows **.

Shoulder shaping
1st row P until 4 sts remain, P2 tog through backs of loops, P2.
2nd and 3rd rows K 1 row, P 1 row.
4th row K2, sl 1, K1, psso, K until 3 sts remain, inc 1, K2.
5th and 6th rows P 1 row, K 1 row.
*Repeat 1st to 6th rows twice.

Shape for neck
1st row P4, cast off 8, P2 tog through backs of loops, P2.
2nd row K2, K2 together.
3rd row P2 tog, P1.

Take 2 remaining sts tog and fasten off.
Rejoin yarn to remaining 4 sts.
1st row K2 tog, K2.
2nd row P1, P2 tog.
Take 2 tog and fasten off.

Right sleeve
Work as for left sleeve until ** is reached.

Shoulder shaping
1st row P2, P2 tog, P to end.
2nd and 3rd rows K 1 row, P 1 row.
4th row K2, inc 1, K until 4 remain, K2 tog, K2.
5th and 6th rows P 1 row, K 1 row.
Repeat from * on left sleeve, reversing shaping.

Collar
Using No. 7 [US No. 6] needles and black yarn, cast on 94 sts.
1st row P2, *K2, P2; repeat from * to end.
2nd row K2, *P2, K2; repeat from * to end.
Rib 22 rows more.

Shape collar
1st row Rib until 10 sts remain, turn.
2nd row Sl 1, rib until 10 sts remain, turn.
3rd row Sl 1, rib until 20 sts remain, turn.
4th row As 3rd.
5th and 6th rows Sl 1, rib until 30 remain, turn.
7th row Sl 1, rib to end.
Cast off firmly in rib.

Pocket tops
(Both alike)
Using No. 7 [US No. 6] needles and black yarn, pick up and K 26 sts from pocket edge.
Work 7 rows of K2, P2 rib.
Cast off in rib.

To make up
Press all parts except the ribbing, working on the wrong side with a warm iron over a damp cloth. Set sleeves into their correct armholes, then join sleeve seams. Sew cast-off edge of collar to neck edge. Make pockets from lining fabric and sew in position, then sew sides of pocket tops to right side of jacket. Press seams. Sew in zipper.

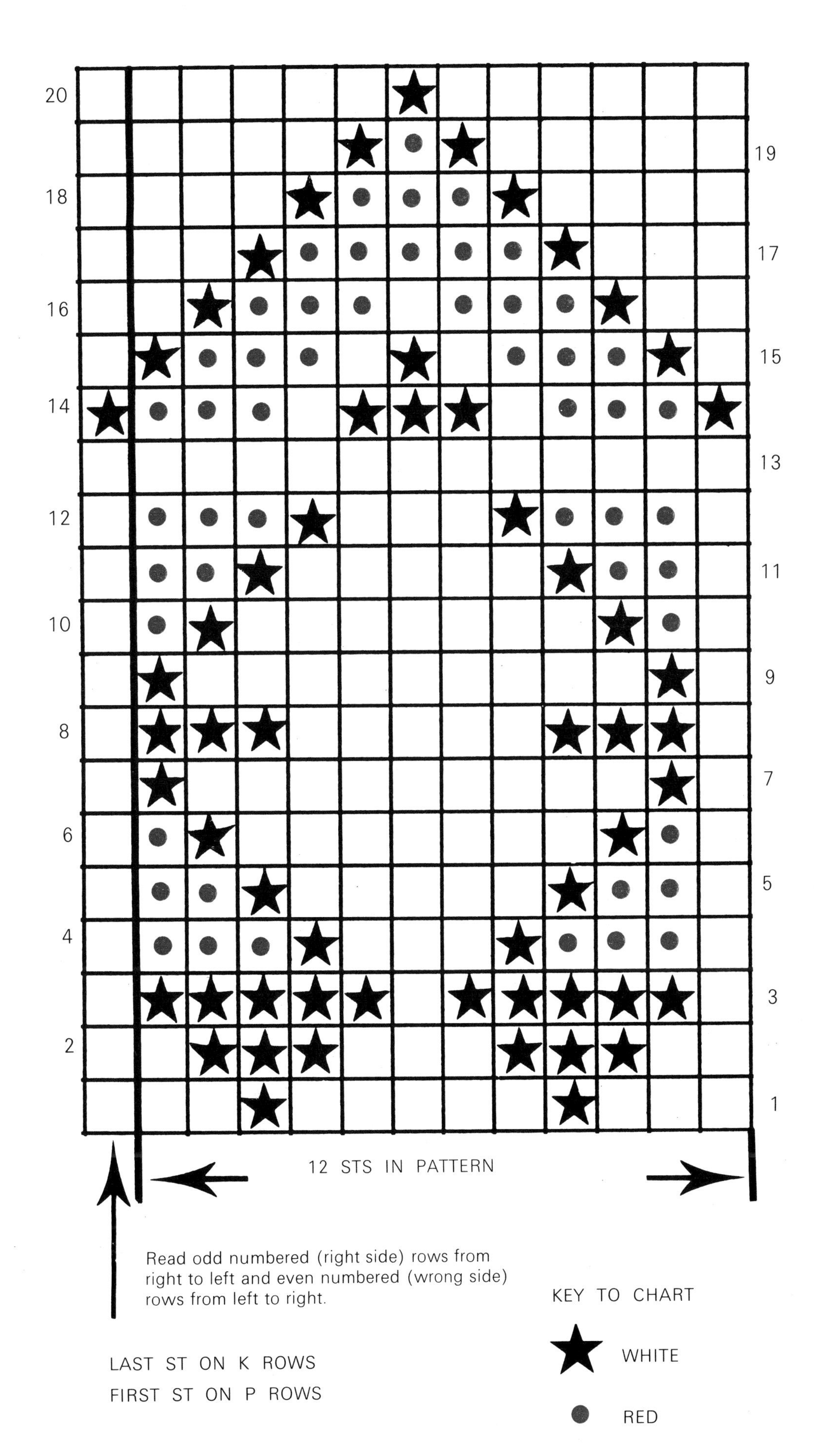

A rose in winter

17th-century Venetian tunic

This tunic is part of a collection of silk garments in the Victoria and Albert Museum, London, and is assumed to have been knitted in Venice during the 17th century.

The tunic is quite small in size – only 22½ins. (57cm.) long, and it is knitted in green silk with a pattern of roses in gold thread. The deep hem is knitted in a checker-board pattern of purl and stocking (stockinette) stitch and the same pattern is worked round the cuffs. The flared inserts at the sides of the tunic are from a different garment and were added later – perhaps to fit the tunic for an increasing girth!

Two rose-patterned panels make up the back of the tunic and two the front. Garments of this period were often made up from rectangular pieces of knitting and it is likely that the demand for hand-knitting had developed to such an extent that knitters found it expedient to knit panels of pattern for the customers to have made up for themselves. Although the Venetian patterning was often ambitious, the standard of the knitting is low and, almost without exception, garments were poorly made.

This beautiful sweater set successfully adapts the complex patterning of the 300-year-old Venetian tunic to a modern garment. The distinctive rose pattern has been used for the fronts, back and sleeves of the cardigan, with a single rose spray on the matching short-sleeved sweater. The crenelated design on the cardigan front edges and hem highlights the prettiness of the flower motif.

The long sleeves of the cardigan are worked with two-colour bands at the shoulders and wrists for a striking geometric contrast. Both garments are knitted in Wendy Tri-nylon 4-ply Crepe yarn in Silvery Shadow and Cameo Cream.

A sweater set that demonstrates how readily a 300-year-old pattern can be adapted for a modern garment. The original 17th century Venetian tunic was knitted in green silk and the roses were in gold thread.

Materials
Sweater: 11(11:12:13) 20gr. [8(8:8:9)oz.] balls of Tricel/Nylon mixture 4-ply yarn in main colour (M) and 1 ball in contrast colour (C).
One pair each of Nos. 11 and 10 [US Nos. 2 and 3] needles.
One set of 4 double-pointed No. 11 [US No. 2] needles for the neck band.
Jacket: 9(10:11:12) 20gr. [7(7:8:8)oz.] balls in main colour and 7(7:8:9) [5(5:6:7)oz.] balls in a contrast colour.
One pair each of Nos. 9, 10 and 11 [US Nos. 4, 3 and 2] needles and a twin-pin or round No. 10 [US No. 3] needle, 30in. [76cm.] in length for border.
2yd. [2m.] of 1-in. wide [2·5cm.] ribbon for facing.

Tension or Gauge: 14 sts to 2in. [5cm.] over the st st (stockinette stitch) using No. 10 [US No. 3] needles.

Sizes
To fit bust sizes 32(34:36:38)in. [81(86:91:97)cm.].

Sweater
Length from shoulder, 19(20:21:22)in. [48(50·5:53:55·5)cm.].
Sleeve seam, 4¾in. [12cm.].

Jacket
Length from shoulder, 22(23:24:25)in. [56(58·5:61·5)cm.].
Sleeve seam, 17in. [43·5cm.].
Note: Figures in parentheses ( ) refer to larger sizes. Where only one figure is given this refers to all sizes.

Sweater Back
Using No. 11 [US No. 2] needles and M, cast on 98(104:110:116) sts and work 32 rows in K1, P1, rib.
Change to No. 10 [US No. 3] needles and beginning with a K row, st st (stockinette stitch) 6 rows.
Continue in st st (stockinette stitch), inc 1 st at each end of next row and every following 6th row until there are 116(122:128:134) sts on the needle.
Continue on these sts until work measures 13(13½:14:14½)in. [33(34:35·5:36·5)cm.], ending with a P row.

Shape armholes
Cast off 7 sts at beg of next 2 rows, then dec 1 st at beg only of the 8 following rows.
On 94(100:106:112) sts continue straight until armhole measures 6(6½:7:7½)in. [15(16·5:18:19)cm.] ending with a P row.

Shape shoulders
Cast off 7(7:7:8) sts at beginning of next 4 rows, then 6(7:8:8) sts on 4 following rows.
Leave remaining 42(44:46:48) sts for neck band.

Front
Work as given for back until there are 116(122:128:134) sts on the needle.
Continue on these sts until work measures 10½(11:11½:12)in. [26·5(28:29:30)cm.], ending with a P row.
Now work the 2-colour motif (see chart) as follows:
1st row K18(21:24:27) and place a marker after last stitch to mark the beginning of motif. Join in C for motif, 10M, 3C, 11M. Place a marker after last stitch to mark end of motif, K to end with M.
2nd row P to marker, then for motif, P9M, 2C, 3M, 1C, 9M, P to end with M.
These 2 rows set the stitches for the motif. Work from the 3rd row to 45th row of motif as shown on chart outlined *but* when work measures same as back to armholes, shape armholes as given on back.
Continue on these 94(100:106:112) sts until the 45th row of motif has been worked.
Break off C and continue with M only until work measures 16½(17:18:18½)in. [42(43:45·5:47)cm.] ending with a K row.
Divide sts for neck and shoulders.
Next row P38(40:42:44) sts, cast off 18(20:22:24) sts, K to end and work on the last set of sts.

Shape neck
1st row Dec 1 st at neck edge.
2nd row Cast off 2, work to end.
Repeat these 2 rows 3 times.
Continue on these 26(28:30:32) sts until armhole measures the same as back, ending at armhole end.

Shape shoulder
Cast off 7(7:7:8) sts at beginning of next row and following alternate row; 6(7:8:8) sts at beginning of next 2 alternate rows and fasten off.
Rejoin M to neck edge of remaining sts and K to end of row.
Complete as first side.

Sleeves
(Both alike)
Using No. 11 [US No. 2] needles and M, cast on 84(88:92:96) sts and work 14 rows in K1, P1 rib.
Change to No. 10 [US No. 3] needles and, beginning with a K row, st st (stockinette stitch) 4 rows. Continue in st st (stockinette stitch) and inc 1 st at each end of the next row and 2 following 4th rows.
On 90(94:98:102) sts st st (stockinette stitch) 21 rows (or for sleeve seam length required), ending with a P row.

Shape top
Cast off 7 sts at beginning of next 2 rows.
Dec 1 st at beg of every row until 40 sts remain, then dec 1 st at each end of every row until 24 sts remain.
Cast off.

Neck band
Join shoulder seams.
Using double-pointed needles and M, K across the 42(44:46:48) sts at back neck edge, pick up and K 27(31:35:37) sts from edges of left front neck edge, 18(20:22:24) sts from cast-off edge at centre front, pick up and K 27(31:35:37) sts from right front neck edge. Distribute these 114(126:138:146) sts on 3 needles and work 9(9:10:10) rounds in K1, P1 rib, then cast off in rib.

To make up
Press all parts except the ribbing lightly on the wrong side with a warm iron over a dry cloth. Set in sleeves. Join sleeve and side seams. Press seams.

Jacket Back
Using No. 11 [US No. 2] needles and M, cast on 124(130:136:142) sts and work 34 rows in K1, P1 rib.
Change to No. 9 [US No. 4] needles and work the two-colour pattern as follows: Join in C.
1st row K18M(21M:24M:3C, 24M), *3C, 24M; repeat from * twice (3 times:3 times:3 times), 3C, 22M(1C:3C, 1M:3C, 4M).
2nd row P20M(1M, 1C, 21M:1C, 3M, 1C, 21M:2M) *2C, 3M, 1C, 21M; repeat from * twice (twice:3 times:4 times), 2C, 3M, 1C, 17M (2C, 3M, 1C, 20M:2C:2C, 3M).
3rd row K17M(20M:2M, 1C, 20M:5M, 1C, 20M), *1C, 5M, 1C, 20M; repeat from * twice (3 times:3 times:3 times), 1C, 5M, 1C, 19M(1C, 1M:1C, 4M:1C, 5M, 1C, 1M).
4th row 20M(1M, 1C, 21M:4M, 1C, 21M:2M), *1C, 4M, 1C, 21M: repeat from * twice(twice:3 times:4 times), 1C, 4M, 1C, 17M(1C, 4M, 1C, 20M:1C, 1M:1C, 4M).
These 4 rows set the stitches for the motif pattern.
Continue in st st (stockinette stitch) across all the sts, work from the 5th to 45th row of chart, on which are marked the beginning and end of rows on all sizes.
46th row P8(11:14:17)M, *3C, 24M, repeat from * ending last repeat with P5(8:11:14)M.
47th row K3(6:9:12)M, *2C, 3M, 1C, 21M; repeat from * ending last repeat with K7(10:13:16)M.
These 2 rows set the motif for the 2nd half of the pattern.
Work from the 48th to 90th row on chart.
These 90 rows form the pattern.
Pattern 10(14:18:22) rows more.

Shape armholes
Continue in pattern and cast off 8 sts at beg of next 2 rows, then dec 1 st at the beg only of the 10 following rows.
Continue on these 98(104:110:116) sts until the 45th pattern row has been worked.
With M, P 1 row. Break off M and continue with C only.
Change to No. 10 [US No. 3] needles.
Beginning with a K row work in st st (stockinette stitch) until armhole measures 6½(7:7½:8)in. [16·5(18:19:20·5)cm.], ending with a P row.

Shape shoulders
Cast off 7(8:9:9) sts at beginning of next 4 rows; 8(8:8:9) sts on 4 following rows.
Cast off remaining 38(40:42:44) sts.

Left front
Using No. 11 [US No. 2] needles and M, cast on 44(48:52:56) sts and work 34 rows in K1, P1 rib, on the last row inc 1 st at each end and 1 in the centre. 47(51:55:59) sts.
Change to No. 9 [US No. 4] needles and join in C.
1st row K10(10:12:13)M, 3C, 24M, 3C, 7(11:13:16)M.
2nd row P5(9:11:14)M, 2C, 3M, 1C, 21M, 2C, 3M, 1C, 9(9:11:12)M.
These 2 rows set the motif for front, pattern 43 rows.
46th row P20M, 3C, 24M(24M, 3C, 24M:2C, 24M, 3C, 24M, 2C:2M, 3C, 24M, 3C, 24M, 3C).
This row sets the stitches for the motif on 2nd half of pattern.
Continue in pattern until the 90th row has been worked, then pattern 10(14:18:22) rows more. Work 1 row more here on right front.

Shape armhole
Cast off 8 sts at beg of next row, then dec 1 st at armhole end of the 5 following alternate rows.
Cont on these 34(38:42:46) sts until the 45th pattern row has been worked.
With M work 1 row.
Using C and No. 10 [US No. 3] needles, st st (stockinette stitch) 7(7:9:11) rows. Work 1 row less here on right front.

Shape neck
Cast off 2(4:4:4) sts at beg of next row, then dec 1 st at neck edge of the 2(2:4:6) following rows.
On 30(32:34:36) sts cont in st st (stockinette stitch) until armhole measures the same as back ending at armhole end.

Shape shoulder
Cast off 7(8:9:9) sts at beg of next row and following alternate row; 8(8:8:9) sts on next 2 alternate rows and fasten off.

Right front
Work as given for left front noting the variations in the rows where indicated.

Sleeves
(both alike)
Using No. 11 [US No. 2] needles and M, cast on 56(60:64:68) sts and work 34 rows in K1, P1 rib.
Change to No. 10 [US No. 3] needles.
Joining in and breaking off colour when necessary continue as follows:
With C, st st (stockinette stitch) 8 rows, inc 1 st at each end of last row.
Work in spot pattern.
1st row K1M, *1C, 2M; repeat from * to end.
2nd row With M, P.
3rd and 4th rows Repeat 1st and 2nd rows.
5th row Repeat 1st row.
6th row With C, P, inc 1 st at each end. 60(64:68:72) sts.
St st (stockinette stitch) 6 rows C, inc 1 st at each end of last row.
Repeat 6 spot pattern rows but begin 1st row with *K1C, 2M. 64(68:72:76) sts.
With C, st st (stockinette stitch) 8 rows, inc 1 st at each end of last row. 66(70:74:78) sts.
Change to No. 9 [US No. 4] needles and work the 2-colour pattern.
1st row K16(18:20:22)M, 3C, 24M, 3C, 20M (22M:24M:24M, 2C).
2nd row P18M(20M:1C, 21M:2M, 1C, 21M), *2C, 3M, 1C, 21M; repeat from * ending 15(17:19:21)M.
3rd row K15(17:19:21)M, *1C, 5M, 1C, 20M; repeat from * ending 17M(19M:20M, 1C:20M, 1C, 2M).
4th row P18M(20M:1C, 21M:2M, 1C, 21M), 1C, 4M, 1C, 21M, 1C, 4M, 1C, 15(17:19:21)M.
5th row K16(18:20:22)M, *1C, 2M, 1C, 23M; repeat from * ending 19M(21M:23M: 1C, 1M).
6th row Inc in 1st st, P11(13:15:17)M, 6C, 2M, 2C, 17M, 6C, 2M, 2C, 16M(18M:17M, 3C:17M, 5C), inc in last st. 68(72:76:80) sts.
These 6 rows set the motif pattern.
Work 39 rows more, inc 1 st at each end of every 6th row, working the inc sts into the pattern as they occur.
46th row P13(15:1:19)M, *3C, 24M; repeat from * ending with 10(12:14:16)M.
47th row K8(10:12:14)M, *2C, 3M, 1C, 21M; repeat from * ending with K12(14:16:18)M.
These 2 rows set the motif for the 2nd half of the pattern.
Continue in pattern until 90 rows of pattern have been completed, still inc each end of every 6th row until 86(90:94:98) sts are on the needle.
Break off C, then with M st st (stockinette stitch) 2 rows. Break off M.
Change to No. 10 [US No. 3] needles.
Join in C and work in st st.

Shape top
Cast off 8 sts at beg of next 2 rows, then dec 1 st at beg of 8 following rows.
Join in M and work 5 rows of spot pattern, still dec 1 st at beg of each row.
Break off M.
With C, st st (stockinette stitch) 11 rows, dec 1 st at beginning of each row.
Join in M and work 5 rows of spot pattern, dec 1 st at beg of each row. Break off M.
With C, st st (stockinette stitch) 3(7:11:15) rows, dec 1 st at beg of each row.
Now dec each end of the next 8 rows.
Cast off remaining 22 sts.

Border
Join shoulder seams. With right side of work facing you and using twin-pins or round needles No. 10 [US No. 3] and M, pick up and K 146(156:166:176) sts from right front ending at neck edge, 90(100:110:115) sts from neck edge, 146(156:166:176) sts from left front. 382(412:442:467) sts.
1st row P146(156:166:176), for corner P1, K1, P1 all in next st, P88(98:108:113), for corner P1, K1, P1 all in next st, P to end.
2nd row *K to corner st, K1, P1, K1 into corner st, rep from * once, K to end.
Note on K rows the corner is worked K1, P1, K1 and on P rows P1, K1, P1.
Work 1 row more, still working corners as set.
Join in C and work 2 rows in C, still working corners.
6th row *K3M, 2C; rep from * 29(31:33:35) times, with M, K1, inc in corner, K1, **2C, 3M; repeat from ** 18(20:22:23) times, 2C, with M, inc in corner, K1M, ***2C, 3M; repeat from *** to end.
7th row P sts as set, inc in corners with M.
Break off C.
With M, K 3 rows, still working corners as before.
Cast off fairly tightly knitwise on wrong side of work.

To make up
Press as for sweater. Set in sleeves.
Join sleeve and side seams. Face border with ribbon, mitring corners at neck edge.
Press seams.

KEY: • CONTRAST COLOUR

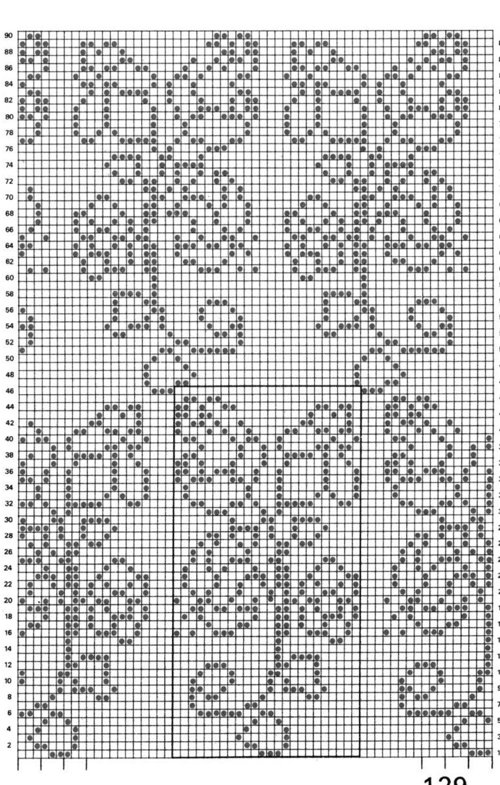

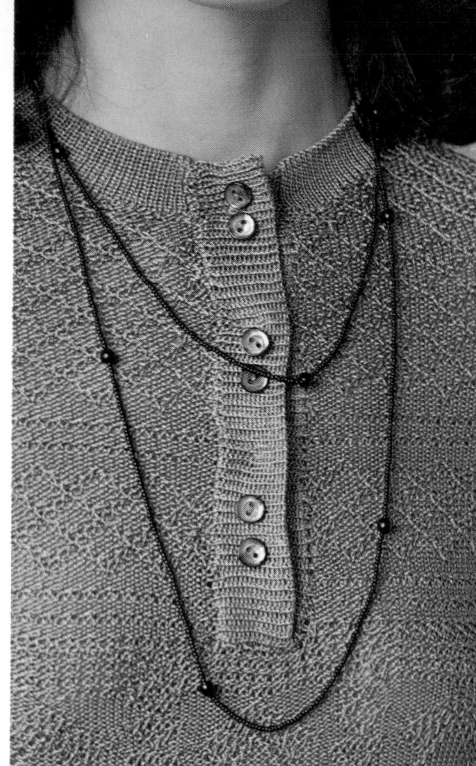

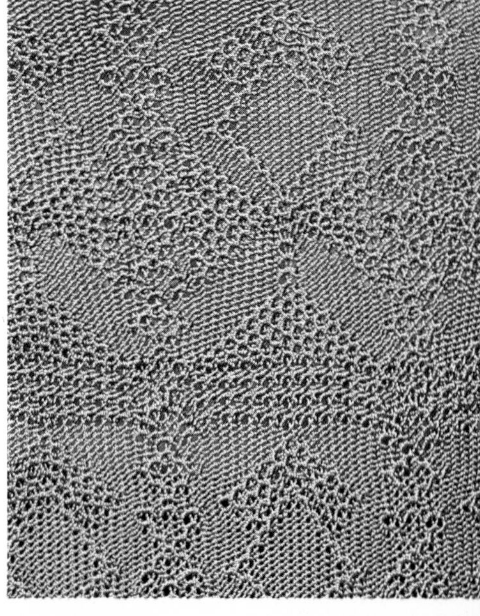

That Royal look

King Charles's Italian shirt

This fine knitted shirt is said to have belonged to King Charles I of England. It was worn during his imprisonment, prior to his execution, and perhaps even on the day of his death. King Charles died in 1649 AD.

The shirt was probably made in Italy, one of the centres of beautiful silk knitting in the 17th century, and it is knitted in a different way from the brocaded type of knitted panel associated with earlier Italian knitting. Not only is the patterning achieved with texture rather than with coloured yarns and threads but the garment has also been cleverly shaped during the process of knitting.

In structure, the shirt is very similar to those garments produced by folk knitters in different parts of the world. It has a small, standing collar, straight armholes and shoulder seams. The yoke area has a different and simpler pattern from the pattern of the main body and sleeves of the garment. The main pattern has much in common with the geometric pattern seen in Egyptian coloured knitting and is separated from the borders by three bands of purl knitting, a device often seen in Jersey and Guernsey knitting.

A third pattern of crosses and diamonds is used to form a narrow vertical band between the motifs of the main pattern and again between the body of the garment and the yoke. It is also used as a detail on the front opening placket.

The main body of the shirt and the sleeves appear to have been knitted "in the round" and the neck band has been knitted on, after the stitches of the front and back have been picked up. The extraordinary detail of this fine piece of knitting includes a row of twelve small buttons which have been worked to match.

The quality of design and workmanship in the shirt indicates not only a tremendous improvement in the standards of Italian knitting between the 16th and 17th centuries but also a change in attitudes to the production of knitted garments.

Hitherto, panels of knitting had been produced as an alternative method to weaving, the garment pieces being cut out and sewn together as with ordinary woven fabric. King Charles's shirt incorporates many refinements of shaping and fit which are only possible with knitting and the form of the garment was obviously dictated by the fact that it was knitted.

An elegant "shirt" for any occasion – or certainly suitable for both day and evening wear. This beautiful knitted design based on a Royal shirt has that unmistakable "quality" look.

This modern interpretation of King Charles I's knitted shirt faithfully reproduces the designs formed by the stitches. A simple trellis pattern forms the yoke with the main body part and the sleeves worked in a complex, raised pattern made up of plain and purl stitches.

This shirt has a similar stand-up collar with a decorative buttoned neck opening, which closes with snap fasteners.

This shirt has been knitted on a domestic knitting machine. Although an experienced knitter could make a similar shirt by hand, the work would be long and require great concentration. A Knitmaster domestic knitting machine was used to make the shirt in grey-coloured Ideal Rayon yarn.

Materials
3(4:4) cones of rayon yarn.
6 small, matching buttons.
3 press fasteners.
For Knitmaster 321 and 323 automatic punch card knitting machines.

Tension or Gauge: 30 sts and 74 rows to 4in. [10cm.] measured over tuck stitch pattern. Tension dial at approximately 6.
Note: Figures in parentheses ( ) refer to the larger sizes. Where there is only one figure this refers to all sizes.

Sizes
To fit bust sizes 32(34:36)in. [81(86:92)cm.]. Purl side is used as right side.

Back
Insert punch card A and lock on row 1. Cast on 144(152:159) sts by hand. Tension dial at 5. K 9 rows. Tension dial at 7, K 1 row. Tension dial at 6. Row counter 000. Release card and set machine for tuck knitting, K 62 rows. Remove card from machine. Insert punch card B and lock on row 1. Set machine for free move and with no yarn in feeder, take Carriage from right to left and left to right. Reset Carriage for tuck knitting, release card, and with yarn in feeder, dec 1 st at both ends of next and every following 27th row, 10 times in all. 124(132:139) sts remain.
K 28 rows without shaping. Row counter 334. Carriage at right. Remove card from machine and insert punch card A and lock on row 1. Set machine for free move and with no yarn in feeder take Carriage from right to left and left to right. Reset Carriage for tuck knitting. Release card and with yarn in feeder* shape armholes.

Shape armholes
Cast off 5 sts beg of next 2 rows, K 2 rows. Cast off 3(4:4) sts beg of next 2 rows, K 2 rows. Cast off 3 sts beg of next 2 rows, K 2 rows. Cast off 2 sts beg of next 2 rows and following 3rd and 4th row, K 4 rows. Dec 1 st at both ends of next and every following 6th row, 5(6:7) times in all. 84(88:93) sts remain. K15(9:3) rows. Remove card from machine and insert punch card C and lock on row 1. Set machine for free move and with no yarn in feeder, take Carriage from right to left and left to right. Reset Carriage for tuck knitting. Release card and with yarn in feeder, K 72(82:90) rows without shaping. Row counter 468(478:486). Carriage at right.

Shape shoulders
Cast off 6 sts beg of next 2 rows, K 2 rows. Cast off 5(6:6) sts beg of next 2 rows, K 2 rows. Cast off 5(5:6) sts beg of next 2 rows, K 2 rows. Cast off 5 sts beg of next 2 rows, K 2 rows. Cast off remaining 42(44:47) sts.

Front
Follow instructions for Back to *. Shape front opening and armholes. Using an odd length of yarn, cast off 10(10:11) sts in centre. Using an odd length of yarn, take 57(61:64) needles at left down into A position.

Right side
Cast off 5 sts beg of next row, K 3 rows. Cast off 3(4:4) sts beg of next row, K 3 rows. Cast off 3 sts beg of next row, K 3 rows. Cast off 2 sts beg of next and following 4th row, K 5 rows. Dec 1 st beg of next and every following 6th row, 5(6:7) times in all. 37(39:41) sts remain. K15(9:3) rows. Remove card from machine and insert punch card C and lock on row 1. Set machine for free move and with no yarn in feeder, take Carriage from right to left and left to right. Reset Carriage for tuck knitting. Release card and with yarn in feeder, knit 45(51:53) rows. Carriage at left.

Shape neck
Cast off 5 sts beg of next row, K 3 rows. Cast off 4 sts beg of next row, K 3 rows. Cast off 2 sts beg of next row, K 3 rows. Dec 1 st beg of next and every following 4th row, 3(4:5) times in all, K6(6:8) rows. Row counter 468(478:486). Carriage at right.

Shape shoulder
Cast off 6 sts beg of next row, K 3 rows. Cast off 5(6:6) sts beg of next row, K 3 rows. Cast off 5(5:6) sts beg of next row, K 3 rows. Cast off 5 sts beg of next row, K 3 rows. Cast off remaining 2 sts. Take Carriage to right of needle bed. Insert punch card A into machine and lock on row 1. Take Carriage from right to left. Release card and work left side as for right side but reverse the shapings by reading left for right and vice versa.

Sleeves
(Both alike)
Insert punch card A and lock on row 1. Cast on 69(71:73) sts by hand. Tension dial at 5, K 4 rows. Row counter 000. Release card and set machine for tuck knitting and K 62 rows. Remove card from machine and insert punch card B and lock on row 1. Set machine for free move and with no yarn in feeder, take Carriage from right to left and left to right. Reset Carriage for tuck knitting, release card and with yarn in feeder inc 1 st at both ends of next and every following 21st(20th:19th) rows, 11(12:13) times in all. 91(95:99) sts altogether. K 23 rows without shaping. (Adjust length at this stage if desired.) Row counter 296(306:314). Carriage at right.

Shape top
Cast off 4 sts beg of next 2 rows, K 2 rows. Cast off 2 sts beg of next 2 rows and following 4th row, 3 times in all, K 5 rows. Dec 1 st at both ends of next and every following 6th row, 9(9:10) times in all, K 3 rows. Dec 1 st at both ends of next and every following 4th row, 1(3:3) times in all, K 3 rows. Cast off 2 sts beg of next 2 rows, K 2 rows. Cast off 3 sts beg of next 2 rows and following 3rd and 4th rows, K 2 rows. Cast off 4 sts beg of next 2 rows, K 2 rows. Cast off 5 sts beg of next 2 rows. Cast off remaining 15(15:17) sts.

Neckband
Join shoulder seams. With plain side facing, pick up 104(110:116) sts evenly around neck edge and place them onto machine. Tension dial at 5. Using main yarn, K 14 rows. Tension dial at 7, K 1 row. Tension dial at 5, K 13 rows. Cast off loosely.

Front bands
(Both alike)
Fold neckband in half and catch down on the inside. With plain side facing, pick up 60(64:68) sts evenly along one front edge from loose row on neckband to end of opening and place onto machine. Inc 1 st at both edges. 62(66:70) sts altogether. Tension dial at 5. Using main yarn, K 16 rows. Tension dial at 7, K 1 row. Tension dial at 5, K 15 rows. Cast off loosely.

To make up
Pin out and steam each piece carefully with a warm iron over a damp cloth. Join side and sleeve seams. Press. Set in sleeves and press again. Fold front bands in half and catch on the inside. Neaten top edge. Neaten lower edges lapping one band over the other. Sew buttons on front flap of neck opening, in groups of two. Sew three press fasteners in position to close opening. Turn up 4 rows around lower edge of sleeves and 10 rows around lower edge of main part and catch down on the inside of the garment.

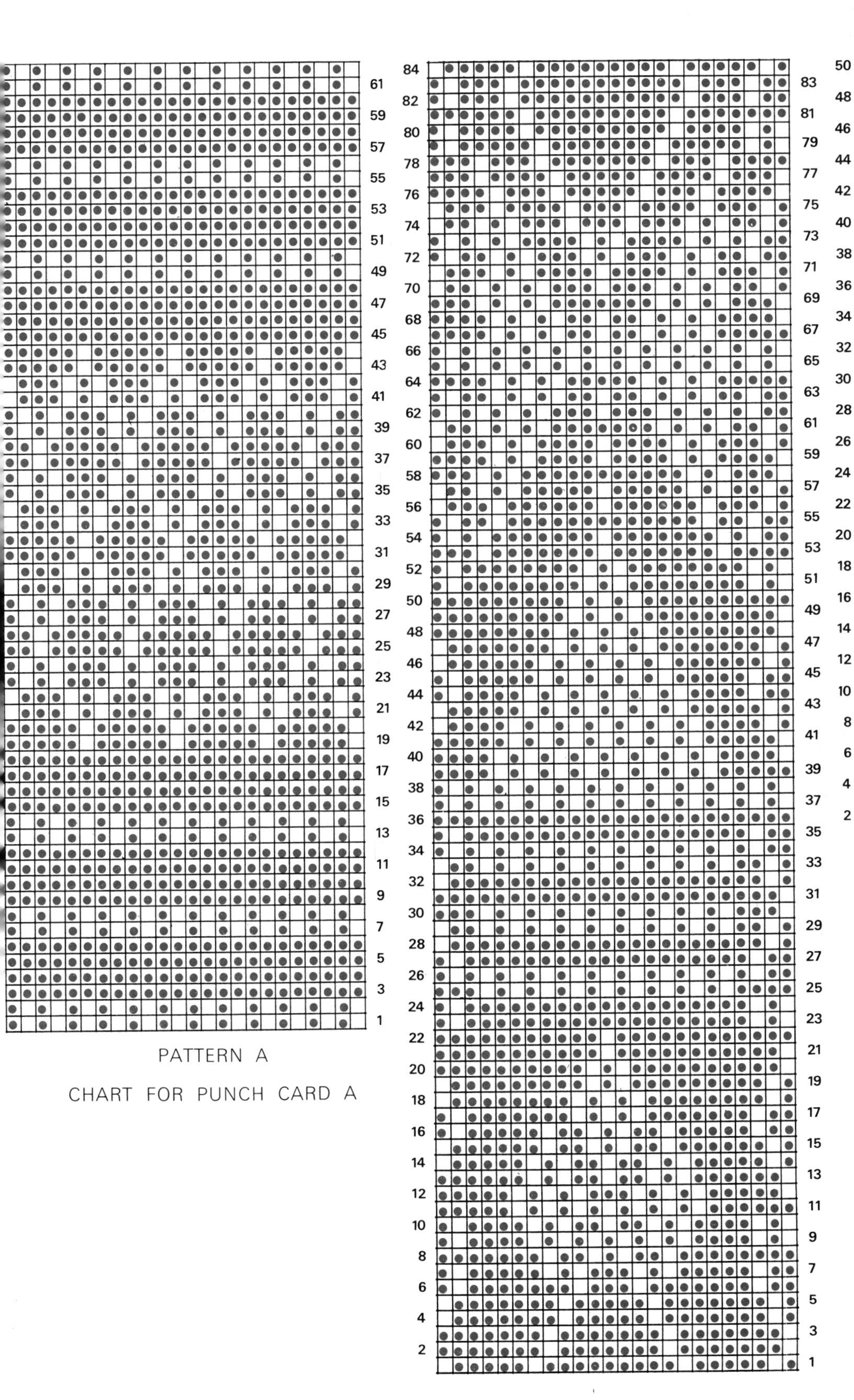

PATTERN A

CHART FOR PUNCH CARD A

PATTERN B

CHART FOR PUNCH CARD B

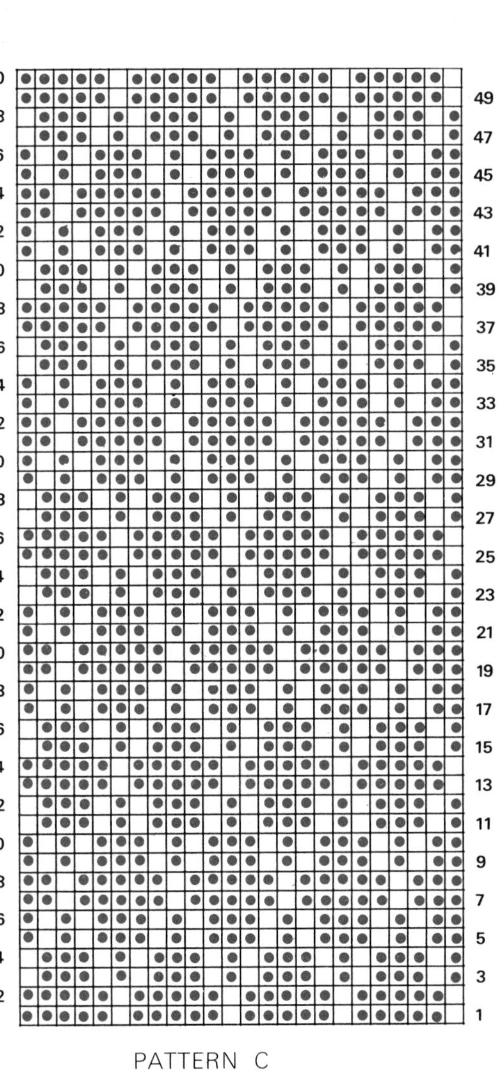

PATTERN C

CHART FOR PUNCH CARD C

A pattern of grace

17th-century Venetian cape

This garment is another example of the almost phenomenal skill of the Italian knitters in the 17th century. The structure of the knitting and the patterning is very much in the character of the Italian jackets on page 126.

The patterning is a brocade-type knitted with a purple silk ground, the motifs picked out in silver gilt and silver thread. The main pattern area of formalized leaf designs is bordered by bands of geometric patterning.

The quality of the knitting in the cape is extremely high but the actual making up of the garment is rather crudely done. The fabric has obviously been knitted in panels and sold to be made up into a cape by the purchaser himself or by a tailor.

The top edge of the garment is gathered onto a coarse tape and, although it has always been referred to as a cape, there is the possibility that it might have been a petticoat piece. During this period of history over-skirts were split at the front to show petticoats of sumptuous embroidery but there is no reason why a petticoat piece should not have been knitted. The ragged edge to the garment is, in fact, fringing and was probably added at a later date.

Modern domestic knitting machines enable home knitters to produce fashion clothes in a comparatively short space of time, especially when complex two-colour patterning is involved. This elegant 3-piece evening suit interprets superbly the beautiful patterning of the Italian cape on this page. The matching v-necked sweater is sleeveless and knitted in stocking stitch. The neckline and armholes are edged with white ribbing.

The casually-styled, long-line jacket uses purl stitch worked vertically rather than horizontally and provides a complete contrast in texture to the patterned skirt.

The suit illustrated was knitted on a Knitmaster domestic knitting machine using standard 4-ply yarn.

A startling effective yet subtle and sophisticated three-piece evening suit. The "maze" patterned skirt brilliantly sets off the simplicity of the sweater and jacket. The effect is coolly attractive – yet delightfully warm for a chilly evening.

Materials
Standard 4-ply yarn in the following quantities:
Cardigan: 3(3:4) 25gr. [3(3:4)oz.] balls in Green, colour 1; 14(15:17) [13(14:15)oz.] balls in White, colour 2.
Shell top: 4(5:6) [4(5:6)oz.] balls in colour 1; 3(3:4) [3(3:4)oz.] balls in colour 2.
Skirt: 17(18:19) [15(16:17)oz.] balls in colour 1; 19(20:22) [17(18:20)oz.] balls in colour 2.
1in. [2·5cm.] wide elastic to fit waist.
7in. [18cm.] skirt zip fastener.
Crochet hook.
For Knitmaster 321 and 323 automatic punch card knitting machines

Tension or Gauge: 28 sts and 38 rows to 4in. [10cm.] measured over stocking stitch (stockinette stitch). Tension dial at 7··.
30 sts and 40 rows to 4in. [10cm.] measured over pattern. Tension dial at 8·.
23 sts and 72 rows to 4in. [10cm.] measured over tuck stitch. Tension dial at 7··.

Sizes
To fit bust sizes 32(34:36)in. [81(86:92)cm.], Waist measurement 23(25:27)in. [58(63·5:69)cm.].
Note: Figures in parentheses ( ) refer to larger sizes. Where there is only one figure this refers to all sizes.

Cardigan back
Insert card 1A into machine and lock on row 1. Using waste yarn, cast on 106(111:117) sts. *K 7 rows (K 1 row extra for right front). Carriage at left. Tension dial at 6··. Row counter 000. Using colour 1, K 12 rows. Tension dial at 8··, K 1 row. Tension dial at 6··, K 12 rows. Turn up a hem.
Tension dial at 7··. Row counter 000. Release card and work in tuck stitch throughout.
Using colour 2, K 40 rows. Dec 1 st at both ends of next and every following 22nd row, 7 times in all. 92(97:103) sts. K 25 rows without shaping. Row counter 198. Inc 1 st at both ends of next and every following 36th row 4 times in all. 100(105:111) sts. K 35 rows without shaping. Row counter 342. Carriage at right.

Shape armholes
Cast off 4 sts at beg of next 2 rows, K 2 rows. Cast off 2 sts at beg of next 2 rows, K 2 rows. Dec 1 st at both ends of next and every following 4th row 3 times in all, K 7 rows. Dec 1 st at both ends of next and every following 8th row 3(4:5) times in all. 76(79:83) sts. K 95(95:97) rows without shaping. Row counter 478(486:496). Carriage at right.

Shape shoulders
Cast off 4 sts at beginning of next 2 rows and every following 3rd and 4th rows 3(4:3) times in all; K 2 rows.
1st and 3rd sizes only: Cast off 3(5) sts at beginning of next 2 rows. K 2 rows.
All sizes: Cast off remaining 46(47:49) sts.

Left front
Insert card 1A into machine and lock on row 1. Using waste yarn, cast on 47(49:52) sts. Follow instructions for back from * to *.
Tension dial at 7··. Row counter 000.
Release card and work in tuck stitch throughout. Using colour 2, K 40 rows. Dec 1 st at right edge on next and every following 22nd row 7 times in all. 40(42:45) sts. K 25 rows without shaping. Row counter 198. Inc 1 st at right edge on next and every following 36th row 4 times in all. 44(46:49) sts. K 8 rows. Row counter 315. Carriage at left.

Shape neck
Dec 1 st at left edge on next and every following 11th row 3 times in all. K 4 rows. Row counter 342. Carriage at right.

Shape armhole
Cast off 4 sts at beg of next row, K 3 rows. Cast off 2 sts at beg of next row, K 1 row. Dec 1 st at left edge on next row, K 1 row. Dec 1 st at right edge on next and every following 4th row 3 times in all. Dec 1 st at left edge on next row, K 6 rows. Dec 1 st at right edge on next row, K 3 rows. Dec 1 st at left edge on next row, K 3 rows. Dec 1 st at right edge on next row, K 6 rows. Dec 1 st at left edge on next row. Dec 1 st at right edge on next row, K 7 rows. Dec 0(1:1) sts at right edge on next row, K 1 row. Dec 1 st at left edge on next row, K 5 rows. Dec 0(0:1) st at right edge on next row, K 4 rows. Dec 1 st at left edge on next and every following 11th row 7(7:8) times in all. K 8(16:15) rows. Row counter 478(486:496). Carriage at right.

Shape shoulder
Cast off 4 sts at beg of next and every following 4th row 3(4:3) times in all, K 3 rows.
1st and 3rd sizes only: Cast off 3(5) sts at beg of next row, K 3 rows.
All sizes: Cast off remaining 2 sts.

Right front
Follow instructions for left front but reverse the shapings by noting alteration in number of rows worked and reading left for right and vice versa.

Sleeves
(Both alike)
Insert card 1A into machine and lock on row 1. Using waste yarn, cast on 48(51:54) sts. Follow instructions for back from * to *.
Tension dial at 7··. Row counter 000.
Release card and work in tuck stitch throughout. Using colour 2, K 6 rows. Inc 1 st at both ends of next and every following 24th(25th:26th) row 11 times in all. 70(73:76) sts. K 23(23:21) rows. Row counter 270(280:288).

Shape top
Cast off 4 sts at beginning of next 2 rows, K 2 rows. Cast off 2 sts at beg of next 2 rows, K 2 rows. Dec 1 st at both ends of next and every following 4th row 5 times in all, K 7 rows. Dec 1 st at both ends of next and every following 8th row 6(7:8) times in all, K 3 rows. Dec 1 st at both ends of next and every following 4th row 3 times in all, K 3 rows. Cast off 2 sts at beg of next 2 rows and following 3rd and 4th rows. K 2 rows. Cast off 4 sts at beg of next 2 rows, K 2 rows. Cast off remaining 14(15:16) sts.

Edging band
Using waste yarn cast on 21 sts, K 8 rows. Tension dial at 6··. Row counter 000. Using colour 1, K until band is long enough to go around front edges of Cardigan. Using waste yarn, K 8 rows. Release from machine.

To make up
Pin out each piece to size and press with a warm iron over a damp cloth. Join side, shoulder and sleeve seams. Set in sleeves. With right sides together, join one edge of band to front edge. Fold in half to inside and catch down other end of band. Graft ends of bands. Give final pressing.

Shell top
Back
Using waste yarn, cast on 125(132:139) sts, K 7 rows. Carriage at left. Tension dial 6··. Row counter 000. Using colour 2, K 12 rows. Tension dial at 8··, K 1 row. Tension dial at 6··, K 12 rows. Turn up hem. Tension dial at 7··. Row counter 000. Using colour 1, K 14 rows. Dec 1 st. (3 sts in) at both ends of next and every following 4th row 9 times in all. 107(114:121) sts. K 1 row. Row counter 048. Inc 1 st (3 sts in) at both ends of next and every following 13th row 5 times in all. 117(124:131) sts. *K 13 rows. Row counter 114. Carriage at right.

Shape armholes
Cast off 7 sts at beg of next 2 rows, 3 sts at beg of next 2 rows and 2 sts at beg of next 4(6:6) rows. Dec 1 st at both ends of next and every following alternate row 7(7:8) times in all. 75(78:83) sts. K 59(63:65) rows without shaping. Row counter 194(200:204). Carriage at right.

Shape neck and shoulders
Using length of colour 1, cast off centre 29(30:31) sts. Using nylon cord, K the 23(24:26) sts to left of centre by hand, taking

the needles down into A position.
K the right side as follows:
Cast off 3(3:4) sts at beg of next row. Cast off 6 sts at beg of next row. Cast off 3(3:4) sts at beg of next row. Cast off 5(6:6) sts at beg of next row. Cast off 4 sts at beg of next row, K 1 row. Cast off remaining 2 sts.
Slide carriage to left. Unravel nylon cord bringing needles to their correct position.
K left side as for right side.

Front
Follow instructions for back to *. K 7 rows. Row counter 108. Carriage at right.

Shape neck
1st and 3rd sizes only: Transfer the centre st to its adjacent needle.
All sizes: Using nylon cord K the 58(62:65) sts to left of centre by hand taking the needles down into A position.
K the right side as follows:
K 1 row. Dec 1 st (3 sts in) at left edge on next and following 3rd row, K 1 row. Row counter 114. Carriage at right.

Shape armhole
Cast off 7 sts at beg of next row. Dec 1 st (3 sts in) at beg of next row. Cast off 3 sts at beg of next row, K 1 row. Cast off 2 sts at beg and dec 1 st (3 sts in) at left edge on next row, K 1 row. Cast off 2 sts at beg of next row. Dec 1 st (3 sts in) at beg of next row. Cast off 1(2:2) sts at beg of next row. K 1 row.**
Dec 1 st at beg and dec 1 st (3 sts in) at left edge on next row, K 1 row. Dec 1 st at beg of next row. Dec 1 st (3 sts in) at beg of next row. Dec 1 st at beg of next row, Knit 1 row.**
Repeat from ** to ** once more.
Dec 0(1:1) sts at beg and dec 1 st (3 sts in) at left edge on next row, K 1 row. Dec 0(0:1) sts at beg of next row. Dec 1 st (3 sts in) at left edge on next and every following 3rd row 15(17:17) times in all. K 12(12:16) rows. Row counter 194(200:204). Carriage at right.

Shape shoulder
Cast off 3(3:4) sts at beg of next and following alternate row, K 1 row. Cast off 4 sts at beg of next row, K 1 row. Cast off remaining 2 sts.
Slide carriage to left. Unravel nylon cord bringing needles to their correct position.
K the left side as for the right side reversing instructions left for right and vice versa.

Neck band
(Two pieces)
Join one shoulder seam, press. Push 122(128:133) needles up to B position. With right side of work facing you, pick up 55(58:59) sts along back neck edge and 67(70:74) sts along front neck edge to centre front and place on needles. *Tension dial at 6··. Row counter 000. Using colour 2, K 1 row. Dec 1 st (3 sts in) at centre front edge on next and every following alternate row 5 times in all, K 1 row. Tension dial at 8··, K 1 row. Tension dial at 6··. K 1 row. Inc 1 st (3 sts in) at centre front edge on next and every following alternate row 5 times in all, K 2 rows. Row counter 024. Using waste yarn, K 8 rows. Release from machine.*
Push 67(71:74) needles up to B position. With right side of work facing you pick up 67(70:74) sts evenly along front neck edge to centre front and place on needles. Follow instructions for neckband from * to *.

Armhole bands
(Both alike)
Join rest of shoulder seam, press.
Push 126(133:140) needles up to B position. With right side of work facing you pick up 126(133:140) sts evenly around armhole edge and place on needles. Tension dial at 6··. Row counter 000. Using colour 2, K 1 row. Dec 1 st (3 sts in) at both ends of next and every following alternate row 5 times in all, K 1 row. Tension dial at 8··, K 1 row. Tension dial at 6··, K 1 row. Inc 1 st (3 sts in) at both ends of next and every following alternate row 5 times in all, K 2 rows. Using waste yarn, K 8 rows. Release from machine.

To make up
Pin out each piece to size and press using a warm iron over a damp cloth. Join side seams. Fold neck and armhole bands in half to the right side of garment and backstitch through the loops of the last row knitted in colour 2. Unravel waste yarn. Give final pressing.

Skirt
Right front and left back panels
Insert card into machine and lock on row 1. Using waste yarn cast on 137(140:144) sts, 61 sts to left of centre and 76(79:83) sts to right of centre. K 6 rows (K 1 row extra for left front and right back only). Carriage at right. Tension dial at 6··. Row counter 000. Using colour 2, K 12 rows. Tension dial at 8··, K 1 row. Tension dial at 6··, K 12 rows. Turn up hem. Carriage at left. Tension dial at 8·. Row counter 000. Release card and with colour 1 in feeder 1 and colour 2 in feeder 2, work in pattern.

Shape lower edge
Always taking the yarn round the first inside needle, push 48 needles at opposite end to carriage to D position on the next row, K 1 row. Push 12 inside needles at opposite end to carriage back to C position on next and every following alternate row 4 times in all. K 2 rows. Dec 1 st at right edge on next and every following 5th row 86 times in all. 51(54:58) sts. K 3 rows. Lock card. Row counter 440. Carriage at right. Tension dial at 6··. Using colour 2, K 10 rows. Tension dial at 8··, K 1 row. Tension dial at 6··, knit 10 rows. Cast off.

Left front and right back panels
Follow instructions for right front and left back panels but reverse the shapings by noting alteration in number of rows worked and reading left for right and vice versa.

To make up
Pin out each piece to size and press using a warm iron over a damp cloth. Join front, back and side seams leaving an 8in. [20cm.] opening in side seam for zip fastener. Fold waistband in half to the inside and stitch.
Insert elastic into waistband and oversew ends. Work 1 row double crochet [US s.c.] along zip opening. Sew in zip fastener. Press again.

CHART FOR PUNCH CARD
KEY: ★ CONTRAST COLOUR

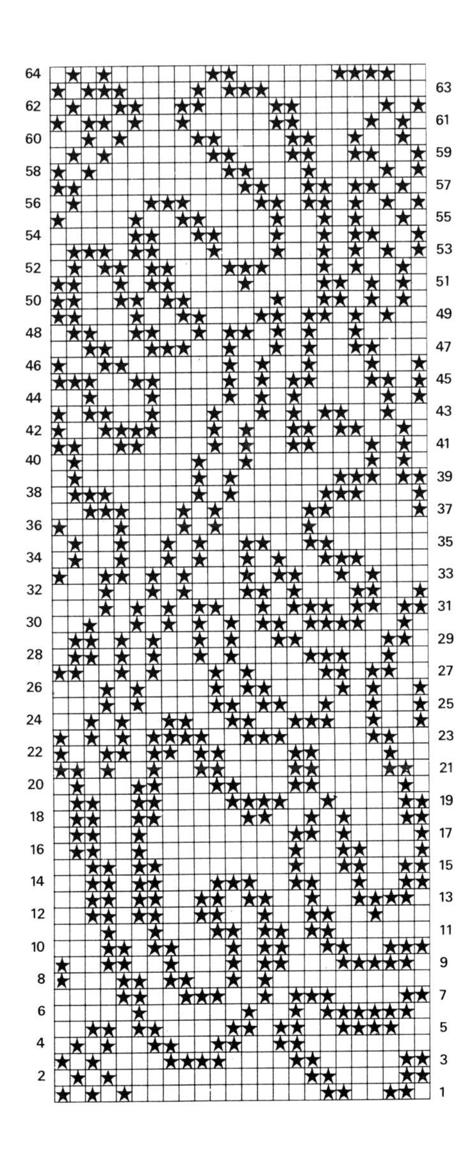

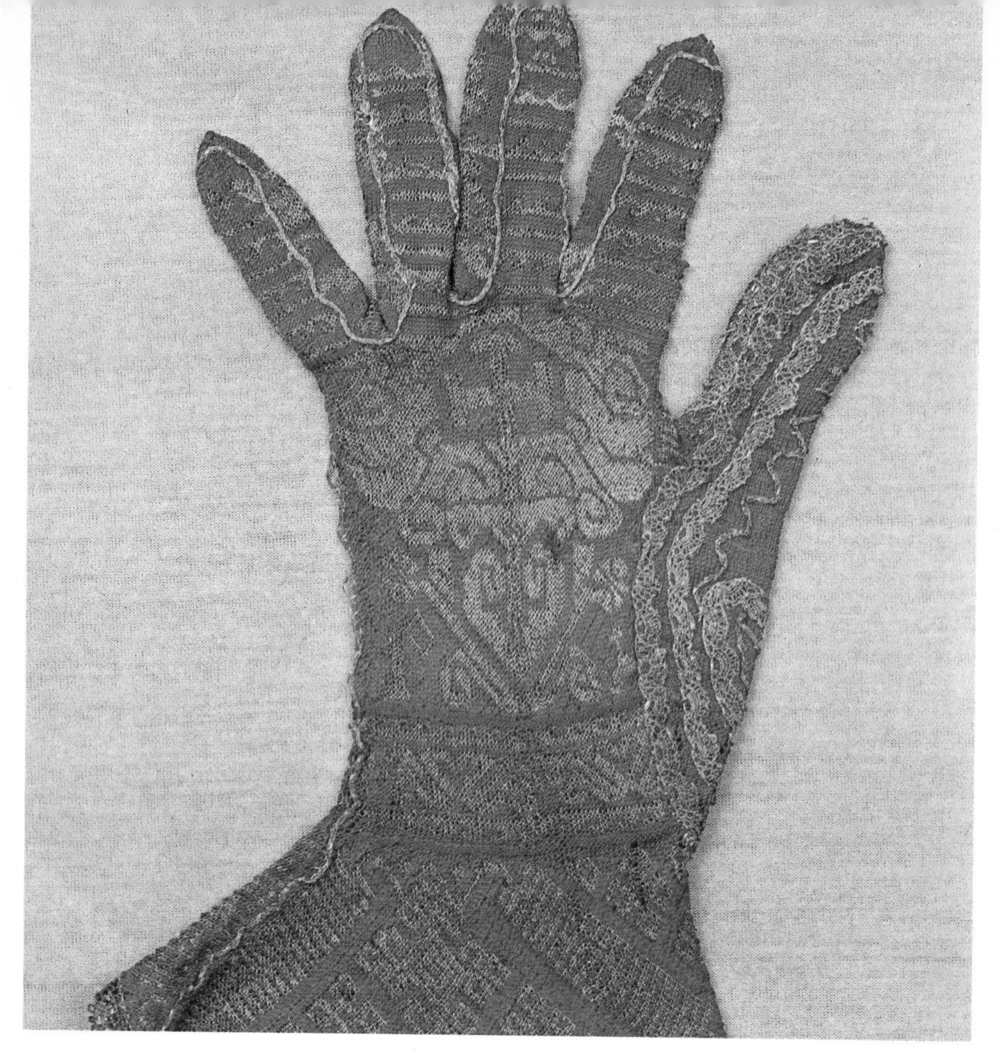

Snug as a glove...

16th-century Spanish altar glove

The group of 16th-century knitting to which this glove belongs is the first major evidence of knitting in Europe. The glove is an accomplished piece of work and suggests that knitting had already become an established craft. Gloves such as this were worn as part of the regalia of a priest and the sumptuousness of this single surviving glove suggests that it was of a pair belonging to a senior member of the church hierarchy.

The glove is knitted in red silk with a silver gilt pattern knitted in. The tension or gauge is quite fine, 25 stitches and 19 rows to one inch (25mm.). The silver gilt thread is knitted in on the back of the work so that there are no long threads to catch the finger tips.

The bands of pattern at the wrist and on the fingers are typical of those found in Arab coloured knitting but the pattern on the gauntlet and on the back of the hand are more advanced in design. The cross of the Christian church can be seen worked into the pattern on the back of the hand.

The glove is trimmed with silver gilt bobbin lace. The lace runs in a double layer round the seam joining the thumb to the side of the glove and along the edge of the gauntlet. Plaited braid is used to outline forchettes on the fingers, the outer side seam of the glove and as additional decoration on the thumb. The use of this braid is interesting because there are, in fact, no forchettes on the fingers and no side seam since the glove is knitted in the round. The braid is used simply to imitate the construction of a leather glove.

The thumb is also knitted in the round and is lined with red knitted silk. The thumb is set into the side of the glove with a small diamond-shaped gusset to give better fit and provide ease of movement. This beautiful glove and others like it were produced in Spain and exported all over Europe, probably via the emissaries of the church. Similar items were occasionally mentioned in English household records and are evidence of the growing trade between the countries of Europe.

A "he-man" sweater which goes to prove how ingeniously ancient knitting designs can be adapted. After all, how many men can claim that their waistcoat or vest owes its origin to a Spanish altar-glove.

The beautiful patterning on this sleeveless vest or waistcoat is directly derived from the patterning which can be seen on the gauntlet and back of the Spanish glove. The way in which the patterning has been used makes this an extremely elegant garment and yet it has the easy-to-live-in look of well-designed modern casual wear.

The back of the waistcoat is knitted in one-colour ribbing thus achieving a very neat fit to the garment.

The garment illustrated was knitted in Emu Scotch Superwash Double Knitting yarn in Chestnut and Aran White.

Materials
11(12:13:13) 25gr. [10(11:12:12)oz.] balls of Double Knitting [knitting worsted] yarn in main colour (A); 4(5:5:6) 25gr. [4(5:5:6]oz.] balls in contrast colour (B).
One pair each of Nos. 11, 10, 9 and 8 [US Nos. 2, 3, 4 and 5] needles.
5 ⅜in. [1cm.] wide buttons.

Tension or Gauge: 11 sts and 15 rows to 2in. [5cm.] over st st (stockinette stitch) using No. 8 [US No. 5] needles.

Special abbreviation for this design:
Up 1 Pick up the loop lying between the needles and knit or purl into the back

Sizes
To fit chest sizes 38(40:42:44)in. [96·5(101·5:106·5:111·5)cm.].
Length from shoulder, 24(24½:25:25½)in. [61(62:63·5:64·5)cm.].
Note: Figures in parentheses ( ) refer to the larger sizes. Where there is only one figure this refers to all sizes.

Back
Using No. 10 [US No. 3] needles and A cast on 134(142:150:158) sts and work in rib as follows:
1st row (right side) K2, *P2, K2; repeat from * to end.
2nd row P2, *K2, P2; repeat from * to end.
Repeat these 2 rows 5 times more.
Change to No. 9 [US No. 4] needles.
Rib 94 rows.

Shape armholes
Cast off 6(7:8:9) sts at beg of next 2 rows.
Cont in rib, dec 1 st at each end of the 7 following rows, then dec 1 st at each end of every alternate row until 94(98:102:106) sts remain.
Rib 47 more rows.

Shape shoulders
Cast off 7 sts at beg of the next 3 rows.
Next row Cast off 7 sts, rib next 12(13:14:15) sts and leave on spare needle until required.
Cast off 40(42:44:46) sts for back neck edge, rib to end and work on this last set of sts.
* Continue to shape shoulder and neck edge.
1st row Cast off 6(7:8:9) sts at beg and dec 1 at end for neck.
2nd row Dec 1, rib to end.
Cast off remaining 5 sts.
Rejoin yarn to neck edge of 13(14:15:16) remaining sts and rib to end of row. Now work from * to end as first side.

Back neck ribbing
With right side of work facing you and using No. 11 [US No. 2] needles and B, pick up and K 50(54:58:62) sts.
Work 7 rows in K2, P2 rib.
Cast off in rib.

Pocket backs
(Two alike)
Using No. 8 [US No. 5] needles and A cast on 28 sts.
Beg with a K row, st st (stockinette stitch) 30 rows.
Leave on a spare needle until required.

Left front
Using No. 8 [US No. 5] needles and A cast on 3 sts. Work the two-colour pattern from the chart in st st (stockinette stitch). (It is not necessary to weave in the yarn but care must be taken not to draw the yarn tightly across the back of the work or it will become puckered.)
1st row K in A.
2nd row Cast on 3 sts in A, K 3A, 2B, inc 1B, 1A in last st (7 sts).
3rd row Cast on 3 sts, 1B, 2A, 2B, 1A, 1B, 2A, inc 1 with B in last st (11 sts).
4th row Cast on 3 sts, 4A, 2B, 4A, 2B, 2A, inc 1 with A in last st (15 sts).
5th row Using B, cast on 3, work to last st, inc 1 (19 sts).
6th row Using A, cast on 3, work to last st, inc 1 (23 sts).
7th row Cast on 3 sts. 1B, *3A, 3B; repeat from * 3 times, inc 1 with A (27 sts).
8th row Cast on 3 sts. 1A, 1B, *2A, 2B, 1A, 1B; repeat from * 3 times, 2A, 1B, inc 1 in 1B, 1A (31 sts).
9th row Cast on 3 sts. 1B, *4A, 2B; repeat from *4 times, 2A, inc 1 in A (35 sts).
10th row Repeat 5th row (39 sts).
11th row Repeat 6th row (43 sts).
12th row Cast on 3 sts. 2B, *3A, 3B; repeat from * 6 times, 1A, inc 1 in A (47 sts).
13th row Using A, cast on 4(6:9:12) sts. 1(3:6:9)A for side edge, *1B, 1A, 1B,** 2A, 2B, 1A, 1B; repeat from ** 6 times, 2A, 2B, inc 1A, 1B, *. 52(54:57:60) sts for full width of front. 51 pattern sts 1(3:6:9) in A.
Now work from the 14th to 44th rows as given on chart, keeping 1(3:6:9) sts in A at side edge.
45th (pocket) row 1(3:6:9)A, 12B, sl next 28 sts onto a stitch holder and leave until required, with B work across the 28 sts of one pocket back, with B work to end.
Work from the 46th to 88th rows as given on chart.
Break off B and continue with A only.
Work 2 rows.

Shape armhole and front edge
Next row Cast off 7(7:8:9) sts for armhole, work until 3 remain, take 2 tog for front, work 1 st.
Dec 1 st at armhole end of each of next 6 rows and dec 1 st at front edge on every 4th of these rows. Dec 1 st at armhole on the next 4(5:6:7) alternate rows still dec 1 st at front edge every 4th row until 20(21:22:23) sts remain.
Continue on these sts until armhole measures same as back ending at armhole end.

Shape shoulder
Cast off 6(7:8:9) sts at beg of next row; 5 sts at beg of 2 following alternate rows.
Work 1 row then cast off remaining 4 sts.

Right front
Work as given for left front until the 12th row has been worked.
13th row Cast on 3 sts. Now work from * to * as 13th row on left front, turn, cast on 1(3:6:9) for side edge and keep these sts in A throughout the pattern rows. 51 pattern sts 1(3:6:9) in A.
Work the 51 sts in pattern as given on chart from the 14th to 44th rows.
45th (pocket) row With B, K11, sl next 28 sts onto a stitch holder and in their place with B, K across the sts of other pocket back, pattern to end.
Beg with the 46th row work from chart over 51 sts until 88th row has been completed.
Break off B.
Work 2 more rows.

Shape front and armhole
1st row K1, K2 tog through back of loops for front edge, K to end.
2nd row Cast off 7(7:8:9) sts. P to end.
Now work from ** to end as given for left front.

Pocket Tops
(two alike)
Using No. 10 [US No. 3] needles and B, K across the 28 sts on stitch holder.
Rib row P1, *K2, P2; repeat from * ending with P1.
Work 5 rows in rib.
Cast off in rib.

Left front edging
With right side of work facing you and using No. 11 [US No. 2] needles and B, pick up and K 52(56:60:64) sts from shoulder to first front dec and place a coloured marker after last st; 74(78:82:86) sts along straight edges of front and place a marker after last st; pick up 26 sts to point, place a marker after last st; pick up

2 sts from cast-on edge and place a marker after last st; pick up 24(28:32:36) sts to side seam edge. 178(190:202:214) sts.

1st row P2, *K2, P2, repeat to end.

2nd (inc) row Rib to 1st marker, up 1 K, rib to 2nd marker, up 1 K, rib to 3rd marker, up 1 K, K2, up 1 K, rib to end.

3rd row Work in rib but purling all new sts.

4th (inc and buttonhole) row Rib to 1st marker, K1, up 1 K, K2, P1. *Cast off 3, rib the next 12(13:14:15) sts; repeat from * 3 times, cast off 3, rib next 3 sts, up 1 K, rib to next marker, K1, up 1 K, K2, up 1 K, rib to end.

5th row Work in rib as 3rd row casting on 3 sts over those stitches cast off to complete buttonholes.

6th row Rib to 1st marker, K2, up 1 P, rib to 2nd marker, up 1 P, rib to 3rd marker, K2, up 1 P, K2, up 1 P, rib to end.

7th row Work in rib knitting all sts made on previous row.

Cast off in rib, following the line of incs with up 1 P as you cast off.

Right front ribbing

Work to match left front omitting buttonholes and beg at side seam edge.

Armhole edgings

(Two alike)

Join shoulder seams.

Using No. 11 [US No. 2] needles and B, pick up and K 118(122:126:130) sts evenly round one armhole.

Work 7 rows in rib as given for back neck ribbing.

Cast off in rib.

To make up

Press back lightly under a damp cloth with a warm iron. Pin fronts out to size taking care to keep the points and press them on wrong side. Join side and armhole band seams. Sew pocket tops to right side of fronts and pocket backs to wrong side of fronts.

Press all seams. Sew on buttons.

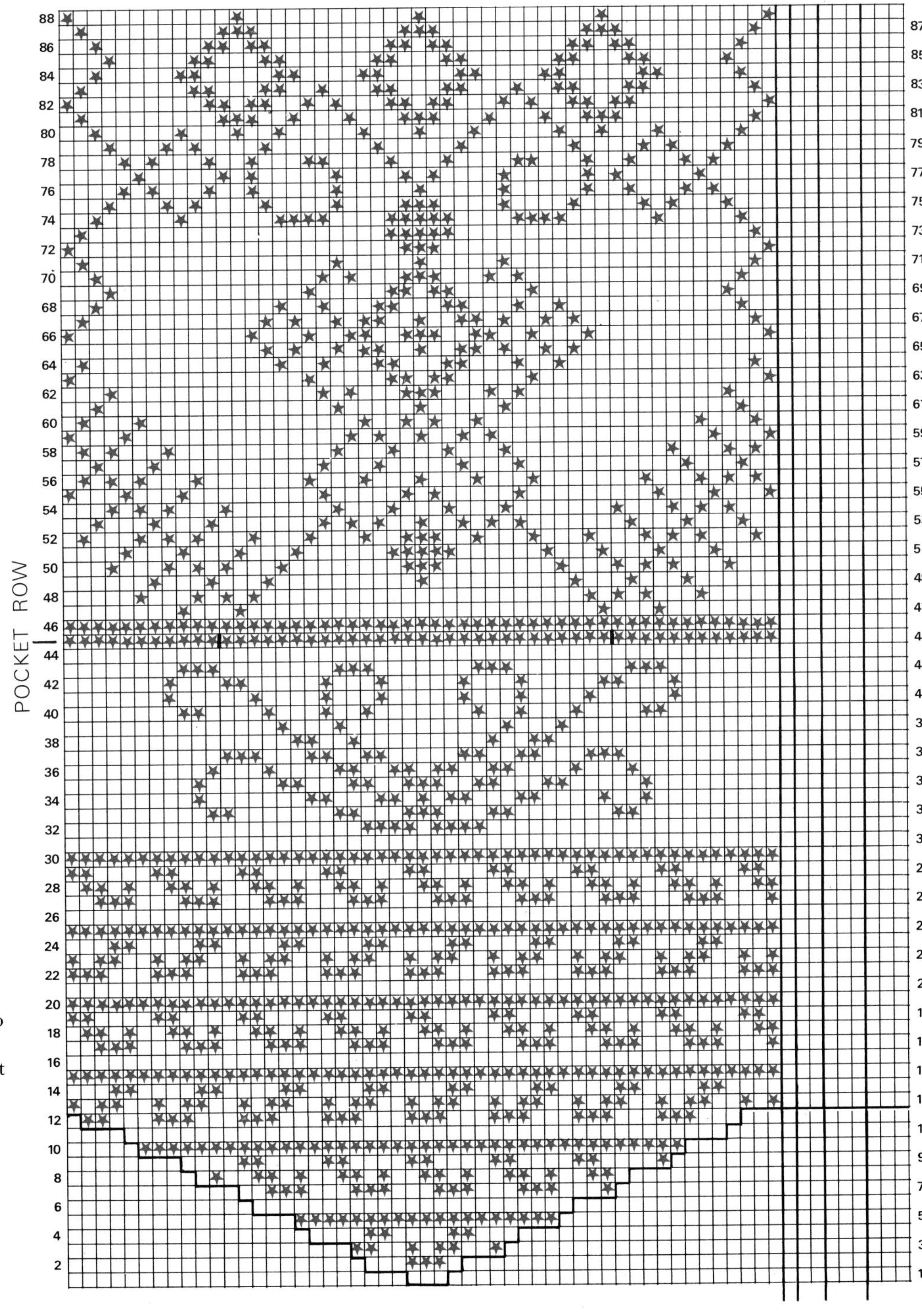

KEY TO CHART

KEY: ✶ CONTRAST COLOUR

Floating a stitch

17th-century silk cap

Compared with other pieces of Italian knitting of the same date, this knitted silk cap is rather unusual. Instead of the brocade-type fabric produced with coloured threads and metallic yarns, the textural pattern of this cap has been created by structure and yarn. The ground is knitted in a matt silk thread with a heavier, shiny yarn used to create the pattern by making a float stitch on the surface of the fabric.

The knitting is of quite a high standard but it is quite impossible to guess in what context the cap was knitted. It has been suggested that it might have been produced by a home knitter rather than a professional. However, the standard of work indicates that caps such as this may easily have been produced by professional knitters, possibly in a different guild from those producing brocade pieces.

The cap was shaped while being knitted and the tip is adorned with a magnificent, complicated-looking tassel.

Knitted caps were popular accessories over a long period of time. They were worn mostly by men throughout the 17th century when many men had shaved their heads clean to allow the heavy and cumbersome wigs to be worn comfortably. Wigs were worn in public and at home in company but caps were substituted when the man was alone.

Similar caps were worn by workmen and artisans and these were much simpler, being knitted in worsted yarn, sometimes striped in bright colours.

"Float stitches", short lengths of yarn which lie on top of the knitted fabric, are the feature of this scoop-necked sleeveless sweater in the same way that the Italian knitted silk cap has the motif "raised" above the background fabric.

The sweater has been cleverly designed so that the background fabric is worked in purl knitting, providing a matt texture as a contrast for the coloured float stitches.

The sweater illustrated is knitted in Wendy 4-ply yarn in School Grey, Black, Aran White, Parisienne Navy and Emerald.

Another example of the ingenuity that can be used in adapting the most unlikely originals for present-day garments. A 17th-century gentleman who used this design on his cap would surely be surprised to see the use designer Anne Gordon has made of it! Nevertheless – it is a most effective adaptation.

Materials
11(11:12:12) 25 gr. [10(10:11:11)oz.] balls of standard 4-ply yarn in Grey, main colour M.
1 ball each of Black (B), White (W), Navy (N) and Emerald (E).
1 pair each of No. 10 and 11 [US Nos. 3 and 2] needles.
1 set of 4 double-pointed No. 11 [US No. 2] needles for neck band.

Tension or Gauge: 14 sts and 18 rows to 2in. [5cm.] over st st (stockinette stitch) on No. 10 [US No. 3] needles.

Sizes
To fit chest sizes 38(40:42:44)in. [97(102:107:112)cm.].
Length from shoulder 24½(25:25½:26)in. [62·5(63·5:64·5:66)cm.].
Note: Figures in parentheses () refer to the larger sizes. Where there is only one figure this refers to all sizes.

Back
Using No. 11 [US no. 2] needles and M, cast on 140(148:156:164) sts and work 30 rows in K1, P1 rib.
Change to No. 10 [US No. 3] needles and beg with a P row, work 112(114:116:118) rows in reversed st st (stockinette stitch).

Shape armholes
Cast off 8(9:10:11) sts at beg of next 2 rows.
Dec 1 st at beg of 14 following rows 110(116:122:128) sts.
Reversed st st (stockinette stitch) 70(72:74:76) rows.

Shape shoulders
Cast off 7(7:8:8) sts at beg of next 4 rows; 7(8:8:9) sts on 4 following rows.
Leave remaining 54(56:58:60) sts until required for neck band.

Front
Work as for back until 29 rows in K1, P1 rib have been worked.
Next row Rib 49(53:57:61) sts, place a marker after last st to mark last st of pattern panel, rib 42 sts for panel and place a marker after last st, rib to end. (Wind each ball of colour into 2 balls.)
Change to No. 10 [US No. 3] needles and work in reversed st st (stockinette stitch) with float st – the float sts are not worked but woven across the front of the centre panel of 42 sts as follows:
1st row With M, P49(53:57:61) sts, for pattern panel, join in Black (B), *Bring B yarn to front of work, P3M, place B yarn behind work, P1M, bring B to front of work, P3M, place B behind work, P14M, join 2nd ball of B and rep from * once to end of panel then P49(53:57:61)M.
2nd row With M, K49(53:57:61) sts, for pattern panel K13M, *place B behind work, K3M, bring B to front of work, K1M, place B behind work, K3M*, K14M, repeat from * to * K1M, to end of panel then K49(53:57:61)M.
These 2 rows set the sts for the pattern panel. Now work from the 3rd to 39th row on chart. Break off B, and join in White (W) and work from the 40th to 78th row of chart.
These 78 rows form the float stitch panel. Repeat them once more using Navy (N) instead of B and Emerald (E) instead of W but when 112(114:116:118) rows from beginning have been completed, shape armholes as given for back.
Cont on 110(116:122:128) sts until the last row of the E pattern has been completed. Break off E and cont with M only.
Reversed st st (stockinette stitch) 1(3:5:5) rows.
Divide sts for neck and shoulders.
Next row K47(49:51:53) sts and leave on spare needle until required, K16(18:20:22) sts and leave for neck band, K to end and work on the last set of sts.

Shape neck
1st row Work until 2 sts remain, K2 tog.
2nd row Cast off 2, work to end.
Repeat these 2 rows twice.
Dec 1 st at neck edge of every row until 28(30:32:34) sts remain.
Cont on these sts until armhole is same depth as back armhole ending with a K row.

Shape shoulder
Cast off 7(7:8:8) sts at beg of row and on following P row, then 7(8:8:9) sts on following 2 P rows. Fasten off.
Rejoin yarn to 47(49:51:53) sts and P to end of row. Complete to match first side.

Armhole bands
(Two alike)
Join shoulder seams.
Using No. 11 [US No. 2] needles and M, pick up and K 186(190:196:202) sts all round one armhole.
Work 9 rows in K1, P1 rib. Cast off in rib.

Neck band
Using set of 4 No. 11 [US No. 2] needles and M, K across the 54(56:58:60) sts from back neck edge, pick up and K64(66:68:72) sts from left front neck edge, K across the 16(18:20:22) sts at centre front, pick up and K64(66:68:72) sts from right front neck edge. 198(206:214:226) sts.
Work 9 *rounds* in K1, P1 rib.
Cast off firmly in rib.

To make up
Press all parts except the ribbing on the wrong side with a warm iron over a damp cloth.
Join side and armhole band seams.
Press seams.

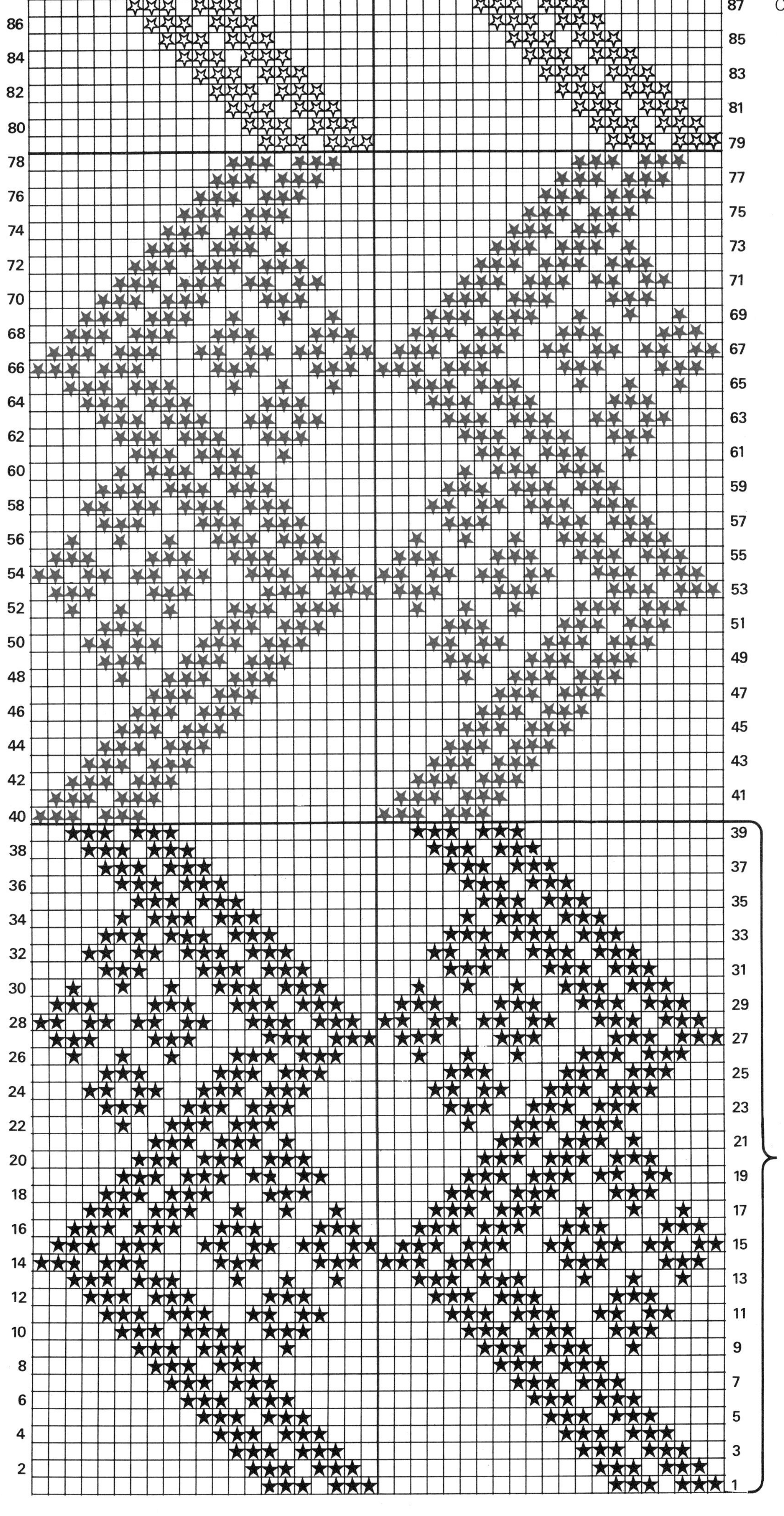

CONTINUE 4 REPEATS OF PATTERN

KEY TO CHART

★ BLACK

★ WHITE

☆ NAVY

From Jacob's dream...

18th-century German knitted carpet

This carpet can be considered a knitting masterpiece. It would have been one of a number of pieces of knitting (usually a bonnet, a pair of gloves, a pair of stockings, a jacket and a carpet), which an apprentice to a knitting guild was required to knit over a period of thirteen weeks to gain full membership of the guild. Knitting guilds were formed in several European countries but only those in Germany seem to have stipulated carpets as part of the skill required of their knitters.

This particular carpet comes from the Alsace area, probably from Strasbourg, and is typical of that district in that it has the eagle of the Habsburg family in each of the upper corners. The Habsburgs granted many of the charters in the area.

However, in some ways, the actual layout of the design of flora and fauna around a central picture of religious derivation is more typical of the carpets of Silesia, although these were often larger, up to 120ins. (205cm.) across.

This carpet is approximately 66ins. (168cm.) square and is made of wool. The centre panel depicts "Jacob's Dream" and the inscription reads *"Hilfe Wirt Gott Ferner Schicken Meinen Feinden Zum Verdruss"* which translated means "God will continue to send help, to mine enemies sorrow". Surrounding this centre piece is a floral border which contains a multitude of rather stylized flowers and fruit, together with peacocks, a unicorn, a deer, a rampant lion, two over-sized unidentifiable birds, two smaller birds, two eagles and, standing under an apple tree, Adam and Eve. Finally, surrounding this, is a double border of geometric pattern into which is inset the date, 1781. The entire carpet is knitted in stocking stitch at a tension or gauge of eight rows to one inch (25mm.).

The size and weight of the carpet indicates that it was produced on a peg frame. Being such a fine work of art, the carpet was probably never used on the floor but was used as a tapestry.

Clearly designed for the Original Man, this striking "bird front" sweater has a gaiety and "swirl" about it guaranteed to catch anyone's eye. And if his name is Jacob, so much the better – for the design surrounded Jacob's Dream. . . .

The richly patterned front of this long-sleeved sweater uses bird and flower motifs from the border of the 18th-century knitted carpet. The original carpet shows the shapes against an ecru-coloured ground, whereas the sweater has dark blue for the background, producing a more brilliant and striking contrast for the colours.

Although 18th-century knitting guild apprentices were required to knit complex patterns by hand, this sweater was knitted on a domestic knitting machine. However, an experienced and enthusiastic craftswoman might decide to reproduce the beauty of this unique sweater in hand knitting, following the pattern chart row by row.

The sweater illustrated was knitted on a Jones knitting machine using 2-ply lambswool yarn.

Materials
In 2-ply lambswool, 5(5:6:6) 50gr. [8(9:9:9)oz.] balls in Navy Blue (colour 1). 2(2:2:2) 50gr. [3(3:3:3)oz.] balls in White (colour 2). 1 50gr. [1oz.] ball each of Tan (colour 3), Turquoise (colour 4), Emerald (colour 5), Beige (colour 6).
For single-bed knitting machines with minimum of 200 needles.

Sizes
To fit chest sizes 36(38:40:42)in. [92(97:102:112)cm.].
Length from back neck, 25½(26:26½:27)in. [65(66:67:69)cm.].
Length of sleeve, 18(18½:19:19½)in. [46(47:49:50)cm.].

Tension or Gauge: 36 sts and 52 rows to 4in. [10cm.] over st st (stockinette stitch) with tension dial at 4 approximately.

Welt Tension or Gauge: (machines without ribbing attachment), dial at 1.

Back
Cast on 172(182:190:200) sts for 2 × 1 rib using colour 1 with tension dial at 1. K 40 rows dial at 5, K 1 row dial at 1, K 40 rows to 3½in. [9cm.]. Turn up hem.
Set machine for main tension and, using colours 1 and 2, K patterned border, working from chart (45 rows). K straight for 176 rows.

Shape armhole
Cast off 8(9:10:10) sts at beg of next 4 rows. Dec 1 st each end of next and every 3rd row until 132(136:140:144) sts remain. K straight for 112(120:126:134) rows.

Shape shoulder
Cast off 5 sts at beg of next 14 rows, cast off 5(6:7:8) sts at beg of next 2 rows, thread up 52(54:56:58) sts.

Front
Knit as for back to patterned 2-colour border then follow chart for main design using 6 colours.

Shape armhole and neck
Still following the chart, shape the armholes as for back and at the same time after 4 rows, thread up sts to left of centre 0 and take off machine, dec 1 st on neck edge on next and every following 4th row 14 times, then every following 5th row until 40(41:42:43) sts remain. Continue knitting until front matches back.

Shape shoulder
Cast off 5(6:7:8) sts at armhole edge every alternate row 7 times then replace left front on machine. Knit as for right front reversing all shaping.

Sleeves
Using colour 1, cast on 80(82:84:86) sts and rib 3½in. [9cm.] cuff, as for main garment. Change to main tension and K 45 rows of 2-colour patterned border, increasing 1 st each end of every 6th row until there are 134(140:146:152) sts. Knit straight for 188(194:202:208) rows, or until sleeve is desired length.

Shape armhole
Cast off 8(9:10:10) sts at beg of next 4 rows, dec 1 st at each end of next and every 3rd row until 68(70:72:74) sts remain.
Cast off 3 sts at beg of next 16 rows, cast off 20(22:24:26) sts.

Neckband
Using colour 1, cast on 116(123:128:135) sts and rib 14 rows as before, dec 1 st on right edge of every alternate row, 6 times; K 14 rows inc 1 st on right edge of every alternate row 6 times. With right side of work facing machine, place left front evenly on machine with band and cast off together.
Repeat band for right front, reversing all shaping.

To make up
Join shoulder seams. Sew in sleeves and press seams. Join sleeve seams and side seams of sweater, sew in sleeves. Sew neck bands to sweater fronts and join centre front.
Press all seams on wrong side.

See Page 154 for colour chart.

WIRT GOTT FERNER SCHICK

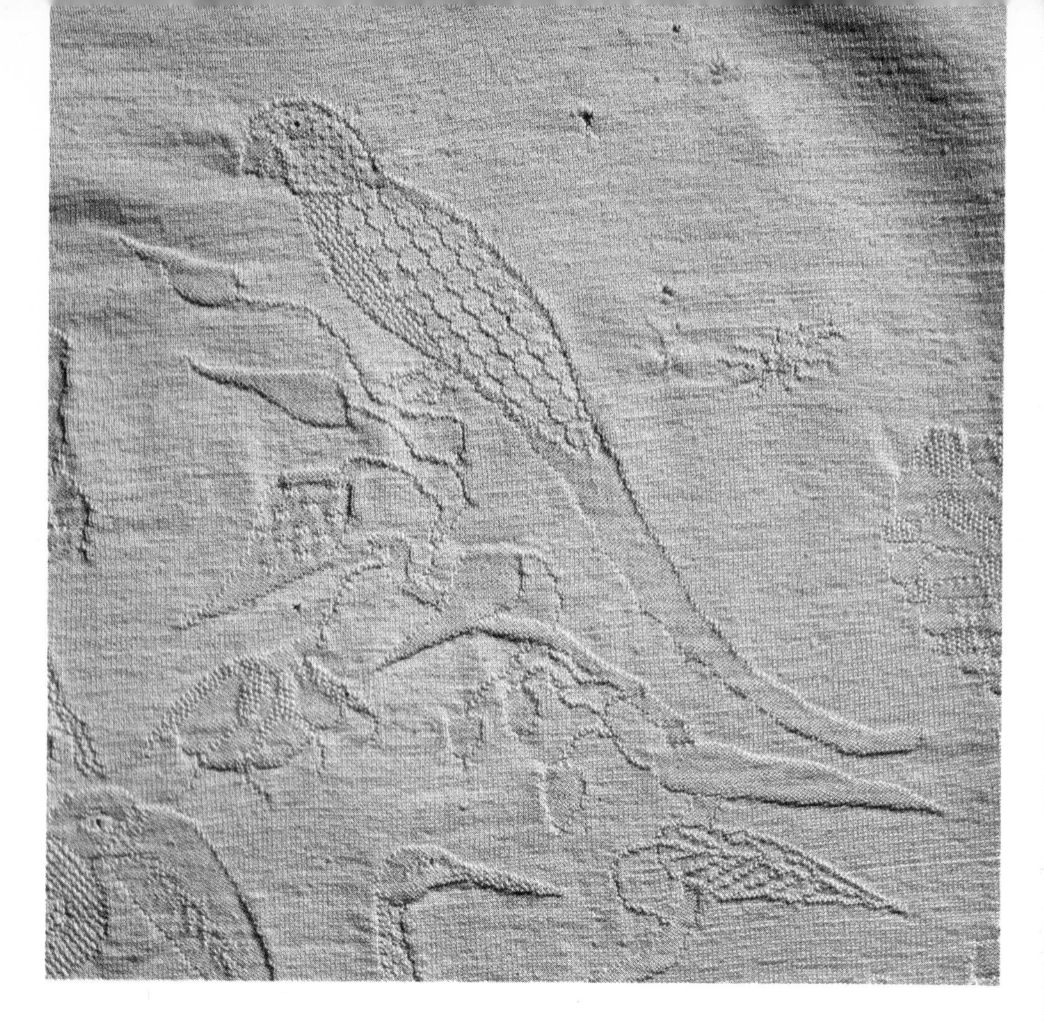

A bird from Holland

Dutch embossed petticoat

The history of this remarkable piece of knitting is not known. Traditionally, it is thought to have originated in Holland and is known as the Dutch embossed petticoat. It is dated as 17th to 18th-century, by which time this type of knitting was certainly known in Holland.

The fabric itself is a wide tube of knitting, 30¼ins. (76·8cm.) deep with a total circumference of 124½ins. (320cm.), and has no seam.

It is a beautiful piece of work which must have been greatly cherished for it is still in very good condition. The knitting is fine, having 22 stitches and 36 rows to one inch (25mm.), and has an estimated 2650 stitches in each row. The pattern is made up entirely of textures, of plain and purl stitches, and takes the form of a multitude of birds and animals of all kinds.

The design of the creatures shows good draughtsmanship, quite apart from the superb knitting.

The top edge of the tube petticoat would have been gathered round the waist and was probably worn over a cotton or linen shift and under a full skirt, providing the bulk to hold out the skirts. Not only did these petticoats provide bulk but, being made of two-ply worsted wool, they also provided warmth, a major consideration in houses with stone-tiled floors and ill-fitting doors and windows.

The bird and animal motifs which form the patterning of the remarkable embossed petticoat from Holland provide modern knitters with a rich variety of designs for all kinds of garments and accessories.

A single bird perched on a leafed branch has been used for the scarf illustrated and faithfully reproduces the original design in plain and purl stitches. The charm of this scarf therefore lies in the textural interest rather than in the use of colour. The scarf is edged with rows of moss stitch.

Pingouin Coton No. 5 in Fougére was used to knit the scarf illustrated.

Allure from a bird scarf. . . . The bird design is at the end of the scarf and is a true copy from a similar bird motif on an 18th century Dutch petticoat. Here is another design which shows the infinite range of possibilities old patterns can provide.

Materials
3 balls of No. 5 Cotton yarn.
One pair each of No. 13 and No. 14 [US No. 0 and 00] needles.

Tension or Gauge: 17 sts and 22 rows to 2in. [5cm.] over the st st (stockinette stitch) using No. 13 [US No. 0] needles.

Size
7¼in. [18·5cm.] wide and 48in. [122cm.] long.

To work the scarf
Using No. 14 [US No. 00] needles, cast on 62 sts and work from chart as follows:
1st row *K1, P1; repeat from * to end.
2nd row *P1, K1; repeat from * to end.
3rd row As 1st row.
This completes the moss stitch border.
Change to No. 13 [US No. 0] needles.
4th row P1, K1, P1 for moss stitch border, K until 3 sts remain, K1, P1, K1 for moss stitch border.
5th row K1, P1, K1, K until 3 sts remain, P1, K1, P1.
6th row As 4th row.
These last 3 rows set the moss stitch borders.
Work the motif from the 7th to 116th row on the chart.
Continue in st st (stockinette stitch) with moss stitch borders until scarf measures approximately 48in. [122cm.] long, ending with a wrong side row.
Change to No. 14 [US No. 00] needles and work 3 rows in moss stitch, then cast off.
Press scarf lightly, with a warm iron over a damp cloth.

KEY TO CHART

KEY ★ PURL ON RIGHT SIDE ROWS

KNIT ON WRONG SIDE ROWS

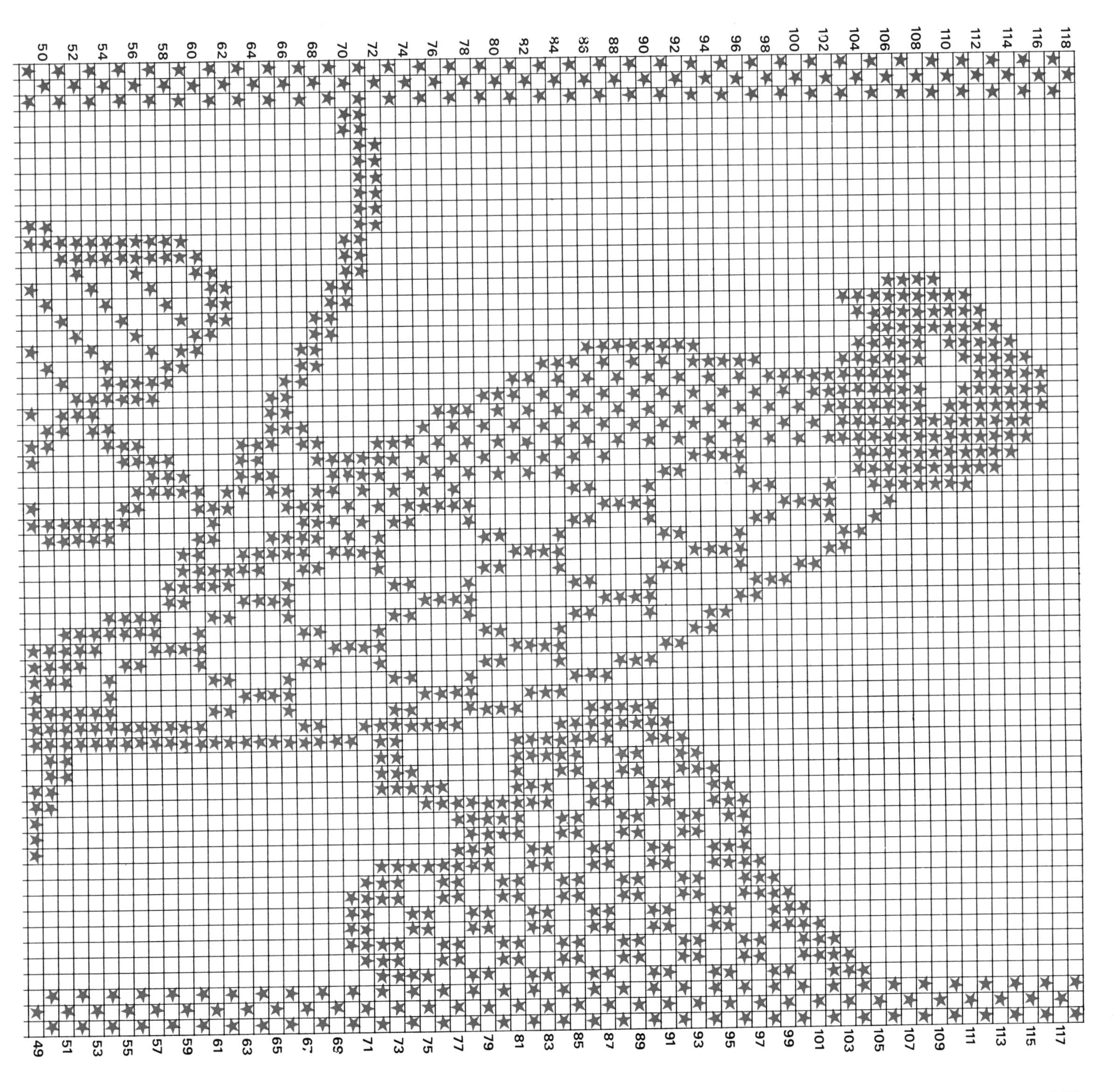

Colour chart for man's birdfront sweater – see page 148

Note: colours used here are for ease of working and do not represent the actual garment colours. Colour 1, for instance is Navy

KEY TO CHART BACKGROUND COLOUR 1 GREY COLOUR 2 PINK COLOUR 3

Blue and Colour 2 is white (see instructions page 148)

BLUE COLOUR 4 GREEN COLOUR 5 ORANGE COLOUR 6

Index

Knitting information

So there we are – twenty-four patterns for dedicated knitters and every one of them is, we hope, the nearest practical adaptation of the original pattern into a wearable and attractive garment that we can devise. We say "dedicated" deliberately, since these patterns do require an above average dedication. That is the secret of their attraction. They are not difficult to knit but the hand-made garments do take time. The knitter, therefore, must feel more involved with the product than in the case of the average commercial pattern. Some of the lace patterns might prove tricky. We have included quite a variety of traditional lace patterns, for example, in the caftan. The caftan, incidentally, probably requires the greatest dedication of them all. After all, it's a lot of knitting in sheer physical terms. Our guess is that a really good knitter could complete her caftan, giving a bearable degree of devotion to it every day, in about six weeks, so there is a target to aim at. Don't feel a duffer if you miss that target. Our title declares that knitting is an art and true art is meant to be a pleasure, not an endurance test. There may be some cunning and skill required on the evening top. Bead knitting – alas – is a dying craft. That – added to the fact that it can be exceedingly beautiful if done properly – is precisely why we are eager to promote it. Nevertheless, if you follow every single line of our instructions you will end up with the garment as described. But you may well decide to be more venturesome in one area. Colour, for example. We have tried wherever possible faithfully to reflect the colours of the original patterns in the original articles. You may well have a preference for a different shade here or there – or even for an entirely different colour. Feel free to adapt. After all, we have very freely adapted the originals so please don't feel we are trying to limit *your* imagination, tastes or inclinations.

FIND YOUR OWN ORIGINALS

Our advice, in general terms, is quite simple. Pick the garment or pattern you like most for your first attempt. Human nature will ensure that you will be prepared to put more effort into something you really like. Then proceed to the ones in the "oh dear, it's marvellous – but could I tackle *that*" category. You will be surprised how quickly confidence grows. So there it is. Twenty-four garments for today from patterns of the past. We hope you will like them. And we certainly hope we have put you on that adventurous and exciting trail of working out your own patterns from even more unusual originals. It all adds a new dimension to gallery trotting and weekend museum viewing.

We are also, on these pages, giving you some essential information you will need when you come to knit your garment. Now, everything is up to you. So reach for your needles at once!

continued on page 160

A law for the "Queen's true subjects . . ."

Queen Elizabeth I's Sumptuary Law revitalized the woollen industry and gave a boost to the knitting trade by clamping down on the manufacture of felt and velvet hats. This extract from the original law begins by deploring the decline in the art of making woollen caps – a decline, says the law, which has been brought about by the popularity of felt hats. The subsequent loss to the woollen industry caused many "good cities and towns to be brought to desolation" and "a great number of people (have been) forced to depend upon foreign wools, to the discomoditie of the Realm".

The law warns that even greater damage to the trade will ensue if a remedy is not quickly found. "It may please the Queen's most excellent majesty, at the lamentable complaints of her said poor subjects, that it be enacted by the authority of this present parliament that no person . . . shall after the feast of the nativity of St John the Baptist . . . make or work any felt or hat . . . or any foreign woollen stuff" unless they serve certain apprenticeship requirements.

In the second main paragraph, the word "knyt" appears as the second to last word in the third line. The paragraph reads: "And be it enacted by the authoritie aforesayd, that from the fyrst daye of Aprill next comming no person whatsoever shall make, sell, or cause to be made or sold, any cappe or other thing of felt but only hattes, nor shall make, sell, or cause to be made or sold, any cappe of any woollen cloth, not knyt. . . ."

For most of the "Queen's true subjects", it was back to the knitting needles!

Cui quidem Bille perlecte et ad plenum intellecte per dictam dnam Reginam ex auctoritate parliamenti predicti sic Responsum est:

La Royne le veult

EXHIBITA est Regine Mati in parliamento predicto Billa quedam formam actus in se continens.

WHERE greate multytudes of the Queenes Maties true Subiectes, vsing the arte of makyng of wollen cappes, are impoverisshed and decayed by the excessyve vse of hattes and feltes, and thereby dyvers good Cities and townes brought to desolation, greate plentie of straunge comodityes, wthout necessitie consumed, and greate number of people enforced to depende vpon the havyng of forraine wolles, to the discomoditie of this Realme, the diminisshing of service to be done to the Queenes Matie, and greatter evident damagies, if remedy be not provided: It maye therefore please the Queenes most Excellent Matie, at the lamentable sute and complaynt of her sayd poore Subiectes, That it be enacted by the authoritye of this present parliament, that no person by hym or her selfe, or by any other, shall after the feast of the Nativity of St John Baptist next comyng, make or worke any felte or hatte, of, or wth any forraine woolle or stuffe, vnlesse suche person shall fyrst have ben apprentice or Covenaunt servaunt to suche mysterie of felt or hatt makyng by the space of seven yeres at the leaste, vpon payne to forfayte all suche hattes or feltes, as he shall make, or cause to be made whyle he worketh contrary to the fourme of this acte, and fyve poundes in money for every monethe that he shall so contynewe.

AND BEE it enacted by the authoritie aforesayd, that from the fyrst daye of Aprill next comyng, no person whatsoever, shall make, sell, or cause to be made or solde, any cappe or other thyng of feltes, but only hattes, nor shall make, sell, or cause to be made or solde, any cappe of any wollen cloth not knyt. And that no person after the sayd fyrst daye of Aprill, shall dye, or cause to be dyed black any cappes wth barke or smacke, but only wth copperas and gall, or wth woad and madder.

AND for the setting of many poore and impotent persons to worke, and for better makyng of cappes, that no person, after the sayd first daye of Aprill, shall thicke or full in any myll, or cause to be thicked or fulled in any myll, any cappe, untyll suche tyme as the same cappe be first well scowred and closed vpon the banke, and half thicked at the leaste in the footestocke. And that no man under the degree of a knyght, or of a lordes sonne, shall after the sayd fyrst daye of Aprill, weare any hatte or upper cappe of velvet, or covered wth velvet, on payne to forfayte for every hatte, cappe, or other thyng to be made, dyed, thycked, fulled, solde or worne, contrary to the meanyng of this acte, tenne shillinges, whereof the one moitye shalbe to the Queenes Matie, her heyres and Successours, the other moitye to suche person then vsyng the feate of cappe making, as will sue for the same, in any Courte of Recorde, wherein no Essoyne, protection, or wager of lawe, for the defendaunt shalbe admytted or allowed.

AND for the better and truer makyng of cappes and hattes wthin this Realme: Bee it enacted by the authoritye aforesayd, that it shalbe lefull to the maister and wardens of the company of haberdasshers, wthin the Citie of london, and to theyr Successours for the tyme beyng, calling to them one of the companye of the cappers, and another of the makers of hattes, as often as neede shall requyre, wthin the sayd Citie, or wthin three myles of the same, to searche all and all maner of cappers and makers of hattes, and the offendours and defaultes by them founde, to correct and punysshe by fynes and otherwyse, as in lyke case they doo other offendours and defautes in the sayd companye. And that it shalbe lefull for all mayors, bayliffes, and other head officers, in all other Cities and townes corporate, to doo the lyke.

PROVIDED ALLWAY, and be it enacted by the authoritye aforesayd, that every hatmaker, that is nowe a maker or worker of hattes, and being a housholder, apprentice, Covenaunt servaunt, or iourneyman, shall or maye, duryng suche persons naturall lyfe, contynewe makyng of hattes and feltes, albeit suche person were not bounden apprentice to the same arte for the space of seven yeres. And be it enacted, that no maister maker of hattes shall take or receyve any apprentices, contrarie to the true meanyng of this acte, that is to saye above two apprentices at one tyme nor those for any lesse tyme then seven yeres at the leaste on payne to suffer for every apprentyce to be taken or retayned agaynst the fourme of thys acte, one monethes imprisonment in the comon gaole, wthout bayle or maynprise. And that every takyng or retayning of apprentices contrarye to this acte shalbe voyde: And also suche person so takyng or retayning shalbe from thensforth dysabled to have any moo apprentices, then one at one tyme.

PROVIDED ALLWAYE that nothing in this acte shall extende to charge any person allowed to be a feltmaker or hatmaker, wth any payne or forfayture, for setting or vsyng his or their owne children to the makyng or workyng of feltes or hattes in his or theyr owne houses. Provided that this acte shall not extende to any makyng of hattes wth worsted yarne, in the Citie of Norwiche.

Knitting information

Abbreviations used in the pattern instructions

Here are the general knitting and crochet abbreviations used in the patterns in this book. Some less familiar ones are occasionally used and where these occur they are given as special abbreviations at the beginning of the instructions.

K	Knit
P	Purl
St(s)	Stitch(es)
Dec	Decrease
Inc	Increase
Tog	Together
Rep	Repeat
Beg	Beginning
Cont	Continue
Foll	Following
Rem	Remaining
Sl	Slip
St st	Stocking stitch (US Stockinette stitch) K on right and P on wrong side rows, working on two needles.
St st	When working on four needles, K every round.
K or P2 tog b	K or P two stitches together through the back of the stitches.
psso	Pass the slipped stitch over.
R st st	Reversed stocking (stockinette) stitch, P on right side and K on wrong side rows.
Up 1 K or P	Pick up the thread that lies between the needles, slip it onto the left-hand needle and K or P into the back of the thus increased stitch.
Yb	Yarn back of work.
Yf	Yarn forward or in front of work.
Yrn	Yarn round the needle.
C3f	Slip next two stitches onto a cable needle and leave at front of work, P1 then K2 from cable needle.
C3b	Slip next stitch onto cable needle and leave at back of work, K2 then P1 from cable needle.
C8	Slip next 4 sts onto cable needle and leave in front of work, K4 then K4 from cable needle.
Ch	Chain in crochet.
DC	Double crochet (US single crochet)
Tr	Treble crochet (US double crochet)

Tension and gauge

To ensure that your garments knit up as we intend, it is important that the yarn you use produces the same tension or gauge as that recommended in the pattern directions.

The stitch tension or gauge gives the number of stitches and rows which should be produced in a given area of knitting and to produce a garment of the correct size it is essential to work to the tension or gauge given.

But some people knit more loosely or tightly than others and if you are one of these, it may be necessary for you to use needles of a different size.

To check your own knitting tension or gauge, cast on 30 stitches using the size of needles and type of yarn recommended. Work the main pattern stitch until the knitting is approximately 4 in (10 cm) deep. Cast off and pin out the knitted swatch smoothly without stretching. Measure 2 in (5 cm) across the swatch and mark it with pins inserted vertically. Measure 2 in (5 cm) down the swatch and mark again with pins.

Count off the number of stitches and rows in the pinned area and then check against the pattern directions.

If you have more stitches and rows than specified in the pattern you are knitting too tightly. Try needles of the next larger size. If your swatch seems to have fewer stitches and rows, try needles of the next smaller size.

Comparative sizes of knitting needles

American	*English*	*Metricated sizes*
15	000	10mm.
13	00	9mm.
12	0	8mm.
11	1	7·5mm.
10½	2	7mm.
10	3	6·5mm.
9	4	6mm.
8	5	5·5mm.
7	6	5mm.
6	7	4·5mm.
5	8	4mm.
4	9	3·75mm.
3	10	3·25mm.
2	11	3mm.
1	12	2·75mm.
0	13	2·25mm.
00	14	2mm.

ACKNOWLEDGEMENTS

Air India, J. Allan Cash, Crown Copyright (Public Records Office), Emu, Greek Tourist Board, *Guernsey and Jersey Patterns* by Gladys Thompson (Dover Publications), Hamburger Kunsthalle, Hayfield, India Tourist Board, Irish Tourist Board, International Wool Secretariat, Knitmaster, Lister, Lord Middleton Collection (Museum of Costume and Textiles, Nottingham), The Mansell Collection, Marnie, Musées Nationaux Paris, the Museum of London, National Gallery, London, National Museum, Wrocklaw, Pingouin, Royal Ontario Museum (by kind permission of The Passold Research Fund), Sirdar, Trinity College Library, Dublin, Victoria and Albert Museum, London, Walker Art Gallery, Liverpool, Wendy Wools.
Photography: Tony Boase, John Carter, Bruce Scott
Charts: Stobart Sutterby